STRANGLING THE CONFEDERACY

STRANGLING
THE
CONFEDERACY

Coastal Operations
of the
American Civil War

KEVIN DOUGHERTY

CASEMATE
Philadelphia & Oxford

Published in the United States of America and Great Britain in 2012 by
CASEMATE PUBLISHERS
908 Darby Road, Havertown, PA 19083
and
10 Hythe Bridge Street, Oxford, OX1 2EW

Copyright 2009 © Kevin Dougherty

ISBN 978-1-61200-092-3
Digital Edition: ISBN 978-1-93514-950-7

Cataloging-in-publication data is available from the Library of Congress
and the British Library.

10 9 8 7 6 5 4 3 2 1

Printed and bound in the United States of America.

For a complete list of Casemate titles please contact:

CASEMATE PUBLISHERS (US)
Telephone (610) 853-9131, Fax (610) 853-9146
E-mail: casemate@casematepublishing.com

CASEMATE PUBLISHERS (UK)
Telephone (01865) 241249, Fax (01865) 794449
E-mail: casemate-uk@casematepublishing.co.uk

CONTENTS

CONTENTS (cont'd)

INTRODUCTION

The Civil War marked a significant increase in cooperation between the Army and Navy. The evolution of this cooperation can be readily seen in the series of operations conducted by Federal forces along the Confederate coast. Beginning with modest operations, in which the Navy dominated the battle and the Army provided an occupying force afterwards, these endeavors grew into truly amphibious assaults with land and naval forces working in tandem. Taken together, these operations can be viewed as comprising a campaign engineered and supervised by a novel creation called the Navy Board, and reflecting a major step in the evolution of joint warfare and planning in U.S. military history.

The operations took advantage of both the superior Federal Navy and the revolution in naval warfare wrought by steam power. They allowed the Federal force to maintain the initiative by determining the time and the place of the attack, and compelled the Confederates to tie up many forces defending the myriad of possible Federal objectives along the vast Southern Coast. At the same time, the operations reflected Federal priorities and the need to allocate finite resources.

The operations were also an important and effective part of the Federal strategy against Confederate logistics. While the Navy blockaded Southern ports, the Army both held terrain and severed rail communications. It was a powerful combination.[1] The result was that as Confederate logistics were weakened, Federal logistics were strengthened.

Rather than being a haphazard consequence, this outcome was the result of some very deliberate effort. Although the Federal commanders did not have the benefit of modern joint doctrinal publications, their actions with regard to the coastal war can be viewed in light of the same considerations today's military planners use when developing a campaign.

Campaign planning is "the process whereby combatant commanders and subordinate joint task force commanders translate national or theater strategy into operational concepts."[2] The national strategy relevant to the Civil War coastal campaign was articulated in April 1861, when President Abraham Lincoln declared a blockade of the Confederacy. Lincoln's goal was to isolate the Confederacy and deny it the diplomatic, informational, military, and economic benefits it would gain from international commerce and access. A special planning body called the Navy Board was convened in June 1861, to develop an effective means of implementing this national strategy.

To help counter the massive scope of the Confederate coastline, Secretary of the Navy Gideon Welles initially divided responsibility between two squadrons, the Atlantic Blockading Squadron and the Gulf Blockading Squadron. The Atlantic Blockading Squadron's area of operations stretched from Alexandria, Virginia to Key West, Florida. The Gulf Blockading Squadron's responsibilities ranged from Key West to the Mexican border.[3] This particular study will examine four distinct campaigns—the Atlantic Blockading Squadron's campaign on the Atlantic, Brigadier General Ambrose Burnside's Expedition along the North Carolina coast, the Peninsula Campaign in Virginia, and the Gulf Blockading Squadron's campaign on the Gulf.

Campaigns are "a series of related major operations aimed at accomplishing strategic and operational objectives within a given time and space."[4] The operations along the Confederate coast all were related in their pursuit of the Federal strategy of isolating the Confederacy. The Atlantic Campaign consists of operations at Hatteras Inlet, Port Royal Sound, Fernandina, and Fort Pulaski. Burnside's Expedition includes Roanoke Island, New Bern, and Fort Macon. By design, the Peninsula Campaign was more of a land attack on Richmond than a part of the coastal campaign, but one of its fringe benefits was the Federal reoccupation of Norfolk, so it is included in this study. The Gulf Campaign involves Ship Island, New Orleans, Pensacola, and Galveston. Three other operations that are part of the overall coastal campaign but proved more difficult challenges for the Federals are Charleston, Mobile Bay, and Fort Fisher, which guarded the Confederate port of Wilmington. These will be discussed as separate operations to highlight their chronological separation from the rest of the campaign.

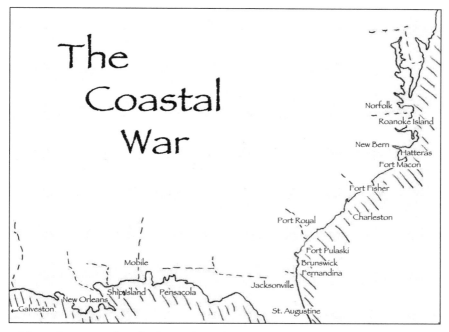

Although seemingly a hodgepodge of indiscriminate battles, the coastal war was actually a well-planned campaign to systematically gain control of the Confederate coast.

Certain themes emerge from each of these campaigns. They include the utility of the Navy Board and its efficiency in planning means of strengthening the blockade, competition for finite resources, a failure to capitalize on success, and various issues involving joint operations and unity of effort. Admiral Samuel Du Pont's Atlantic Campaign is singularly important because it would not be until Major General Ulysses Grant's Vicksburg Campaign of 1863 that another Federal commander conducted a true campaign that successfully achieved a clearly defined strategic objective; in Du Pont's case tightening and improving the blockade.[5] Burnside's Expedition is important because it marks the growing role of the Army in coastal operations. The Army would no longer merely occupy what the Navy had compelled to surrender, but would now project power inland and further weaken Confederate logistics. The objective of the Peninsula Campaign was Richmond, and it failed in this regard, in part because of a lack of unity of effort between the Army and the Navy. However, by reoccupying Norfolk, the Peninsula Campaign was beneficial to the Atlantic Blockading Squadron. The centerpiece of the Gulf Campaign was capturing the key city of New Orleans. Federal possession of New Orleans not only reduced blockade running, it was also a major step toward controlling the Mississippi River and cutting the Confederacy in two. The Gulf Campaign allowed the Federals to take the war to the Deep South long before an overland advance was possible.

Each specific operation within the campaigns also offers its own unique lessons for the student of joint operations, as well as showing a stage in the evolution of Army-Navy capabilities and cooperation. In the Atlantic Campaign, Hatteras Inlet, North Carolina, was the first such venture attempted, and it was appropriately limited in scope. It was by far a Navy-dominated affair, and one in which the possibilities of the steam engine began to become apparent.

Port Royal Sound, South Carolina, was much more ambitious and reflected the Federals' growing confidence in coastal warfare. Even more so than Hatteras Inlet, Port Royal Sound was a Navy show. Indeed, it was one that clearly demonstrated just how much the steam engine had altered the historic balance between the ship and the fort.

Fernandina, Florida, offered the outstanding southern port that the Navy Board had originally envisioned as the Atlantic blockade's southern base. However, as Du Pont easily captured Fernandina and other ports within his large geographic command, the Army began to feel itself overextended. Indeed after occupying Jacksonville, the Army then abandoned it, forcing Du Pont to withdraw as well. Jacksonville marked the limitations of joint cooperation in the Atlantic Campaign.

This string of successes had given the Federals the southern base they needed and had cleared the Confederate coast from Charleston, South Carolina, down to Savannah, Georgia, where the mighty Fort Pulaski guarded the Savannah River. Fort Pulaski's thick walls were considered impregnable, and indeed, up to this point in history, cannon had been unable to breach masonry walls at distances of over 1,000 yards. However, technological advances in rifled artillery changed this relationship, just as steam power had done to the relationship between ship and fort.

It remained for the Burnside Expedition, starting with its Roanoke

Island, North Carolina operation, for the Federal Army and Navy to work simultaneously rather than sequentially. This endeavor was truly an amphibious assault, featuring innovative techniques in landing and naval gunfire. Nonetheless, the Federal force did not advance inland after this initial success.

Eventually, the Federals would exploit their possession of Hatteras Inlet by attacking New Bern, North Carolina. New Bern was not just a port, but one with important rail lines stretching first to Goldsboro, and from there to Richmond. New Bern showed another dimension of the logistical impact of coastal war.

With the Confederate loss of New Bern, Fort Macon was isolated and fell easily to the Federals after a short siege. However, it would also mark the premature end of the Burnside Expedition. Just as Burnside appeared to be unstoppable in his effort to introduce a new front to the war, the failing Peninsula Campaign required his resources to be shifted elsewhere. From a joint perspective, one of the issues that plagued the Peninsula Campaign was a lack of unity of effort between the Army and the Navy.

Nonetheless, in spite of its overall failure, the Peninsula Campaign resulted in the reoccupation of Norfolk, Virginia. Of additional importance was the fact that the Confederates evacuated Norfolk on the Atlantic on the same day they evacuated Pensacola, Florida, on the Gulf. Both blockading squadrons thus gained important ports within Southern territory.

The Gulf Campaign began with Ship Island, a modest operation against little Confederate resistance. However, possession of this strategic point off the Mississippi coast helped give the blockade a more convenient base from which to conduct operations in the Gulf than the previously closest Federal possession at Key West, Florida. More importantly, Ship Island would provide a critical staging area for future operations against New Orleans.

New Orleans was the South's largest city, a key shipbuilding facility and a wealthy cotton distribution center, yet the Confederate efforts to defend it certainly did not reflect this importance. Convinced that an attack would come from upriver rather than from the Gulf, the Confederate defenses were plagued by poor decisions, competing priorities, inattention, and lack of cooperation. In the end, the Federal

Navy had little difficulty making its way past the two forts designed to stop it and captured the city for the Army to then occupy. While the Army's role may have been secondary, its presence made the Navy's more stunning tactic possible.

After their victory at New Orleans, the Federals appeared to be preparing to attack Mobile Bay, Alabama. This threat was too much for the Confederates at Pensacola, who abandoned their position there, realizing that they lacked the resources to defend such far-flung points of their nation. Pensacola then became the headquarters for the Gulf Blockading Squadron.

Although remote from the heartland of the Confederacy, Galveston was an important port to Texas, and increasingly important to the Confederacy after the loss of New Orleans. While Galveston initially fell to the Federals after only token resistance, the Confederates recaptured it in a daring joint Army-Navy attack. It was the only major port to be recaptured by the Confederates, and it remained in their hands until the end of the war. This Federal setback was indicative of how the Gulf Campaign was running out of steam.

In fact, both the Atlantic and Gulf Campaigns enjoyed initial success but gradually began to culminate: to reach that "point in time and space where the attacker's effective combat power no longer exceeds that of the defender's, or the attacker's momentum is no longer sustainable, or both."[6] A combination of eroding unity of effort, ineffective future planning, and strengthened Confederate defenses all conspired against Federal success. Three Confederate strongholds, Charleston, Mobile Bay, and Fort Fisher, North Carolina, proved to be particularly troublesome for the Federals. Thus, although Charleston and Fort Fisher were part of the overall Atlantic Campaign and Mobile Bay was part of the Gulf Campaign, they are treated as separate operations here because their resistance distanced them from the chronology of the easier targets of the campaigns.

Charleston, as not just an important port but also the very birthplace of secession, was a much-desired target for the Federals. However, its strong forts, torpedoes, and natural defenses allowed it to withstand numerous attacks and a lengthy siege. In the end, Charleston succumbed not to a joint attack from the sea, but to a much later land attack during Major General William Sherman's

Carolina Campaign. Charleston is the lone example in this study of a Confederate fort that did not fall to the Federal joint Army-Navy attacks. Its strength was the result of the change in Confederate coastal defense strategy after Port Royal and shows what may have been possible if the Confederates had been able to focus their efforts on a limited number of strategic points.

Early Federal action against Mobile Bay fell victim to higher priorities elsewhere. When Admiral David Farragut eventually ordered, "Damn the torpedoes! Full speed ahead" and ran past the position's strong forts, the military significance was almost moot. However, the victory, combined with Sherman's capture of Atlanta, had the political impact of securing Lincoln's re-election and thus ensuring the Civil War would end in Confederate surrender.

The culmination of the coastal war was at Fort Fisher, which guarded the last open Confederate port at Wilmington, North Carolina. The first Federal attempt there ended in failure, in no small part due to the inability of the Army and Navy commanders to work together. A change in Army leadership brought excellent cooperation between the two components, illustrating the necessity of unity of effort. With the Federal victory at Fort Fisher, the coastal war was over. It was also apparent just how far Army-Navy operations had advanced throughout the course of the war.

The book concludes with a section called "The Coastal War and the Elements of Operational Design." The elements of operational design are the tools modern-day military planners use to construct campaigns. This analysis shows that while there were some shortcomings, particularly in unity of effort and planning sequels, the Navy Board was well ahead of its time in terms of translating a national strategic objective into a military campaign. The coastal operations envisioned by the Navy Board made a marked contribution to the ultimate Federal victory. Nonetheless, each of the four campaigns studied here eventually reached its point of culmination. This fact indicates that the Navy Board was perhaps disbanded before its work was complete.

THE KEY FEDERALS

Alexander Bache (1806–1867) was, on the eve of the Civil War, one of America's most famous scientists and educators. He was a great-grandson of Benjamin Franklin and a West Point graduate. Bache came up with the initial idea of a Navy Board that would guide the strategic planning of the blockade. He would become the only civilian member of the Board.

Bache was well prepared for this duty. He had previously served on the Lighthouse Board and other Navy boards, and was the founder of the National Academy of Sciences. As superintendent of the Coast Survey, Bache had provided the Department of the Navy with charts and maps on almost a daily basis. He was also critical in recommending the Navy Board's membership.[1]

John Barnard (1815–1882) graduated second from the West Point class of 1833, and served in various engineering positions in the Mexican War, and as an engineering professor and superintendent at West Point. Barnard was the engineer in charge of the defenses of Washington when, as a major, he became one of the four members of the Navy Board. Barnard's principal duty on the Board was to provide engineering expertise on coastal defenses and topography, but, as an Army officer, he was also able to provide some informal liaison between the Army and the Navy. The junior member of the Navy Board, Barnard ultimately rose to the rank of major general.[2]

Ambrose Burnside (1824–1881) graduated 18th of 30 in the West Point class of 1847. He served in the Mexican and Indian Wars and then resigned in 1853 to manufacture firearms in Rhode Island. In

1856, he invented a breech-loading rifle, the fourth model of which was bought by the government for use during the Civil War. In the process, however, Burnside's Bristol Rifle Works went bankrupt and Burnside lost almost everything he had. Still, he refused help from his friends and went west in search of employment.

There, his West Point classmate George McClellan, vice-president of the Illinois Central Railroad, offered Burnside the position of cashier of the Illinois Land Office. McClellan even allowed Burnside and his wife to live in the McClellans's residence. McClellan's kindness paid off. Burnside was able to recover financially and pay off his Rhode Island debts. In June 1860, he was promoted to treasurer of the railroad. [3]

Burnside entered the Civil War as a colonel of the 1st Rhode Island Volunteers. He commanded a brigade at Manassas and was promoted to brigadier general.[4]

Major General Ambrose Burnside commanded the Army of the Potomac during the ill-fated Battle of Fredericksburg, but his earlier performance on the North Carolina coast was much more inspired.
Photograph courtesy of the Library of Congress, Prints & Photographs Division.

After Manassas, most of the 90-day enlistments of the men of the 1st Rhode Island expired, and the men returned home. Burnside was left without an active command, but he did not remain idle during this period. He began developing the concept for raising an amphibious force to attack the Confederate coast, a concept that would become reality in the form of the Burnside Expedition.[5]

Burnside was likeable, modest, and simple—qualities that would help him cooperate and achieve unity of effort with his naval counterparts.[6] He would eventually rise to command of the Army of the Potomac, a position for which he was unqualified, and he is sadly best remembered for his disastrous defeat at Fredericksburg. In his expedition to North Carolina, however, he would perform well. Indeed at Roanoke Island, Richard Sauers concludes, "Burnside illustrated all the traits of a good Civil War commander."[7]

Benjamin Butler (1818–1893) was an astute criminal lawyer and active politician before the war. His political connections netted him a brigadier generalship in the Massachusetts militia on April 17, 1861, and on May 16 he became the first major general of United States Volunteers appointed by President Abraham Lincoln.[8]

Butler was associated with a string of military controversies and blunders to include defeat at Big Bethel, issuance of the infamous "Woman Order" in New Orleans, and allowing his Army to be bottled up at Bermuda Hundred. However, in spite of his military ineptitude, he was so politically powerful that Lincoln dared not relieve him until after the 1864 elections.

Butler's success at Hatteras Inlet in August 1861 helped him gain a much-inflated reputation as a strategist. In actuality, the Navy had carried the day, and Butler's troops merely occupied the forts after the Confederates evacuated them. Nonetheless, Butler then returned to Massachusetts to recruit an expedition to operate in the Gulf, which resulted in his commanding the Army contingent at Ship Island that was earmarked to support the naval assault on New Orleans. On May 1, 1862, he occupied New Orleans after Admiral David Farragut had reduced its defenses. He served as controversial military administrator of the city, earning the nickname "Beast Butler" in the South. He also entered into a feud with Rear Admiral David Porter over Porter's contribution to the battle; a feud which would still be simmering when the two served together at Fort Fisher.[9]

Late in 1863, Butler took command of what became the Army of the James. It was in this capacity that he exercised his command prerogative and chose to personally lead the first attack on Fort Fisher in December 1864. His fixation on the idea of an exploding powder ship, his subsequent feeble attack, and his inability to cooperate with Porter led to a miserable failure and the end of his military career.[10]

On January 8, 1865, Butler was relieved of command, and he later appeared before the Joint Congressional Committee on the Conduct of the War to defend his actions at Fort Fisher. In the midst of the proceedings, newspaper boys could be heard announcing that Fort Fisher had fallen. Butler protested, "Impossible! It is a mistake, Sir," but he was wrong. Ever resilient, Butler was able to turn even this potential embarrassment to his favor. Referred to affectionately by a colleague as "the smartest damned rascal that ever lived,"[11] Butler was able to cast a portion of the blame on Porter and have the Committee conclude that "the determination of General Butler not to assault the fort seems to have been fully justifiable by all the facts and circumstances then known or afterward ascertained."[12] His military career was still over, but Butler had once again triumphed politically.

Major General Benjamin Butler proved to be a difficult partner in joint operations at New Orleans and Fort Fisher.

Photograph courtesy of the Library of Congress, Prints & Photographs Division.

John Dahlgren (1809–1870) was appointed a midshipman in 1826 and served 16 years as an ordnance officer. During that time he invented the Dahlgren gun, a rifled cannon, and boat howitzers with iron carriages. Dahlgren's boat howitzers were the finest guns of their time and were used by both Federals and Confederates throughout the Civil War. They remained in active service in the U.S. Navy until the 1880s and were copied throughout the world.

Dahlgren took command of the Washington Naval Yard on April 22,

1861. He was promoted to captain on July 16, 1862, and appointed Chief of the Ordnance Bureau on July 18. Many felt Dahlgren was nothing but a shore officer, sharing Admiral Samuel Du Pont's assessment that Dahlgren "chose one line in the walks of the profession [scientific ordnance work] while [Admiral Andrew] Foote and I chose another [sea duty]; he was licking cream while we were eating dirt."[13]

Dahlgren ruthlessly exploited his ordnance achievements and his close relationship with President Lincoln, and on February 7, 1863, he was promoted to Rear Admiral. When Du Pont was relieved as commander of the South Atlantic Blockading Squadron, Dahlgren, in spite of his lack of experience with sea command, became his replacement on July 6. In that capacity, Dahlgren launched several attacks and siege operations against Charleston, South Carolina, but was unable to capture it.[14]

Charles Henry Davis (1807–1877) entered the Navy as a midshipman in 1817 and served in the Pacific, the Mediterranean, the South Atlantic, and along the New England coast, eventually advancing to the rank of commander. He was a prominent astronomer, and as head of the Naval Almanac had produced navigational and astronomical tables for the Navy. He had served with Alexander Bache on various Navy boards, and Bache tapped Davis to be a member and secretary of the Navy Board. He was promoted to captain in November 1861 and served as Du Pont's chief of staff and Flag Captain during the Port Royal Expedition.[15]

Samuel Du Pont (1803–1865) became a midshipman in 1815 and served in European waters, the West Indies, along the South American coast, in the Mediterranean, and in the Mexican War.[16] In the latter conflict, he gained valuable experience in blockade duty, and Daniel Ammen believes that it was this quality that led to Du Pont's selection to serve as president of the Navy Board in June 1861.[17] In this capacity, Du Pont was instrumental in planning the strategy for the blockade and coastal war.

Du Pont was promoted to flag officer in September 1861, and in October he commanded the fleet that captured Port Royal Sound. In this operation, he expanded on Silas Stringham's technique of firing while moving, and explicitly demonstrated that the fort was no longer intrinsically superior to the ship.

From there, Du Pont continued to ravage the Confederacy's Atlantic Coast. Ultimately, growing tension between Du Pont and his Army counterparts, as well as stiff Confederate defenses at Charleston, caused Du Pont's campaign to culminate. At Charleston, Du Pont suffered a series of repulses by the Confederate defenders, and he became increasingly cautious and continually at odds with President Lincoln and Secretary of the Navy, Gideon Welles. Du Pont was relieved from his command and served out the war on various boards and commissions.

Du Pont was a true military professional, but also a man who was thin-skinned and jealous of his reputation. He was a firm believer in joint operations, understanding the concept more clearly than any other Federal commander, except perhaps Lieutenant General Ulysses Grant or Admiral David Porter.[18]

A member of the talented Delaware manufacturing family, Du Pont is described by Bruce Catton as "a sailor whose social and financial standing was quite impeccable."[19] His fall from grace after Charleston leads his biographer, Kevin Weddle, to term him "Lincoln's tragic admiral" and calls his story "one of the most heartbreaking of the Civil War."[20]

David Farragut (1801–1870) became a midshipman at age nine, and by age twelve he was serving as a prize master. He fought aboard the *Essex* in the War of 1812 under Captain David Porter (father of the Civil War admiral, David Dixon Porter) and served most of the Mexican War on blockade duty. In 1855, he was promoted to captain. By the time of the Civil War, many senior naval officers considered Farragut to be a capable officer, but were unsure of his ability to lead a large force because he had not previously commanded one.[21]

Another doubt surrounding Farragut was his ties to the South. Although he was a staunch Unionist, Farragut was born near Knoxville, Tennessee, and had married a woman from Norfolk, Virginia. Additionally, at the time Farragut was being considered for command of the West Gulf Blockading Squadron, he had a brother in

New Orleans and a sister in Pascagoula, Mississippi, and the husband of his cousin was commanding the Confederate flotilla below New Orleans. Secretary of the Navy Welles was willing to overlook these concerns because of his favorable impression of Farragut in Mexico and his willingness to abandon his Norfolk home.[22]

Welles's trust would prove to be well placed. Indeed in Farragut, Welles found a man who "has prompt, energetic, excellent qualities, but no fondness for written details or self-laudation; does but one thing at a time, but does that strong and well; is better fitted to lead an expedition through danger and difficulty than to command an extensive blockade; is a good officer in a great emergency, will more willingly take risks in order to obtain great results than any other officer in high position in either Navy or Army, and, unlike most of them, prefers that others should tell the story of his well-doing rather than relate it himself."[23]

Admiral David Farragut demonstrated outstanding leadership at New Orleans, but the lack of planning for a follow-on operation limited the potential of the victory.
Photograph courtesy of the Library of Congress, Prints & Photographs Division.

Gustavus Fox (1821–1883) was appointed a midshipman in 1838 and served in the Mexican War. He tired of peacetime service and resigned in 1856.

At the outbreak of the Civil War, officers who had resigned in peacetime were ineligible to be restored to their former places in the Navy, so Fox and others like him were recommissioned as acting lieutenants. Fox became skipper of the tug, *Yankee*, at Hampton Roads and soon made a name for himself as a vocal critic of the

Federal failure at Fort Sumter. To both quiet Fox and mollify certain of his patrons, President Lincoln asked Secretary of the Navy Welles to give Fox some responsible job in the Navy Department. On May 8, 1861, Fox received orders appointing him as Chief Clerk of the Navy Department. His duties there were the equivalent of what is now performed by the entire Office of the Chief of Naval Operations. Fox became the Assistant Secretary of the Navy when the post was established later that summer.

Fox approached his duties with zeal and seemingly boundless energy, possessing what Commander Charles Davis called "a gigantic capacity for work." Fox was a godsend to Welles and the Navy Department. With a broad network of friends, Fox made things happen using a deft combination of aggressiveness and tact. Welles gave Fox a wide latitude and counted on his counsel for critical command appointments, strategic planning, and executing the Department's technical business. President Lincoln shared Welles's high opinion of Fox, and Admiral Dahlgren once said, "Captain Fox, *he* is the Navy Department."[24]

Fox, however, would become a champion of the naval parochialism that conflicted with Du Pont's quest for joint action at Charleston. As the two debated the proper course, Fox told Du Pont, "… the crowning act of this war ought to be by the Navy. I feel that my duties are two fold; first, to beat our southern friends; second, to beat the Army."[25] Although Fox and Du Pont were friends, such a view clashed poignantly with Du Pont who argued, "I have never had but one opinion—that the capture of Charleston should be effected by a joint operation of the Army and Navy… we should be willing to share the laurels."[26]

Quincy Adams Gillmore (1825–1888) graduated first in the West Point class of 1849. He supervised harbor construction, taught engineering, and served as quartermaster at West Point before the Civil War. On August 6, 1861, he was promoted to captain and went on to serve as Chief Engineer on the Port Royal Expedition. In that capacity, he directed the bombardment of Fort Pulaski, Georgia, which was the first time in history that long-distance rifled artillery defeated a masonry fort. He was appointed major general on July 10,

1863, and commanded the X Corps and the Department of the South at Charleston, where he was unable to replicate his Fort Pulaski success.

Louis Goldsborough (1805–1873) was warranted as a midshipman at age seven and actually entered the service four years later. By the time of the Civil War, he had been a sailor for almost his entire life. He had made cruises in the Mediterranean and the Pacific, commanded the *Ohio* during the Mexican War, served with Commodore Matthew Perry at Tuxpan in 1847, and been superintendent of the U.S. Naval Academy. In September 1861, he was appointed commander of the North Atlantic Blockading Squadron after Silas Stringham resigned. Goldsborough stood six feet and four inches tall, weighed 300 pounds, and had a red beard that accented his round face.[27] Shelby Foote describes him as "a big, slack-bodied regular of the type called 'barnacles.'"[28] Ivan Musicant writes that Goldsborough looked "every inch the stern Amish elder."[29]

Goldsborough could be parochial—he once declared, "The Navy must end the war! The Army cannot do it!"—but in February 1862, he and Burnside achieved exemplary unity of effort at Roanoke Island.[30] Unfortunately, Goldsborough and Major General George McClellan would later fail miserably to achieve such cooperation during the Virginia Peninsula Campaign from April to July, 1862. Nonetheless, Goldsborough joined Farragut, Du Pont, and Andrew Foote on July 16 in being promoted as the first Rear Admirals in the history of the U.S. Navy. However, Goldsborough's pride was wounded when the Department of the Navy created an independent James River Flotilla, and he resigned as commander of the North Atlantic Blockading Squadron.[31] He then performed administrative duties for the Navy Department and became commander of the European Squadron toward the end of the war.

David Hunter (1802–1886) graduated from West Point in 1822. He served in the Army on the frontier but then resigned his commission to speculate in real estate, only to rejoin the Army and serve as a paymaster during the Mexican War. While serving at Fort Leavenworth, Kansas, in 1860, Hunter established correspondence with Abraham Lincoln on secession rumors and was invited to make the inaugural journey with Lincoln to Washington. His relationship with Lincoln helped Hunter receive an appointment as the fourth ranking volunteer general on May 17, 1861.[32]

In March 1862, Hunter replaced Brigadier General Thomas Sherman as commander of the newly created Department of the South. The next month, Fort Pulaski fell to troops under his command. Hunter's force was defeated at Secessionville on June 16 in an attempt to take Charleston, after which he suspended further operations.

Hunter's career would be characterized by controversy. He had a reputation for being "independent in thought and action," and his relations with his naval counterpart Samuel Du Pont would steadily deteriorate.[33] In May 1862, Hunter would issue an order freeing slaves in his jurisdiction which President Lincoln would have to quickly rescind.

David Dixon Porter (1813–1891) was the son of War of 1812 hero Commodore David Porter, brother of Federal naval officer William Porter, and cousin of Federal Major General Fitz John Porter. He had sailed with his father to the West Indies to suppress piracy in 1824, and was commissioned a midshipman in the Mexican Navy in 1827. In 1829, he joined the United States Navy. He served in the Mediterranean, the South Atlantic, and the Gulf during the Mexican War.[34]

Along the way, Porter also picked up valuable knowledge about New Orleans, probably more so than any other officer in the Federal Navy. He had served with the Coastal Survey, lived for a short time in New Orleans as a recruiting officer during the Mexican War, and captained the mail steamer *Crescent City* on her regular runs between New York, Havana, and New Orleans.[35]

In April 1862, Porter would get a chance to put this personal knowledge of New Orleans to work, commanding 19 mortar boats as part of his foster brother's (Admiral David Farragut's) naval assault on the city. Porter fired a total of 2,997 shells at Fort Jackson but did little damage.[36] Later, he would have to relearn this lesson, that large bombardments are not necessarily effective, at the first battle of Fort Fisher.

Porter had a volatile and self-seeking personality. A fellow officer wrote, "Porter would assassinate the reputation of anyone in his way."[37] Indeed, after New Orleans, Porter became entangled in a squabble with Major General Benjamin Butler. These continuing tensions would preclude effective cooperation between the two commanders at the first battle of Fort Fisher.

But Porter had shown that under the proper circumstances his brash character could accommodate teamwork. Ulysses Grant wrote of Vicksburg that, "The navy under Porter was all it could be, during the entire campaign. . . . The most perfect harmony reigned between the two arms of the service. There never was a request made, that I am aware of, either of the flag-officer or any of his subordinates, that was not promptly complied with."[38] In the second attack on Fort Fisher, Porter would find in Major General Alfred Terry an Army counterpart with whom he could repeat this cooperation.

Rear Admiral David Porter figured prominently in both the Atlantic and Gulf Campaigns. In many ways ambitious and parochial, he also showed a willingness to cooperate in the second attack on Fort Fisher.
Photograph courtesy of the Library of Congress, Prints & Photographs Division.

Stephen Rowan (1805–1890) was one of the Navy's elder statesmen, and his experience would make him a valuable asset to Admiral Goldsborough. Rowan was born in Ireland and began his sea service when he was 15. He served in the Pacific and the Mediterranean prior to the Mexican War, where he displayed solid leadership of one of the naval battalions ashore in California.[39]

At Roanoke Island, Rowan provided close naval gunfire in

support of Burnside's landing, and at New Bern he was the ranking naval officer after Goldsborough was recalled to Hampton Roads to deal with the *Virginia*. Rowan served out the war on blockading duty off the North and South Carolina coasts.

Thomas Sherman (1813–1879), known as "the other General Sherman," graduated from West Point in 1836 and served in Florida and Mexico. He was appointed a brigadier general of volunteers on May 17, 1861, and commanded the Army contingent of the Port Royal Expedition from September 19, 1861, to March 15, 1862. He had a reputation for driving his men hard and maintaining firm discipline.[40]

As the campaign progressed, Sherman would develop an increasingly tense relationship with his naval counterpart, Samuel Du Pont. However, when Sherman was replaced by Major General David Hunter on the eve of the bombardment of Fort Pulaski, even Du Pont allowed that Sherman had "ploughed, harrowed, sowed, and it does seem hard that when the crop was about being harvested he is not even allowed to participate in a *secondary* position."[41]

Silas Stringham (1798–1876) was, like Goldsborough, a veteran sailor. He had entered the Navy as a midshipman in 1809 and served in the War of 1812, the Algerine (Second Barbary) War, the West Indies, the Mexican War, and the Mediterranean.[42] Also like Goldsborough, Stringham had a temper. Bruce Catton describes him as "lean [and] irritable."[43]

On May 1, 1861, Stringham was given command of all blockading forces "from the capes of the Chesapeake to the southern extremities of Florida," and in early August he was ordered to take Hatteras Inlet.[44] At Hatteras Inlet, Stringham excelled. Colonel Rush Hawkins wrote, "Stringham fought this action with admirable skill, worthy of a great commander." Although Du Pont generally gets the credit for his larger and more dramatic maneuver at Port Royal Sound, it was actually Stringham at Hatteras Inlet who first took advantage of steam power to fire while on the move.[45]

Unfortunately, Stringham did not get along well with his superiors. Du Pont complained that Stringham "has eleven ships in

Hampton Roads and *three ports uncovered... he... has evidently the sulks about something."* When Gustavus Fox sent a critical letter questioning some of Stringham's decisions, Stringham considered it an insult and tendered his resignation. He was transferred to the retired list but promoted to Rear Admiral in July 1862. He re-entered active service as commandant of the Boston Navy Yard.[46]

Alfred Terry (1827–1890) had graduated from Yale and practiced law in Connecticut until he was commissioned as a colonel in the militia on May 7, 1861. He led the 2nd Connecticut Regiment at Manassas and later gained valuable experience in coastal operations at Port Royal, Fort Pulaski, and Charleston. Though not a professional soldier, Terry advanced to corps command in Butler's Army of the James by demonstrated ability and was promoted to brigadier general on April 25, 1862.[47]

His most valuable attribute at Fort Fisher was what the *Dictionary of American Biography* describes as his "ability to cooperate with superiors, equals, or subordinates."[48] Rod Gragg writes that as commander of the second Fort Fisher expedition, Terry was "the perfect choice: a seasoned combat commander whose proven competence in joint operations reduced the worrisome risk of another failure at Fort Fisher. His easygoing nature would ensure cooperation with the volatile Admiral Porter, and Terry was respected and liked by the officers and men of the Army of the James."[49]

Before Fort Fisher, Terry was "an unspectacular soldier... but a sound one."[50] After his dramatic success at Fort Fisher, he would be one of just 15 Army officers to receive the "Thanks of Congress."[51]

Gideon Welles (1802–1878) spent most of his pre-Civil War life as a newspaper editor, a Democrat, and a postmaster. He held a minor post as head of the Naval Bureau of Provisions and Clothing during the Mexican War, but otherwise was largely untrained in naval matters. In 1854, he became a Republican and campaigned for Lincoln's election. Lincoln looked past Welles's lack of naval expertise and, seeing his administrative abilities and capability of evaluating and molding public opinion, made him his Secretary of the Navy.

Welles was intensely loyal to Lincoln and a mainstay in his cabinet. Lincoln returned Welles's trust by giving the Navy Department unparalleled freedom from political influence. Welles was stubborn, practical, thrifty, and dutiful. His elderly appearance, including a heavy beard and a wig, helped earn him the nickname "Father Neptune," but he displayed an energy that belied his countenance.

Welles initially argued against the blockade, fearing both foreign intervention and a scarcity of resources to complete the task, but once Lincoln's decision was made, Welles supported it. The incident is indicative of Welles's position in the cabinet. Chester Hearn notes, "Lincoln did not always agree with [Welles], but he always listened."[52]

THE KEY CONFEDERATES

Pierre Gustave Toutant Beauregard (1818–1893) graduated second in the West Point class of 1838. He served as an engineer in Mexico and was the superintendent of West Point for just six days, being reassigned on January 28, 1861, on account of his Southern sympathies. He resigned from the U.S. Army on February 20 and won early fame as the hero of both Fort Sumter and First Manassas.

On August 3 he was promoted to full general, and in early 1862 he was transferred west, where he served as General Albert Sidney Johnston's second-in-command at Shiloh. When Johnston was killed, Beauregard assumed command. Beauregard went on sick leave in June, turning his command over to Braxton Bragg. President Jefferson Davis accused Beauregard of leaving his post without authority and relieved him of command. Upon his recovery, Beauregard returned to Charleston and assumed responsibility for the defenses of the Carolina and Georgia coasts.[1]

Lawrence Branch (1820–1862) was a North Carolina newspaper editor and politician. He was appointed brigadier general on November 16, 1861, and commanded the forces at New Bern. Branch was a natural leader but one without military training. Consequently, he was prone to overlook details of military significance. At New Bern, this would equate to leaving a gap in his defensive line. Later, at Mechanicsville, it would be failing to report his knowledge of Major General Stonewall Jackson's movements to General Robert E. Lee, who desperately needed that information.[2]

George Hollins (1799–1878) was a native of Maryland, but a well-known figure in New Orleans. He had joined the Navy as a 15-year-old and fought with Stephen Decatur against the British in the War of 1812. At age 62, when the Civil War broke out, Hollins still looked combative, exuded the energy of a much younger man, and maintained a reputation as a fighter. He resigned his commission in the Federal Navy on June 8, 1861, and on June 20 was appointed a captain in the Confederate Navy. He quickly proved his aggressive reputation by leading a raid to capture the *St. Nicholas*, a Federal side-wheeler moored in the lower Potomac, and then used her to capture three more prizes in the Chesapeake Bay.

Hollins's knack for getting things done caught the attention of Secretary of the Navy Stephen Mallory, who appointed Hollins to commodore and sent him to New Orleans with instructions to build a navy and remove the blockade. This monumental task was easier said than done, but Hollins was able to piece together six vessels into what he dubbed the "Mosquito Fleet."

Hollins saw the threat to New Orleans differently than did his Army counterpart, Major General Daniel Twiggs. Twiggs, and most Confederate officials in Richmond, viewed the threat as coming from upriver. Hollins, on the other hand, was most concerned about the Federal Navy slipping into the Mississippi from the Gulf and attacking from downriver. There is little evidence that the pair ever conferred to try to resolve their strategic differences.

Hollins would endure other difficulties at New Orleans with ship-building, supplies, command arrangements, and his relationship with Mallory. After New Orleans fell, his testimony against Mallory would be minimized by a pro-Mallory investigating committee.[3]

William Lamb (1835–1909) was a native Virginian who studied law at the College of William and Mary. After graduation, he served as a newspaper editor and followed politics closely. In 1858, he helped organize a militia company with which he would see limited combat early in the Civil War. In 1861, Lamb was promoted to major and ordered to Wilmington as chief quartermaster for the District of Cape Fear. In that capacity, he set about building Fort Anderson on the west bank of the Cape Fear. He proved himself to be very capable as an engineer.

Lamb was promoted to colonel, and on July 4, 1862, he was ordered across the river to command Fort Fisher. Rod Gragg writes, "Lamb was Fort Fisher's creator as well as its commander. No one knew the fort like Lamb."[4]

The Confederacy collapsed before Lamb's promotion to general was confirmed, and many histories of the war ignore his contributions. Nonetheless, for those who study him, it is readily apparent why Lamb was "the Hero of Fort Fisher" to a generation of Southerners.[5]

Robert E. Lee (1807–1870) would, of course, eventually become the commander of the Army of Northern Virginia and one of the most distinguished generals in American history, but during the early stages of the Civil War, his reputation was much less luminous. He had led an unsuccessful campaign in western Virginia, which climaxed in defeat at Cheat Mountain in September 1861. In October, Lee returned to Richmond, but did not stay long. With indications of Federal plans to attack Port Royal Sound, President Jefferson Davis ordered Lee to assume command of a newly formed department comprising the coasts of South Carolina, Georgia, and north Florida. Lee arrived at his new post on November 7, the same day Port Royal was captured by the Federals. He remained in this position until March 1862, when Davis summoned him back to Richmond to serve as his military advisor. When General Joe Johnston was wounded at Seven Pines, Lee assumed command and repulsed McClellan's Peninsula Campaign.

Lee appreciated the problems of defending the vast Confederate coast and worked hard to consolidate and strengthen the effort. The difficulty of this undertaking was compounded with the loss of Fort Pulaski, in whose thick masonry walls Lee had placed great confidence.

Even as commander of the Army of Northern Virginia, Lee could not escape the coastal war. In the summer of 1864, he sent word to Colonel Lamb that Fort Fisher must be held. Without Wilmington open to blockade runners, Lee could not sustain his army.[6] Lee experienced the coastal war both directly in South Carolina and indirectly in Virginia.

Mansfield Lovell (1822–1884) was born in Washington, DC, and graduated ninth in the West Point class of 1842. He served in the Mexican War as an artillery lieutenant, was wounded, and was brevetted to captain. He resigned from the Army in 1854, and, with his close friend and West Point classmate Gustavus Smith, he established a business in New York City that promptly failed. Smith went on to become the city's commissioner of streets and offered Lovell the post of deputy.

Lovell was slow in joining the Confederacy, waiting until after the Battle of First Manassas. He overcame this late start in part thanks to Smith's lobbying on his behalf, and on September 25, 1861, Lovell was sent to New Orleans to help Major General Daniel Twiggs with the defense of New Orleans. While Lovell was on his way, Twiggs asked to be relieved. When Lovell reached New Orleans on October 17, he learned he had been promoted to major general and named Twiggs's successor as commander of Department No. 1.[7]

At 39 years of age, Lovell was viewed by some as a welcome change from the old and infirm Twiggs, but others viewed his appointment askance. Braxton Bragg, who had coveted the position, wrote Governor Thomas Moore, "How do you get along with your new-fledged Major General fresh from the lecture room of New York where he has been . . . instructing the very men he will have to oppose?"[8]

Lovell's reputation suffered greatly from the loss of New Orleans, although a

Major General Mansfield Lovell inherited an unwieldy situation at New Orleans and was unable to make the corrections necessary to sufficiently improve the city's defenses.
Photograph courtesy of the Library of Congress, Prints & Photographs Division.

court of inquiry would vindicate him on July 9, 1863. In the meantime, however, he would show the same lack of initiative he was accused of at New Orleans in his poor performance at Corinth, Mississippi.

John Bankhead Magruder (1810–1871) graduated from West Point in 1830 and served in the Seminole and Mexican Wars. His victory at Big Bethel on June 10, 1861, catapulted him to immediate fame, and he was promoted to brigadier general on June 17 and major general on October 7. However, he was cautious and bumbling during the Seven Days Battles, and was sent from Virginia to the Department of Texas in November 1862. There, he somewhat redeemed himself by the daring, surprise recapture of Galveston on January 1, 1863.

After the Civil War, Magruder initially fled to Mexico, but he soon returned to Houston where he died in 1871. Considered by many to be a humbug for his lackluster performance on the Virginia Peninsula, the people of Galveston remembered Magruder as a hero and savior of the city. They removed Magruder from his modest burial site in Houston to Galveston's Trinity Episcopal Cemetery, where an impressive obelisk marks his grave.[9]

Stephen Mallory (1813–1873) was born in Trinidad, but grew up in Florida. When he was 19, he became the inspector of customs at Key West. He later studied law, became a judge, and fought in the Seminole War. He was a Florida senator at the outbreak of the Civil War, and in that capacity he negotiated the "armistice" surrounding Fort Pickens.

As a senator, Mallory had been chairman of the Senate Committee on Naval Affairs, but Jefferson Davis seems to have selected Mallory to be his Secretary of the Navy primarily out of a desire to have a Floridian in the cabinet. Indeed, Mallory came with some baggage. He was not an ardent secessionist, and he had a reputation for associating with women of questionable virtue. As it turned out, Mallory was the only one of Davis's cabinet appointees whose confirmation Congress delayed. Nonetheless, he became a good Secretary of the Navy and was one of only two cabinet members to serve in the same post throughout the life of the Confederacy (Postmaster General John Reagan was the other).

Mallory had an innovative mind, but creating a Confederate Navy from scratch was a tall order. He had inherited just five vessels from the seceded states, and President Davis seemed to have little interest in naval matters. Nonetheless, Mallory saw early on the importance of ironclads and was instrumental in the conversion of the *Merrimack* into the ironclad *Virginia*. In other endeavors, such as failing to anticipate the attack on New Orleans from the south, Mallory was less successful.[10]

Stephen Mallory attempted to bring some creativity and vision to the fledgling Confederate Navy but faced an uphill challenge in the process.
Photograph courtesy of the Library of Congress, Prints & Photographs Division.

John Mitchell (dates unknown) had originally been sent to New Orleans to assist Flag Officer George Hollins, but when Mallory dispatched Hollins upriver, Mitchell became commander of the slim naval forces around the Confederate forts. Mitchell's Army counterparts criticized him for a failure to cooperate with them, but a board of inquiry would exonerate him on March 17, 1862. He was the husband of the cousin of David Farragut, the man who would command the Federal naval forces attacking New Orleans.[11]

Leon Smith (?–1869) was one of the more colorful personalities of the coastal war. Born in New England (probably Maine), Smith went to sea at age 13 and was a captain by the age of 20. In the 1850s, he commanded one of the Southern Mail steamships that ran from Galveston to New Orleans. He had also worked on steamships in California and served in the Texas Navy during that republic's struggle for independence. In February 1861, when Texas seceded from the Union, Smith commanded the ship that took Colonel John S. "Rip" Ford to Brownsville to take military possession of the Rio Grande.

Smith had met John Magruder during Magruder's old Army days in the West. Reconnecting at Galveston, Magruder quickly added Smith to his staff and gave him the task of rounding up all the steamboats available along the bayous emptying into Galveston Bay. Smith proved resourceful and imaginative—"an artist in steamboat management" according to Virgil Jones.[12] During the recapture of Galveston, the daring Smith was integral to Magruder's success.

Smith never held an official commission in the Confederate Navy but was most often referred to in official reports as a Navy captain or an Army major. He ultimately became the head of Lieutenant General Edmund Kirby Smith's Naval Bureau in the Trans-Mississippi Department. As late as April 1865, Smith was trying gamely to break the Federal blockade and re-establish communications between Shreveport, Louisiana, and the outside world.[13] A marker erected in his honor in Galveston in 1965 calls him the "Lion" of Texas coastal defense during the Civil War.

Josiah Tattnall (1795–1871) joined the Navy in 1812 as a midshipman and fought in the Algerine War, against pirates in the West Indies, and in the Mexican War. He was commissioned senior flag officer in the Georgia Navy on February 28, 1861, and in March was named captain in the Confederate States Navy. Virgil Jones describes Tattnall as "the beau ideal of a naval officer, tall, florid-faced, blue-eyed, genial, modest, courtly, but punctilious to a point of honor."[14]

Tattnall was responsible for the naval defenses of Georgia and South Carolina. At Port Royal Sound, he battled his former messmate Samuel Du Pont in "the old Navy." In March 1862, he would replace the wounded Franklin Buchanan as captain of the *Virginia*. After having to destroy the ironclad to prevent its capture, Tattnall returned to the naval defenses of Georgia.[15]

Moses White (1835–1865) began his studies at the College of William and Mary but then transferred to West Point, where he graduated second in the class of 1858. White was commissioned as an ordnance officer but soon developed epilepsy. Nevertheless, he served in ordnance posts in Louisiana and New Mexico until 1860, when his deteriorating health forced him to take a sick leave of absence.

When his home state of Mississippi seceded, White resigned his commission in the U.S. Army and was appointed a first lieutenant in the Confederate Corps of Artillery. He served as an ordnance officer on the staff of Major General Leonidas Polk until September 30, 1861. At that time, White was promoted to the temporary rank of lieutenant colonel and ordered to take command of the defenses at Fort Macon, North Carolina. During the ensuing siege, White faced challenges from scarce resources, disgruntled subordinates, and his precarious health.[16]

Henry Wise (1806–1876) was a career politician, serving in the House of Representatives from 1833 to 1844, as Minister to Brazil from 1844 to 1847, and as fire-eating governor of Virginia from 1856 to 1860. He was appointed brigadier general on June 5, 1861, and raised an independent legion to help defend the western part of Virginia.

Wise lacked both military skill and the ability to cooperate with others. He has few champions, and most observers highlight his abrasive personality. Clifford Dowdey describes him as "a high-spirited self-glamorizer."[17] Richard Sauers concludes Wise was "not used to taking orders."[18] The *Dictionary of American Biography* characterizes him as "lacking in moderation and judgment

Brigadier General Henry Wise had an irascible personality that served him poorly at Roanoke Island and elsewhere.
Photograph courtesy of the Library of Congress, Prints & Photographs Division.

. . . one of the last great individualists in Virginia history."[19] Even as governor, he was frequently at odds with the General Assembly, and his programs were regularly vetoed.[20]

These personality flaws contributed to a petty rivalry Wise played out with Brigadier General John Floyd in the Kanawha Valley in southwestern Virginia in 1861. Sauers writes that this incident "foreshadowed Wise's actions in North Carolina," where he had difficulty cooperating with Captain William Lynch, his naval counterpart, in the defense of Roanoke Island.[21]

THE BLOCKADE AND THE NAVY BOARD

On April 19, six days after Fort Sumter, President Lincoln issued a proclamation declaring the blockade of the Southern States from South Carolina to Texas. On April 27, the blockade was extended to Virginia and North Carolina. The purpose of the blockade was to isolate the Confederacy from European trade. The terms of the proclamation were:

> Now therefore I, Abraham Lincoln, President of the United States . . . have further deemed it advisable to set on foot a blockade of the ports within the States aforesaid, in pursuance of the laws of the United States and of the Law of Nations in such case provided. For this purpose a competent force will be posted so as to prevent entrance and exit of vessels from the ports aforesaid. If, therefore, with a view to violate such blockade, a vessel shall approach or shall attempt to leave any of the said ports, she will be duly warned by the commander of one of the blockading vessels, who will endorse on her register the fact and date of such warning, and if the same vessel shall again attempt to enter or leave the blockaded port, she will be captured, and sent to the nearest convenient port for such proceedings against her, and her cargo as prize, as may be deemed advisable.

Declaring a blockade and making it effective, however, were two different things. With 189 harbor and river openings along the 3,549 miles of Confederate shoreline between the Potomac and the Rio Grande, clearly some focus was needed. In fact, much of the South's seacoast had water too shallow for all but small craft. More importantly, only ten seaports had rail or water connections with the Confederate interior: Norfolk, Virginia; New Bern and Wilmington, North Carolina; Charleston, South Carolina; Savannah, Georgia; Fernandina, Jacksonville, and Pensacola, Florida; Mobile, Alabama; and New Orleans, Louisiana.[1] These locations would become the focus of the Federal effort.

Responsibility for the Federal blockade strategy rested with the Navy Board (also called the Blockade Board, the Strategy Board, and the Committee on Conference) that Secretary of the Navy Gideon Welles created in June 1861, to study the conduct of the blockade and to devise ways of improving its efficiency. The Board had four members. Captain Samuel Du Pont, a professional naval officer and member of the famous Delaware manufacturing family, was its head. Professor A. D. Bache, the second member, was superintendent of the Coast Survey and brought to the Board specialized knowledge of the Confederate coast. The third member, Major John Barnard, was an Army engineer who contributed engineering and fortification expertise and provided some liaison between the Army and the Board. Commander Charles Davis was the fourth member and served as the Board's secretary.[2]

Du Pont's biographer Kevin Weddle notes that the Navy Board was a "largely successful attempt by the United States Navy to produce a military (naval) strategy that was fully coordinated with the national strategy and government policies."[3] The Board fulfilled the functions of modern-day campaign plans, which were designed to arrange military operations within a given time and space, to accomplish strategic and operational goals.[4] As Weddle explains, "the board created a roadmap for the Union navy to conduct a major portion of its early strategic responsibilities and stood as the role model for later naval boards and commissions."[5]

Du Pont was an excellent choice as the Board's president, because he was one of the few officers in the Federal Navy who had previous experience with blockading during the Mexican War.[6] An early part of the United States' strategy then had been to blockade ports on

Mexico's Gulf and Pacific coasts to prevent arms and ammunition from entering the country from Europe.[7] Accordingly, in July and August 1846, John Drake Sloat and Robert Stockton, successive Commanders of the Pacific Squadron, established control of the Pacific coast from San Francisco to San Diego. On August 19, Stockton ordered Joseph Hull to blockade Mazatlan and Du Pont to blockade San Blas, about 125 miles south of Mazatlan. Stockton's aim was to seize Acapulco, about 500 miles south of Mazatlan, and use it in support of a joint Army-Navy expedition into Mexico. Thus began Du Pont's experience with blockading, an experience he would repeat on a much larger scale in the Civil War.

The First Blockade of Mexico. On September 2, Du Pont, commanding the *Cyane,* captured two Mexican vessels in the harbor of San Blas. He then sailed north to the pearl-fishing town of La Paz, where he seized nine small boats and secured a promise of neutrality from the governor of Baja California. Moving north some 150 miles to Loreto, Du Pont seized two schooners on October 1, and, on October 7, he shelled Guaymas and burned a brig there. On November 13, Du Pont followed Hull to San Francisco to replenish his dwindling supplies.[8] Because of logistical considerations, the blockade had to be lifted.

The first blockade of Mexico's west coast had lasted only about four weeks. Its ineffectiveness taught Du Pont two key lessons: a blockading force must have enough ships to adequately cover all ports, and blockading ships had to be sustained with supplies and maintenance facilities to enable them to remain on station for extended periods. Weddle notes, "These experiences would serve [Du Pont] well during the Civil War."[9] But first, the Navy would try again off California.

Another Failure. Orders for a second blockade were issued on December 24. Again, it would be an ineffective effort. As other ships left the blockade to restock supplies at San Francisco, Du Pont was left by himself. To provide the friendly inhabitants of La Paz and San Jose del Cabo with some semblance of protection, Du Pont resorted to sailing the *Cyane* back and forth between San Jose and Mazatlan. This opened Mazatlan to commerce, breaking the blockade. Eventually, Du Pont sailed to Hawaii for more supplies.[10]

These experiences showed Du Pont firsthand the practical difficulties of a blockade. Such an undertaking is very resource-intensive in terms of both ships and supplies. To maintain the blockade, ships cannot abandon their positions to get supplies. Either the resupply points must be close enough to facilitate the blockade or additional ships must come in to replace the departing ones. Again, Du Pont would carry these lessons into the Civil War. Mexico had given Du Pont "a foretaste, on a most limited scale, of the duty which he was later to undertake on a grand scale off the south Atlantic coast of the Confederate states."[11] Indeed, two days before Du Pont arrived in Washington to assume his duties on the Board, he recalled his previous blockading experience in a letter to a friend: "During the Mexican War I had two hard years' work at it, with endless correspondence with naval and diplomatic functionaries, for I established the first blockade on the western coast."[12]

In spite of these personal credentials, Du Pont ran the Board without stifling creative thought. He and his colleagues issued six primary and four supplemental reports on the status of the Confederate coast and how best to influence it. Their findings formed the basis for future naval and amphibious operations. In the process, Du Pont was able to apply what he had learned in Mexico: blockades were long, drawn-out affairs that were difficult to manage, coordinate, and maintain.[13]

To avoid having to lift the blockade in order to conduct resupply operations as he had experienced in Mexico, Du Pont knew he would need some strategically located land bases. At first the Federals had only Hampton Roads, Virginia, and Key West, Florida, available to them. These widely separated bases made it almost impossible to maintain an effective blockade. Indeed, in the early days of the war, "some ships spent nearly as much time going to and from these bases for supply and repair as they did on blockade duty."[14] This situation would be exacerbated in foul weather when blockading ships would need ports of refuge along the stormy Atlantic. Clearly, the Navy would need additional bases for the blockading squadron to both shut down Confederate blockade running and to resupply the Federal ships.

Shelby Foote writes, "Out of this double necessity the blockade gained a new dimension, one in which the army would have a share. Not only could harbor entrances be patrolled; the harbors themselves might be seized, thus reducing the number of points to be guarded and at the same time freeing ships for duty elsewhere."[15] Thus was born a strategy that would result in a series of Army-Navy operations directed against critical locations along the Southern coast.

The Board's Reports. Secretary Welles's initial guidance to the Board was expansive. He instructed Du Pont:

> The Navy Department is desirous to condense all the information in the archives of the Government which may be considered useful to the Blockading Squadrons; and the Board are therefore requested to prepare such matters as in their judgment may seem necessary: first, extending from the Chesapeake to Key West; second, from Key West to the extreme Southern point of Texas. It is imperative that two or more points should be taken possession of on the Atlantic Coast, and Fernandina and Port Royal are spoken of. Perhaps others will occur to the board. All facts bearing on such a contemplated movement are desired at an early moment. Subsequently, similar points in the Gulf of Mexico will be considered. It is also very desirable that the practicability of closing all the Southern ports by mechanical means should be fully discussed and reported upon.[16]

Welles was clear that he expected the Board to tackle two of the blockade's key challenges: a lack of local information and a lack of logistical bases. Welles had also ordered the Board to plan for the seizure of additional bases, first in the Atlantic and then in the Gulf.[17] It was a far-reaching task, but Welles's guidance was clear and helpful.

The Board held its first meeting on June 27, 1861. Du Pont's goals were to determine how the blockading squadrons should best execute their missions. He was shocked that squadron commanders seemed content to merely cruise aimlessly up and down the coast with a few vessels. Du Pont knew a system was required, what Bache called a "manual" for blockading. Du Pont also recognized the need for joint expeditions to seize logistical bases both to support the blockade, and to be used as springboards to launch ground operations into the Confederate interior. The Board discussed the need for ground troops to seize and hold such bases. Du Pont had clearly defined that the Board's job was to provide the necessary operational and strategic direction for the blockade and its supporting joint operations.[18]

The Board presented its first two reports to Welles on July 5 and 13. The first report confirmed the need for additional bases stating, "It seems to be indispensable that there should exist a convenient coal depot on the southern extremity of the line of Atlantic blockades... [and it] might be used not only as a coal depot for coal, but as a depot for provisions and common stores, as a harbor of refuge, and as a general rendezvous, or headquarters, for that part of the coast."[19] Fernandina, Florida, was the Board's recommendation to meet this requirement.

The second report focused on the need for a second base farther north. First, the Board recommended closing the inlets between the Cape Hatteras barrier islands. Then it examined three potential bases along the South Carolinia coast: Port Royal Sound, Bull's Bay, and Saint Helena Sound. Seizing a base deep in the South would be risky and would require a formidable ground and naval force, but the strategic payoff would be great. Although the Board recognized the superiority of the harbor at Port Royal Sound, it also assumed the Confederates would mount a difficult defense there. Thus, the Board recommended seizing Bull's Bay.

The Board issued two more reports on July 19 and 29. Perhaps the most important of the many recommendations in these reports was that responsibility for the Atlantic blockade be divided between two squadrons. This arrangement would streamline command and control, and reduce the burdens placed on the commanders. Later, the Board would recommend the Gulf Blockading Squadron also be divided into two separate commands.[20]

On August 6, the Board issued its first report on the Gulf. The geographic complexities of the Mississippi River Delta made this region particularly difficult to blockade, and the Board was quick to point out that "the blockade of the river . . . does not close the port [of New Orleans]." Because the capture of New Orleans would require such a large naval and military force, the Board recommended that action against New Orleans be delayed until "we are prepared to ascend the river with vessels of war sufficiently protected to contend with the forts." In the meantime, the Board recommended seizing Ship Island, a barrier island midway between New Orleans and Mobile. Ship Island would serve as the headquarters and logistical base for the Gulf Blockading Squadron, and would be useful as a jumping-off point for any future attack against either New Orleans or Mobile.[21]

Du Pont's stellar work on the Board catapulted him ahead of several more senior officers when it came time to select a commander for the important Port Royal Expedition. It also caused him to divide his attention between the Board and his sea command, and it was not until September 3 that the Board completed its second Gulf report. This report summarized the geography and topography of the rest of the Gulf, including the Florida Keys and the entire coast of Texas. Finally on September 19, the Board made its last report, which supplemented the first Gulf report by carefully outlining the defenses of Ship Island. Du Pont was now fully engaged in his Port Royal Expedition duties, but he asked the Department of the Navy to allow the Board to make one more report—the manual for the conduct of blockading. Secretary Welles failed to act on Du Pont's request, and this report was never finished.[22]

The Navy Board was a resounding success. Indeed, the Department of the Navy accepted most of the Board's recommendations. Welles split the Atlantic Blockading Squadron into the North and South Atlantic Blockading Squadrons, commanded respectively by Flag Officer Louis Goldsborough and Du Pont. Likewise, the Gulf Blockading Squadron was divided into the East and West Gulf Blockading Squadrons under Flag Officers William McKean and David Farragut respectively. The Lincoln Administration and the War and Navy Departments also took swift action on the Board's recommendations for joint operations, seizing Hatteras Inlet in August 1861, Port Royal and Ship Island in November, and Fernandina in March 1862. Welles also used the model of the Navy Board to establish other boards and commissions, such as the Board of Ironclad Vessels and the Board of Naval Examiners. Finally, the Board succeeded in its mission of condensing the wealth of information on the Confederate coast into a useable form that was readily available to the squadron commanders. In praising the work of the Navy Board, Weddle argues that, "the Civil War saw no comparable organization, staff, or agency that systematically formulated naval or military strategy."[23] Du Pont and his colleagues had done their work well.

The Atlantic Campaign

Hatteras Inlet

Port Royal Sound

Fernandina and Jacksonville

Fort Pulaski

HATTERAS INLET:
THE PATTERN IS FORMED

The first of the sites identified by the Navy Board's second report had been Hatteras Inlet, off the North Carolina coast. There, a string of barrier islands and reefs made the wide shallows of Pamlico and Albemarle Sounds an ideal anchorage for raiders and blockade runners, and Confederate privateers and ships of the North Carolina Navy had been attacking Northern shipping from these protected harbors. Furthermore, the sea outside of the barrier islands was frequently too rough for a blockading fleet to be kept on station. Secretary of the Navy Welles wrote blockade commander Flag Officer Silas Stringham, "There is no portion of the coast which you are guarding which requires greater vigilance or where well directed efforts would be more highly appreciated by the Government and country than North Carolina, which has been the resort of pirates and their abettors."[1] The only way to put this Confederate haven out of business was to seize it. In so doing, Hatteras Inlet would become the first joint Army-Navy operation of the Civil War.[2]

Hatteras Inlet was a break in the barrier islands that protected Pamlico Sound. To defend it, the Confederates had begun work on two forts, Fort Hatteras and Fort Clark. These were hastily built earthworks equipped with cannon from the Gosport Navy Yard in Norfolk, but otherwise still under construction. Of the two, Fort Hatteras was by far the larger, sitting on an elevation that allowed it to both command the harbor and protect the smaller Fort Clark. The Federals had fairly good descriptions of the forts from the captains of ships that had been captured by the Confederates, held at Hatteras Island, and then released. These men reported that the Confederate forts were not well armed and could be taken with little or no loss of life.[3]

To deal with Hatteras Inlet, the Federals mounted an operation Shelby Foote describes as "modest in scope but effective in execution."[4] It would be a predominantly naval affair with Stringham commanding a squadron of 7 warships with 158 guns, 4 transports, and a steam tug. In the transports were nearly 900 troops under the command of Major General Benjamin Butler. Butler had recently been removed from command at Fort Monroe, Virginia, after his poor performance at Big Bethel. Tactical command would belong to Colonel Rush Hawkins of the 9th New York Volunteers, a Zouave regiment.[5]

Naval Dominance. The Federal force left Hampton Roads on August 26, 1861, and arrived off Hatteras on the 28th. That morning, the Federals landed some 300 men and two 12-pounder guns well north of the Confederate forts. It was a difficult landing through rough water, and some boats capsized. The troops landed without fresh water or provisions, and their ammunition was ruined in the surf. As the seas became even rougher, they were cut off from communications with the fleet. Nonetheless, they advanced toward Fort Clark, but their services would be of little need.[6]

In fact, Hatteras Inlet would be a Navy dominated affair. Civil War historian Mark Boatner writes that the Federal success "resulted almost entirely from the effectiveness of Stringham's bombardment,"[7] and Foote agrees that, "the army had almost nothing to do."[8] Indeed, this appears to have been the plan from the start. Butler's troops received neither special training nor any plan for an orderly landing. They were simply loaded on their transports and sent forward. Even the planning decision to provide the men with only ten days' rations suggests anticipation of a limited Army role.[9] Later, Federal operations would involve simultaneous Army and Navy action, but at Hatteras Inlet the Army was largely just along for the ride.

In the meantime, Stringham first directed his attention at Fort Clark. With superior ordnance, the Federal ships remained outside the range of the Confederate guns and rained nine and eleven-inch shells upon the fort at a rate of seven per minute. Before long, the Confederates abandoned Fort Clark and withdrew to Fort Hatteras.

Federal troops then took possession of the vacated fort.[10]

At 8:30 the next morning, Stringham began his bombardment of Fort Hatteras. The ships ran past the fort, firing as they went, and then came around again on a different course, making it hard for the Confederate gunners to get their range. Colonel Hawkins observed that, "Instead of anchoring his ships, [Stringham] kept them moving during the whole range of the enemy's works, delivered his fire, generally with surprising accuracy, while the gunners in the forts were compelled to make an on-the-wing shot with pieces of heavy ordnance, and in most instances their shot fell short."[11] Steam power, by freeing ships from the restrictions of wind and current, had made this technique of firing while moving possible, and it represented an important innovation in Federal naval warfare. It would be a technique later exploited with even greater effect by Du Pont at Port Royal Sound.[12]

Military historian Russell Weigley considers Stringham's success to have had an even more far-reaching and revolutionary impact. It had long been held as a military dictum that coastal forts were superior to ships; so much so that one gun on land was considered to be equal to four on water. The entire coastal defense of the United States had been planned according to this precept. Hatteras Inlet suggested that advances in ships and their weaponry may have now negated the fort's inherent advantage. Weigley writes, "This was a bad discovery for the Confederacy, which had inherited the traditional United States system of coastal defense."[13]

The result at Fort Hatteras was a decidedly unequal contest that Confederate apologist E. A. Pollard describes as follows: "Assaulted by nearly a hundred heavy cannon, the fort was unable to reach effectively with its feeble thirty-two pounders, the ships which lay at a safe distance pouring from their ten-inch rifle pivot guns a storm of shells upon the bomb-proofs and batteries."[14] These were exactly the odds the Federals had sought. Pollard credits the Federal "prodigality of preparation and care to ensure victory,"[15] and Philip Van Doren Stern writes that, "Every preparation had been made for [the Federal Navy] to overwhelm the two not very strong forts."[16] This attack was the first such venture attempted by the Federals, and they wanted to be sure it succeeded.

Fort Hatteras never stood a chance, and at about noon the Confederates surrendered. The Federals captured 670 prisoners and 35 cannon. The only Federal casualty was a member of the landing party wounded at Fort Clark by friendly naval gunfire. Most of the Federal troops and three of the ships were left to hold the forts, and the remainder returned to Fort Monroe with the Confederate prisoners.[17]

Opportunity Lost? The victory at Hatteras Inlet helped somewhat assuage the Federal disaster at First Manassas five weeks earlier. It also gave the Federals a foothold along the Southern coast, provided new support for blockading squadrons, and meant the Federals now possessed the main passage to the North Carolina sounds.[18] But with Hatteras Inlet now in their possession, the next question for the Federals was what to do with it. The original plan was merely to block the passage using sunken hulks, but Butler and Stringham convinced Secretary Welles to keep the channel open for future operations. Some argued that Hatteras Inlet should be used as a base from which to invade North Carolina, but President Lincoln opposed this idea, insisting that the main business of naval operations on the Atlantic coast was to blockade ports and establish coaling and supply stations for the Federal fleet. Invasion was to be left to the inland armies.[19]

Bruce Catton laments this decision, assessing that, "The government apparently had not done its advance planning very carefully, and for the time being neither the army nor the navy was prepared to do anything but hold the captured position."[20] Catton sees much greater possibilities. He argues that successes such as Hatteras Inlet gave the Federal force:

> an excellent chance to move inland from places it had seized along the coastline and seriously disrupt the operations of the entire Confederacy. They could have cut off, without too much difficulty, the railroads leading from the Deep South to Richmond, and could probably have occupied Georgia two or three years ahead of schedule. They could have left the Confederate Government in Richmond profoundly handicapped and probably, or at least

possibly, could have shortened the war substantially by making an effort to cut the main lines of communication and production in the deeper South. But the Union forces did not do these things. They attempted to seize Richmond head-on, ran into the Confederacy's best generals and best army, and paid

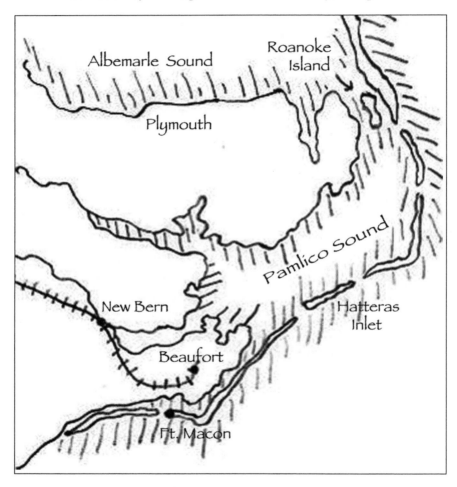

The capture of Hatteras Inlet gave the Federals access to a strategic position that was ripe for exploitation into the Confederate interior. The Federals failed to avail themselves of this possibility.

a terrible price in blood and suffering for the attempt thus made.[21]

In spite of this complaint, Catton admits that Hatteras Inlet "did set a pattern, and important results would grow from it."[22] These included additional Army-Navy operations against the Confederate coast at places such as Port Royal, Roanoke Island, and New Bern. Indeed, the Roanoke Island operation would actually attack through Hatteras Inlet. Furthermore, Hatteras Inlet fueled the imagination of Army of the Potomac commander Major General George McClellan, who would query Colonel Hawkins about the Army-Navy concept's applicability for what would eventually become McClellan's Virginia Peninsula Campaign.[23] Indeed, Hatteras Inlet had set a pattern for much bigger things to come. In the words of Bern Anderson, it marked the very "birth of joint action."[24]

PORT ROYAL SOUND: THE TRIUMPH OF THE PLAN

After Hatteras Inlet, the Federals seized Ship Island, Mississippi, without any significant Confederate resistance. With these two successes along the Confederate coast, the Federals were now prepared to try something a little more ambitious. The target for the third and final Army-Navy operation of 1861 would be Port Royal Sound, South Carolina, another location highlighted in the Navy Board's second report. Neither the Hatteras Island nor the Ship Island operation had given the Federal fleet the large, deep-water harbor it needed in order to maintain a year-round blockade of key ports such as Wilmington, Charleston, and Savannah. Port Royal represented such a prize. It was the finest natural harbor on the Southern coast and could accommodate any navy in the world. Furthermore, from Port Royal the Federals could also gain access to a series of inland waterways from which to blockade the coast from just below Charleston to the Saint Johns River in Florida, without having to risk the uncertainties of the Atlantic. In effect, the Federals could block the neck of the bottle out of which the Confederate vessels had to emerge.[1]

The Stakes Increase. The Navy Board knew that Port Royal would be its biggest effort to date, and that success would require a strong force and the element of surprise. Thus, the Navy Board would take no chances. The Board president himself, Captain Samuel Du Pont, would head the expedition and the Board secretary, Commander Charles Davis, would serve as Du Pont's chief of staff. The fleet would consist of 74 vessels, including transports for a land force of 12,000 men. The warships given to Du Pont were the Navy's best, and his fleet, dubbed "The Great Southern Expedition" in the Northern press, represented the largest assembled to date under the American flag. As an added precaution designed to preserve secrecy, the formal orders were purposely vague about the target.[2]

Army of the Potomac commander Major General George McClellan objected to Du Pont's request for troops, considering the Port Royal expedition to be a sideshow and a distraction from his efforts to build his own army. President Lincoln, however, overruled McClellan and ordered that the troops be given to Du Pont. Brigadier General Thomas Sherman ("the other General Sherman") was appointed as their commander. Orders were very specific about the Army-Navy relationship. Both Du Pont and Sherman were told that Army officers could not command Navy forces, and that Navy officers could not command Army forces except when embarked in naval vessels. Instead of a formal command relationship, both Du Pont and Sherman were encouraged to cooperate with each other. Furthermore, Lincoln ordered that the operation must begin in October.[3]

Ominous Beginnings. On October 20, Du Pont and his fleet put out of Hampton Roads, Virginia, heading south, but the hope for surprise did not last for long. Northern newspapers had given the Confederates notice by speculating as to the fleet's objective. As soon as Du Pont left Hampton Roads, the Confederate government alerted its coastal defenses that the force had sailed, and on November 1, Confederate Secretary of War Judah Benjamin received intimation that the Federals were bound for Port Royal. In fact, on November 4, the Port Royal defenders were telegraphed that, "The enemy's expedition is intended for Port Royal." For some time, President Davis had felt that the Southern coast needed additional defenses, and this new development was just the impetus he needed to act. On November 6, he reorganized the coasts of South Carolina, Georgia, and north Florida into a single department and named General Robert E. Lee as its commander.[4]

In addition to this loss of surprise, the Federals were dealt a cruel blow by the weather. On November 1, Du Pont ran into a gale off Hatteras that caused two of his ships to go down, and a third to have to throw its guns overboard to keep from foundering. By November 2, the fleet was so scattered that Du Pont could see only one other sail from the deck of his flagship, the *Wabash*. Equipment losses were heavy, including ammunition and many of the surfboats that Du Pont and Sherman had counted on to land the troops. Nonetheless, the fleet continued southward. Two days later the weather was clear, and Du Pont dropped anchor off the bar at Port Royal. By then, 25 of his ships had rejoined him, and reinforcements from the squadron at Charleston and stragglers from the original party continued to filter in. Then, Du Pont spent two more days replacing the Confederate-destroyed channel markers—a process greatly facilitated by Commander Davis's experience with the Coast Survey—crossing the bar, completing his attack plan, and holding a final conference with his captains to outline his order of battle. At 8:00 a.m. on November 7, the same day Lee arrived at his new post in Charleston, Du Pont attacked.[5]

The Shifting Balance. Du Pont had studied closely Flag Officer Silas Stringham's battle at Hatteras Inlet, as well as the battles at Odessa and Sevastopol during the Crimean War. In the Crimea, the ships had failed against the forts, but they had come close enough that, when considered along with Stringham's victory, Du Pont felt that the old dictum of the superiority of the fort over the ship might be broken. The key elements working to change the historic balance were the shell gun and the steam engine. Port Royal Sound was big enough to allow maneuver, and Du Pont planned to use his steam engines to keep his ships moving in an elliptical pattern that would keep the two Confederate forts, Fort Walker and Fort Beauregard, under continuous fire. However, unlike Stringham, Du Pont would not be able to outrange the Confederate batteries.[6]

Defending the harbor and the approaches to Beaufort, the two Confederate sand forts were less than three miles apart, but their artillery was of such small caliber and inferior quality that ships could move between them and still stay out of range of both. Fort Walker was located to the south on Hilton Head and had 16 guns mounted, most of which were 32 pounders. The cannon were mounted on the parapet, a measure that increased their range but likewise increased their vulnerability. Fort Beauregard was located to the north at Bay Point and had eight small guns. Inside the forts and in the immediate vicinity were about 3,000 men commanded by Brigadier General Thomas Dayton. The defenders had a blissfully uninformed confidence about them.[7]

Fort Beauregard and its eight small guns proved no match for the superior Federal firepower and maneuver at Port Royal Sound.
Photograph courtesy of the Library of Congress, Prints & Photographs Division.

In addition to these land defenses, Du Pont would have to contend with a Confederate flotilla of three tugs, each mounting one gun, and a converted river steamer. Although this fleet was of dubious quality, it was commanded by Commodore Josiah Tattnall, who Du Pont knew from "the old Navy" as a bold and capable officer. In fact, Tattnall had been Du Pont's nominal squadron commander during his voyage to China in 1857–1858 aboard the *Minnesota*. The forts, however, were Du Pont's principal concern.[8]

Originally, Du Pont had planned a joint operation to reduce the forts, but the bad weather had changed things. The three brigades under Sherman were still somewhat seasick from the rough weather, and more importantly, nearly all their landing craft had been lost in the storm. Thus, with the help of Davis, Du Pont developed a modified plan that would make Port Royal, like Hatteras Inlet before it, a Navy show. In the words of Shelby Foote, Port Royal "was to be a job for the naval force alone... The most [Du Pont] would ask of the army was that it stand by to help pick up the pieces."[9] The key to success in a Navy-only attack would be to keep the fleet moving at all times.[10]

A Brilliant Plan. At 8:00 a.m. on November 7, the attack began. Du Pont had divided his force into a main squadron of nine of his heaviest frigates and sloops, and a flanking squadron of five gunboats. With the *Wabash* in the lead, the Federals entered the sound in parallel columns and began receiving fire from the forts. Du Pont's plan was for the lighter squadron to operate on the right and pass midway between the two forts, both drawing and returning fire. At a point two and a half miles beyond Fort Beauregard, the flanking squadron would turn in a circuit to the left and close in on Fort Walker, meeting it on its weakest side and simultaneously enfilading its two water faces. Once past Fort Walker, the squadrons were to swing in the

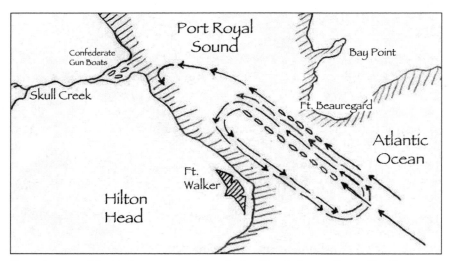

By using an elliptical pattern to attack the Confederate forts, Du Pont made maximum use of steam power and superior ordnance.

direction of Fort Beauregard and repeat the elliptical pattern as often as necessary.[11] Du Pont instructed his ships to be ready to peel off and engage targets of opportunity, including the Confederate ships, as they presented themselves.

As this maneuver was unfolding, Tattnall brought his Confederate flotilla down the sound and engaged the *Wabash*. Du Pont's gunboats went after him, and Tattnall beat a hasty retreat three miles northwest of Fort Walker and took refuge at the mouth of Skull Creek. Dipping his pennant three times in a jaunty salute to his old messmate, Tattnall was bottled up by the Federal gunboats and out of the fight for good.

In the meantime, the main Federal squadron was executing its elliptical pattern, advancing about two miles beyond the entrance of the sound on the Fort Beauregard side and then turning left and returning on the Fort Walker side. Such a course gave the ships the advantage of opening fire on the inland and weaker side of the fort, and of enfilading the main battery before coming abreast of it. With each pass, the squadron widened its course so as to bring its guns closer to the target. These constant changes in speed, range, and deflection made the Federal fleet extremely hard for the Confederate gunners to engage.[12] One Confederate lamented, "No sooner did we obtain [the enemy's] range when it would be changed, and time after time rechanged, while the deep water permitted him to choose his position and fire shot after shot and shell after shell, with the precision of target practice."[13] With a bit of understatement, E.A. Pollard admits that "This manoeuvre doubtless disturbed the aim of the artillerists in the forts."[14]

To make matters worse, the Confederate gunners had more problems than just the moving targets. They were low on ammunition, and some of what they had was the wrong size for their guns. Additionally, they had inferior powder and defective fuses.[15] General Dayton confessed to being unable to provide, "Not a ripple upon the broad expanse of water to disturb the accuracy of fire from the broad decks of that magnificent armada . . . advancing in battle array to vomit forth its iron hail with all the spiteful energy of long-suppressed rage and conscious strength."[16] The Confederates were clearly at a disadvantage.

But what had made this so, even more than the disparity in arms, was Du Pont's brilliant scheme of maneuver. Fort Walker had been built to defend against an attacking force moving straight in from the sea. Thus, its northern flank was its weakest, a fact that Du Pont had learned from reconnaissance. Du Pont's plan took full advantage of this condition.

Confederate resistance did not last long. As Du Pont began his third ellipse, he received word that Fort Walker had been abandoned. At 2:20 p.m., a naval landing party raised the United States flag over the wreckage, and by nightfall Army troops had landed and occupied the fort. Fort Beauregard, which was merely an adjunct to Fort Walker, lowered its flag at sunset, and early the next morning Federal troops crossed the water and occupied it as well. In the words of Foote, for the Confederates "the fight had been lost from the moment Du Pont had conceived his plan of attack."[17]

The Federals lost 8 killed and 23 wounded. The Confederates lost about 100 total. The victory gave the Federals an excellent harbor that became the home base for the South Atlantic Blockading Squadron for the remainder of the war. Moreover, it struck a blow in both the sentimental heartland of secession and in an important cotton-producing region. Within three days, the Federals moved up the rivers and inlets, and occupied the towns of Beaufort and Port Royal. The Federals were now in a position to threaten either Charleston or Savannah, and the local population was thrown into a panic. Confederate confidence was shattered. By December, planters along the Georgia-South Carolina coast were burning cotton to prevent its capture.[18]

Confederate Response. The new department commander, General Robert E. Lee, had arrived too late to do anything about Port Royal, but he accepted its lessons and made adjustments as he could. As Emory Thomas notes, "Nature seemed to conspire against Confederate capacity to defend this coastal region. Barrier islands lay miles from the mainland separated from the major landmass by salt marshes, sounds, and meandering tidal streams, and separated from each other by wide channels. The Federal navy enjoyed dominance in these waterways as in the near-shore waters and ocean beyond. To defend this coast, the Confederates would have to mount batteries of guns everywhere and the new nation (or any nation for that matter) did not have enough guns with enough range to cover every channel, sound, and creek."[19] Thus, Lee concluded that his enemy "can be thrown with great celerity against any point, and far outnumbers any force we can bring against it in the field." This fact confirmed for Lee that the Confederacy could not use a merely defensive strategy. It simply was not strong enough to defend everywhere.[20] Du Pont's biographer Kevin Weddle asserts that "in the space of less than two weeks, the entire Confederate strategy for the defense of its coasts changed because of Du Pont's success at Port Royal."[21]

Such logic would later influence Lee, as commander of the Army of Northern Virginia, to adopt his strategy of the offensive-defensive. In the current emergency, it led him to initiate three measures: strengthening the defenses at Fort Pulaski, Georgia, and Charleston in order to withstand a more serious bombardment than they had been built to sustain, obstruct the waterways that might be used by Federal ships, and to assemble the scattered Confederate forces at the most probable points of Federal attack.[22] Later, Lee would put into effect a longer-range plan by ordering the withdrawal inland of garrisons and guns on outlying positions. This move was part of Lee's plan to hold only key locations such as Charleston. Finally, at Savannah and along the southern part of the Charleston and Savannah Railroad, Lee built a strong defensive line upon which he could concentrate his forces. This would force the Federal Army to fight without the assistance of its powerful Navy.[23] In spite of these efforts, the advantage clearly lay with the Federals.

An Advantage Not Exploited. Sherman briefly considered sending his troops inland and turning "left or right to one of the cities."[24] Doing so would have presented the Confederates with the prospect of a three-front war, but, in spite of his reputation for driving his men hard, Sherman was deterred by "the winding and shallow creeks" and the inexperience of his troops. He did not press his advantage and therefore missed an opportunity. In fact, from the Army point of view, the battle of Port Royal Sound was largely inconsequential in that the Federals never used the port to stage a major offensive. Bern Anderson writes that, "the war might have taken an entirely different course if the Army had chosen to exploit its opportunities in that region."[25] Instead, Theodore Rosengarten concludes that, "What was lost, therefore, in November, 1861, was not the strategic position both sides imagined it to be, but simply the homeland of the old Sea Island families."[26]

Port Royal Experiment. This demographic change, however, was in itself very important. If the Federal military did not fully exploit the Port Royal victory, hosts of social activists did. With the sudden departure of their masters, many blacks were faced with a future for which they had no way of being prepared. Soon many Northerners with a strong moral commitment to abolition descended on the Sea Islands to help the former slaves transition to freedom.

In what became known as the Port Royal Experiment, the region became the cradle of South Carolina's first black schools and free labor initiatives. It also served as a fertile recruiting ground for black soldiers. Although the Emancipation Proclamation was yet to come, the Port Royal Experiment helped place the war in a broader moral conscious. W. Scott Poole writes, "Secession may have begun on the South Carolina coast but it is as true that in this same region the war for the Union became the war against slavery."[27]

The Federal victory at Port Royal allowed newly free slaves like these gain previously unknown independence and opportunity.
Photograph courtesy of the Library of Congress.

FERNANDINA AND JACKSONVILLE:
THE ARMY IS OVEREXTENDED

After his success at Port Royal, Du Pont began reconnoitering the adjacent coastline. As he spread out from Port Royal, he turned his attention to Fernandina, Florida, which lay 25 miles north of the Saint Johns River near the Georgia border. Indeed, Secretary Welles's order convening the Navy Board had specified, "It is imperative that two or more points should be taken possession of on the Atlantic Coast, and Fernandina and Port Royal are spoken of."[1] The first report of the Navy Board, issued in July 1861, stated, "It seems to be indispensable that there should exist a convenient coal depot on the southern extremity of the line of Atlantic blockades... [and it] might be used not only as a coal depot for coal, but as a depot for provisions and common stores, as a harbor of refuge, and as a general rendezvous, or headquarters, for that part of the coast."[2] The Board determined that the best location for this southern base was Fernandina.

The main ship channel over the St. Mary's Bar into Fernandina could accommodate vessels with a 20-foot draught at high tide, deep enough for all but the largest of the Federal Navy's ships. If seized rapidly, the docks and buildings of the unfinished Florida Railroad would provide ready facilities to store coal and repair ships. Fernandina also boasted a healthy climate, with ample wood and fresh water. The area had only a small population, and its isolation by surrounding marshes would simplify its defense once it was captured. The Board felt a force of 3,000 men could take and hold it.[3]

Scant Defenses. The Confederate government never really gave much serious attention to the defense of Florida. The state was sparsely populated and its three coastal towns, Fernandina, Jacksonville, and

St. Augustine, were all relatively unimportant. After the losses of Forts Henry and Donelson in February 1862, Florida received even less priority, and its defensive lines were drawn even tighter. Pursuant to his post-Port Royal strategy, on February 19, General Lee ordered all coastal forces to secure their artillery and to withdraw. The local Confederates took steps to comply, but a lack of transportation forced them to leave half their ordnance behind. Initially, the Federals did not know about the Confederate withdrawal, but Fernandina was now virtually unprotected.[4]

What little defenses Fernandina had were built around Fort Clinch, which contained six batteries that commanded the main ship channel. Among those given pause by these defenses was Admiral David Porter, who after the war claimed the batteries were so well protected by sand hills and vegetation that "striking them from the sea would [be] almost a matter of chance."[5] In addition, there was a battery of four guns on the south end of Cumberland Island aimed across the channel inside the bar. Still further back was a concealed battery in the town itself, which controlled the anchorage. All these defenses were facilitated by a very crooked channel and shallow bar. Based on these advantages, Lee had once considered Fernandina easily defendable from naval attack. Porter was not quite as impressed, but concluded the defenses would be able to make "it warm work for the Navy."[6]

On March 2, 1862, Du Pont dispatched 17 armed vessels under the command of Commodore S. W. Godon to lay anchor off St. Andrew's Island, 20 miles north of the entrance to Fernandina. In addition, six transports carried an Army brigade commanded by Brigadier General Horatio Wright. The plan was to attack by moving through the sound behind Cumberland Island to avoid any Confederate batteries until the ships reached the flank and rear of Fort Clinch.[7] While the vessels examined the channel and waited for the tide, they learned from residents of Cumberland Island that the Confederates had hastily abandoned Fernandina and were currently in the process of evacuating what war materials they could salvage. Porter concluded, "Such was the moral effect of the Port Royal victory, that there seemed to be a stampede along the coast as soon as our naval vessels made appearance."[8] Du Pont agreed, observing that the string of successful Federal operations had the Confederates "flying about like moths around a lamp."[9]

Armed with this new intelligence, Du Pont detached the light gunboats and draught steamers under Commander Percival Drayton and ordered them to push ahead to try to interrupt the Confederate retreat. On entering Fernandina Harbor, Drayton sent an officer to secure Fort Clinch. The Confederates fired a few parting musket shots and then escaped on a train. Drayton gave chase along the river and fired several shells at the fleeing locomotive, but the train escaped across the railroad bridge at Kingsley's Creek. Commander C. R. P. Rodgers pushed ahead with the steam launches, captured the Confederate *Darlington* laden with military supplies, and seized the drawbridge of the railroad. Rodgers later ascended the St. Mary's River, drove away the Confederate pickets, and captured the town of St. Mary's. In all, the Federals captured thirteen guns, including an 80-pounder and a 120-pounder.[10]

Many Federal naval officers felt the Confederates had shown poor judgment in abandoning their works. Rodgers, for example, believed that the Navy might have taken heavy casualties crossing the unmarked bar under fire from Fort Clinch. Dayton agreed, writing, "they ought to have been able to keep out all the fleets of the Union combined, the bar being a very difficult one, and its turns bringing vessels directly under batteries almost end on for miles."[11]

Continued Operations. Such speculation notwithstanding, Brigadier General Wright entered Fernandina Harbor on March 4 and landed his brigade. Leaving the Army in charge of occupying the fortifications at Fernandina, Du Pont continued his operations against the coast. The easy conquest of Fernandina had convinced him to tackle Jacksonville, about 30 miles from the bar up the narrow and twisting Saint Johns River. He dispatched the *Ottawa, Seneca, Pembina, Huron, Isaac Smith,* and *Ellen* for this work. Along the way, the Federals landed troops at Mayport Mills, about three miles upriver, and secured the guns there. Fleeing Confederates burned eight sawmills, over four million board feet of lumber, some ironworks, and a gunboat under construction to avoid their falling into Federal hands. On March 12, the Navy captured Saint Johns Bluff, about five miles above Mayport Mills, and then moved on to Jacksonville. The local authorities there greeted the Federals with a flag of truce.[12]

While this part of his fleet was securing the Saint Johns River, Du Pont also learned that the Confederates had abandoned Brunswick, Georgia, and on March 7 he sent the *Mohican, Pocahontas,* and *Potomska* to secure that location. En route, he found the Confederates had abandoned two strong earthworks on St. Simon's Island, and two even stronger batteries on Jekyll Island. On March 9, the Federals pressed on up the Brunswick River and captured Brunswick, denying the Confederates the terminus of the Brunswick and Florida Railroad, another valuable logistical connection.[13]

On March 11, Du Pont ordered the *Wabash* south to St. Augustine to reconnoiter, and then sent Commander Rodgers ashore in a boat with a flag of truce. Rodgers found a white flag flying over Fort Marion, and the city officials met Rodgers and placed the town under his control. Du Pont's instructions were to guarantee the inhabitants kind treatment if they would accept Federal authority and act in good faith. He even allowed municipal authority to remain in the hands of the citizens.[14] St. Augustine itself was of little importance because it mainly served as a resort for invalids, and its harbor could accommodate only the most shallow draught vessels. It did shelter a couple blockade runners, so its capture made some contribution to the blockade.[15]

Indeed, Du Pont's overall successes greatly facilitated the Federal effort to isolate the Confederacy from the outside world. The geography of the coastline and the fact that the Confederates lacked the resources necessary to defend the inlets allowed Du Pont to maintain a close or inside blockade. Possession of places like Fernandina, St. Augustine, Jacksonville, and Brunswick gave him even greater access to the inland waterways with little fear of the enemy. He now anchored his small and shallow draught vessels directly in the fairways of the inlets. Under these conditions, a lightly armed gunboat usually could control the approaches and effectively close or constrict blockade running. By April, Du Pont had eight major waterways under an inside blockade, and this arrangement virtually stopped any potential trade at these locations.[16] The Confederates could see the futility of trying to hold or recover the exposed harbors and inlets in the area, and they confined future operations to the interior where the Federal Navy could not follow them.[17]

Fort Marion was designed to defend St. Augustine, but the Confederates there offered no resistance to Federal occupation.
Photograph courtesy of the Library of Congress.

Cooperation Unravels. Up to this point, events had unfolded with unanticipated ease and speed for the Federals. Both Du Pont and Sherman made arrangements to secure Fernandina, but beyond that, the command relationship seemed to show signs of stress. Robert Browning believes that the geographical scope of the Army and Navy's operations may have led to the friction. Sherman had no specific orders after the capture of Fernandina and no defined area of command. Du Pont, on the other hand, had much broader guidance with an area stretching as far south as Cape Canaveral and carte blanche to capture anything he could. Thus, when Du Pont pressed on to Jacksonville, he found Sherman "lukewarm," and as Du Pont continued to St. Augustine, Sherman became "disappointed."[18]

As far as St. Augustine was concerned, Du Pont thought, "I could not only take St. Augustine—of course without asking him [Sherman] if I please—but hold it too." Du Pont thus proceeded to garrison St. Augustine with a battalion of marines, much to Sherman's chagrin. Sherman responded by dispatching two companies commanded by a lieutenant colonel in order to outrank Du Pont's marine major. Du Pont then withdrew his marines and sent them back to Washington.

Army-Navy relations were rapidly turning sour.[19]

At the end of March, Major General David Hunter replaced Sherman as commander of the newly created Department of the South. While Du Pont's objective was to capture as much territory as possible, the Army was rapidly beginning to feel overextended. Hunter ordered the withdrawal of troops from Jacksonville, an act that forced the Navy to abandon both the town and the river and withdraw its gunboats to the mouth of the Saint Johns River. This development disappointed not just Du Pont, but also those Jacksonville residents who had "committed themselves to the Union cause." When the Federal garrison departed on April 9, the Confederates immediately reoccupied Jacksonville.[20]

Hunter would make an ill-conceived attack on Jacksonville almost a year later on March 10, 1863, only to then evacuate the town on March 27. Hunter's antics were exasperating to Du Pont, who was under orders to take as many ports as possible. They also caused Du Pont to realize he could not depend on Hunter to be a part of the attack on Charleston, South Carolina, then being considered.[21] Jacksonville would be the site of guerrilla fighting and brown water naval operations until February 7, 1864, when Federal forces occupied it for the fourth and final time.[22] But, as frustrating as Hunter's first abandonment of Jacksonville would be to Du Pont, continued Federal possession of Fernandina offered the promise of facilitating upcoming operations against nearby Fort Pulaski, Georgia.[23]

Brigadier General Thomas Sherman began to lose his characteristic energy as the coastal operations continued. He was eventually replaced by Major General David Hunter. Photograph courtesy of the Library of Congress.

FORT PULASKI: RIFLED ARTILLERY'S FIRST BREACH OF MASONRY

The Federal victory at Port Royal led to a Confederate withdrawal from the entire coastal area south of Charleston stretching down to Savannah, Georgia, one of the South's largest and most important cities. It had a population of about 14,000, and had exported nearly $20 million worth of cotton and lumber before the war.[1] To protect this vibrant commercial center, Fort Pulaski sat on Cockspur Island at the mouth of the Savannah River. It was in a natural defensive position for guarding the seaward approaches to Savannah, some 18 miles inland. As a young engineer officer between 1829 and 1830, Robert E. Lee had worked on the construction of Fort Pulaski, and it was a position in which he had great confidence. It was also a place that he knew would be a target for the Federals.

Confidence in the Thick Walls of Fort Pulaski. Interest in the military aspect of Cockspur Island dates back to 1761, when the British built Fort George there. After the War of 1812, General Simon Bernard began devising a plan for a system of 26 forts from which to defend the American coastline. Fort Pulaski, named after American Revolutionary War hero Count Casimir Pulaski, who was mortally wounded in the siege of Savannah in 1779, was one such fort. In 1829, Lieutenant Robert E. Lee surveyed the fort site and designed the dike system to ensure the necessary drainage. Then in 1831, Lieutenant Joseph K. F. Mansfield began supervising the actual construction of the fort.

By 1847, the basic structure of Fort Pulaski was finished. It encompassed approximately 5 acres and could mount up to 146 guns.

The fort was surrounded by a moat that was 7 feet deep and 35 feet wide. But what would prove to be the greatest obstacle to would-be attackers were the fort's brick walls, which were 7-1/2 feet thick and 35 feet high. It was this barrier that caused the defenders to be so confident. In fact, in November 1861, Lee inspected Fort Pulaski and assured Colonel Charles Olmstead, the Confederate commander there, that the Federal guns on Tybee Island could "make it pretty warm for you here with shells, but they cannot breach your walls at that distance." Lee's remarks were not the result of overconfidence, wishful thinking, or personal attachment. Brigadier General Joseph Totten, the Federal Army's chief engineer, agreed that "the work could not be reduced in a month's firing with any number of guns of manageable calibers."[2]

A Difficult Beginning. In December, Sherman and Du Pont had agreed to launch a powerful coup de main against Savannah, hoping that the capture of the city would cause the Confederates to abandon all the forts south of St. Simon's Island and Brunswick. By this point, the relationship between the commanders was extremely tense, and the planned attack on Fort Pulaski would fail to achieve anything close to the cooperation it would require. Neither man was clearly in charge, which presented a major obstacle. Even Sherman recognized if either he or Du Pont had been given overall authority, more would have been accomplished.[3]

Instead, things muddled along from bad to worse. Du Pont dispatched his trusted subordinate Commodore John Rodgers to conduct reconnaissance, and Rodgers concluded that the Wall's Cut channel was too shallow to risk running gunboats without first being marked. Knowing that the Army would consider him "uncooperative," Du Pont still refused to supply Sherman with any vessels until the channel could be buoyed or staked. Sherman, however, was powerless to do anything without Du Pont, because the general was still waiting for the light-draught steam transports the War Department had promised him. Sherman claimed that if he had the necessary transportation he would attack without the Navy, but the point was moot. Instead, Sherman could only complain that the plan failed to materialize for a "want of cooperation of the navy."[4]

Rather than the planned coup de main, Sherman and Du Pont finally agreed to make a "strong feint" against Savannah, hoping it would draw Confederate troops away from Fernandina, the next Federal objective. The feint consisted of two squadrons of warships, one probing to the south of Savannah and one to the north, followed by three regiments of soldiers aboard Army transports.

When the Confederates saw the warships, they were convinced the Federals were launching a major assault on Fort Pulaski, and Flag Officer Tattnall responded with an expedition to resupply the fort with six months' worth of provisions. To do so he would have to run between the two Federal fleets. Tattnall succeeded in his mission, showing the Federals that the Navy could not prevent communication with Fort Pulaski from its positions on the river during the feint. In a future operation, the Federals would have to secure Wilmington Island to accomplish this purpose. But if the feint failed in this aspect, it did accomplish its goal of unnerving the Confederates. In the meantime, Major General George McClellan sent instructions that the War Department did not consider Savannah to be worth putting under siege and instead instructed Sherman to concentrate his forces on Fort Pulaski, Fernandina, and maybe St. Augustine. On February 14, McClellan sent another message promising to send Sherman a siege train of heavy guns to be used in reducing Fort Pulaski.[5]

Changing Technology. The reason that Sherman would need such powerful guns, and the fact that so encouraged Lee, was that so far in the history of warfare there was not a single instance in which cannon and mortar had breached heavy masonry walls at ranges beyond 1,000 yards. Even after occupying Tybee Island, the Federals would be over a mile away from Fort Pulaski.

But such a condition did not deter Captain Quincy Gillmore, the engineering officer that Sherman ordered to take charge of the investment and bombardment of the Confederate stronghold. An 1849 graduate of West Point, Gillmore had both supervised harbor fortifications and taught engineering before the Civil War, so he knew what he was up against at Fort Pulaski. Nonetheless, he was a staunch believer in the power and accuracy of rifled cannon. Fort Pulaski would give him an opportunity to test his theories.

Gillmore decided to locate his batteries on the northwestern tip of Tybee Island. Throughout February and March, Gillmore's men wrestled with 36 siege guns and mortars, some weighing 8-1/2 tons. Moving them into position was no easy task. Gillmore's work parties constructed a sturdy two and a half mile road over which to transport the guns. To avoid detection by the Confederates, work along the last mile was conducted only at night and in virtual silence. The effort was superintended by Lieutenant Horace Porter, who stated he could "pay no greater tribute to the patriotism" of his work party. Porter reported "they toiled night after night, often in a drenching rain, under the guns of the fort, speaking only in whispers, and directed entirely by the sound of a whistle, without uttering a murmur."[6]

For their efforts, the Federals were able to position eleven siege batteries within two miles of Fort Pulaski. The critical element of this array were nine rifled cannon, a mix of 30-pounder Parrot guns and James guns converted from smoothbores, located at Batteries Sigel and McClellan about a mile southeast of the Confederate position. The superior accuracy, range, and penetrating capability of these rifled pieces were Gillmore's ace in the hole.

Just after sunrise on April 10, the Federals sent an officer to Fort Pulaski demanding its surrender. Olmstead refused the offer, stating that he was there "to defend the fort, not to surrender it."[7] At 8:15, Gillmore obliged and initiated his bombardment with a single 13-inch mortar fired from Battery Halleck, located in about the middle of his line. By 9:30, Gillmore's mortars were firing at 15-minute intervals and his artillery at two or three times that rate. The Federal Columbiads from Batteries Lyon and Lincoln and the rifled cannons concentrated on the southeast angle of the fort. The rifled pieces first pounded the Confederate guns on the parapet, and then shifted to the walls to loosen the brickwork for the Columbiads. Gillmore liked what he saw. By 1:00 he reported, "it became evident that, unless our guns should suffer seriously from the enemy's fire, a breach would be effected." He could already see "that the rifled projectiles were surely eating their way into the scarp of the *pan-coupe* and adjacent south-east face."[8]

By and large, Du Pont and Sherman had experienced relatively little friction while the siege batteries were being prepared. At the end of March, however, Sherman was replaced by Major General David Hunter. Du Pont would later have difficulties with the new general, but for the time being he found him "peculiar, fussy, interfering, *coarse*, although energetic and anxious to please the Navy."[9] Indeed, although the bombardment was mostly an Army operation, Hunter suggested some slight naval participation. Commodore Rodgers brought a detachment from the *Wabash* to Tybee Island on April 10, too late to take part in the firing that day, but on the 11th he added his battery of four rifled guns to the shelling. Gillmore noted that the Navy gunners' "skill and experience were applied with telling effect."[10]

At first the defenders responded with respectable fires, but the accurate Federal shelling quickly dismounted or rendered unserviceable gun after Confederate gun. This suppression contributed to the fact that not a single Federal gun was hit by return fire. By nightfall, the southeast angle of the fort was dangerously damaged. Two embrasures had been enlarged, and the wall had been reduced to half its original seven and a half foot thickness. Olmstead recalled, "shots were shrieking through the air in every direction, while the ear was deafened by the tremendous explosions."

Confederate efforts to remount their guns and repair their positions proved fruitless. The Federals began concentrating their fires on enlarging the breach, and by noon shells were passing through the opening and exploding against the northwest powder magazine. With 40,000 pounds of powder just waiting to ignite, Olmstead had little choice. At 2:30 he raised a white sheet over Fort Pulaski.[11]

During the 30-hour bombardment, each side suffered one fatality. The Federals took some 360 prisoners, about a dozen of which were wounded. Most of Gillmore's men had been New Englanders, and when one captured Confederate made the inevitable allusion to wooden nutmegs, a Connecticut artilleryman pointed to a 10-inch shell that had pierced the fort and told him, "We don't make them of wood any longer."[12]

In the process of silencing 16 of the Confederates' 20 guns, the Federals had fired 5,275 rounds. By the end of the bombardment, the once-imposing moat was so filled with debris it could be crossed without getting wet. Gillmore reported that his mortars "were from some cause practically inefficient," leaving the impressive results to be from the breaching power of his artillery alone. Less than half of the Federal expenditure of ordnance had come from rifled guns, but these more accurate and powerful pieces had done a disproportionate amount of the work.[13]

Gillmore noted that his success represented "the first example, in actual warfare, of the breaching power of rifled ordnance at long range."[14] It "caused a sensation throughout the world in proving many modern fortifications vulnerable to artillery." Specifically, the implications were disastrous for the Confederacy, whose coastal defense system was built around forts such as Fort Pulaski. First, Hatteras Inlet and Roanoke Island had demonstrated that steam power had reversed the historic balance between ship and fort. Now, Fort Pulaski had shown the vulnerability of masonry to rifled artillery. As Daniel Brown concludes, "An entire defense system, which had taken nearly fifty years to perfect, was made obsolete in less than two days."[15] On a more local basis, the Savannah River was now closed to blockade running. Showing a remarkable understanding of the overall strategy of the Navy Board, Gillmore concluded that this victory "set free for service elsewhere the naval force which had been employed there."[16]

However, exactly what would happen next remained in doubt. The main channels of the Savannah River were now open to the larger warships, and the river served as a thoroughfare to the city of Savannah. Still, the Federals did not push up the river. Instead, past experience made Du Pont wonder if the Army would even hang on to Fort Pulaski.

Hunter and Du Pont really had no plans to exploit the situation. This time it was Du Pont's turn to feel a little hesitant. Rumors of a looming Confederate ironclad gave him a fear of being overmatched, and numerous demands on the squadron, coupled with many ships under repair, left him feeling stretched a little thin.[17] Indeed, the city of Savannah itself would not fall until December 21, 1864, when Major General William Sherman captured it at the end of his March to the Sea.

For the time being, however, Du Pont was under increasing pressure, including scrutiny from the Senate Committee on Naval Affairs to keep the blockade as strict as possible. The Committee was particularly interested in the blockade of the port of Charleston.[18] Up until now, the Peninsula Campaign in Virginia had consumed the Navy's resources, but by September, Du Pont would be ready to focus on the Committee's interest.[19] Charleston, however, would prove to be a much tougher challenge than anything Du Pont had experienced thus far.

The powerful effects of rifled artillery left the seemingly impregnable masonry walls of Fort Pulaski a pile of rubble.
Photograph courtesy of the Library of Congress, Prints & Photographs Division.

The
Burnside
Expedition

Roanoke Island

New Bern

Fort Macon

ROANOKE ISLAND:
AMPHIBIOUS PROVING GROUND

Roanoke Island—a few may recall the name as the site of Sir Walter Raleigh's "Lost Colony" and the birthplace of Virginia Dare, the first English child born in the Western Hemisphere, but this mysterious footnote in America's colonial past was also the site of an important—but often overlooked—battle during the Civil War. It was the beginning of the "Burnside Expedition," a campaign that took Army-Navy cooperation to the next level and greatly expanded the logistical impact of the coastal war.

Roanoke Island was an operation which Clifford Dowdey attests involved "the first amphibian force used on the Western continent."[1] It was an operation which Ivan Musicant describes "as neat a combined [more precisely, "joint"] operation as any executed over the course of the entire war."[2] It was an operation which Shelby Foote claims resulted in "arousing the immediate apprehension of every rebel posted within gunshot of salt water. No beach was safe. This newly bred amphibious beast, like some monster out of mythology—half Army, half Navy: an improbable, unholy combination if ever there was one—might come splashing ashore at any point from here on down."[3] Even allowing for poetic license in the exclamations of Messieurs Dowdey, Musicant, and Foote, such bold statements should pique the interest of any student of joint operations. Indeed, what the battle of Roanoke Island offers is an excellent example of how the absence of traditional command structures and doctrine can be overcome by unity of effort and innovative thinking.

Strategic Significance. Roanoke Island's importance lay in its strategic location. Twelve miles long by three miles wide, it lies just off the eastern tip of a low-lying marshy peninsula that divides the Albemarle Sound and the Pamlico Sound on the North Carolina coast. By capturing Hatteras Inlet in August, the Federals controlled Pamlico Sound, the lower of the two bodies of water. This victory had given them year-round anchorage and access to New Bern, the principal eastern depot on the vital railroad supply line to Richmond and the Confederate armies in Virginia. This yet unexploited threat was bad enough, but what was even worse for the Confederates was what might happen if the Federals controlled Albemarle Sound. From there, Norfolk and the critical Gosport Navy Yard would be exposed to an attack from the rear. Key to this defense was Roanoke Island, which Foote describes as "a loose-fitting cork plugging the neck of a bottle called Albemarle Sound. Nothing that went by water could get in there without getting past the cork."[4]

The Defenders. As obvious as this fact was, the Confederates did little to strengthen the defenses of Roanoke Island. The island lay within the command of Major General Benjamin Huger, who, after the loss of Fort Hatteras, ordered a regiment of troops to garrison and fortify Roanoke Island with the help of some North Carolina state militia. Then, in an effort to relieve himself of responsibility for the defense of Roanoke Island, Huger initiated an extensive dialogue with the Confederate War Department over the boundaries of his department. Emory Thomas writes, "While the War Office gerrymandered military departments, work on the island's defenses proceeded indifferently."[5] Finally, in late December 1861, Judah Benjamin succeeded Leroy Pope Walker as the Confederacy's Secretary of War and assigned Brigadier General Henry Wise to Roanoke Island and Huger's department.

Wise was a political general who had served as the fire-eating governor of Virginia, and had previously had difficulty cooperating with other commanders in western Virginia.[6] He owed his rank to his political influence and his ability to raise a "legion" or brigade. However, even a man of Wise's meager military talent could perceive the seriousness of the situation and, as Herman Hattaway and Archer

Jones write, he "decided to try to help by doing what he did best, politicking, in Norfolk with Huger and in Richmond with governmental officials, seeking more troops, supplies, and equipment."[7] Huger and Benjamin responded with expressions of concern but little in the way of tangible support. Indeed, Wise would later complain that Benjamin had provided "Nothing! Nothing! Nothing!"[8] Wise, however, became seriously ill with pleurisy, and practical command of Roanoke Island's defenses fell to Colonel Henry Shaw.

At Shaw's immediate disposal were 1,500 soldiers who Wise would later describe as "undrilled, unpaid, not sufficiently clothed and quartered, and... miserably armed with old flint muskets in bad order."[9] This number would eventually increase to 2,500 as Wise's command continued to trickle in, but even this force would be woefully deficient. The Confederate artillery was misplaced, antiquated, and undersupplied. The troops were so unprepared that as the Federal infantry was beginning its attack, a Confederate captain was still training the crew manning the battery that defended the most critical approach.[10] Wise concluded, "In a word, the defenses were a sad farce of ignorance and neglect combined, inexcusable in any or all who were responsible for them."[11]

The naval component of the Confederate defenses was equally inauspicious. It consisted of two side-wheel steamers, six tiny gunboats, and a floating artillery battery all commanded by Captain William Lynch. Wise had little respect for his naval partners and was critical of Lynch.[12] He contemptuously dubbed Lynch's flotilla the "Mosquito Fleet" and assessed it as "perfectly imbecile."[13] Lynch could be equally partisan. Upon observing the Federal advance through Hatteras Inlet on January 20, Lynch steamed back to Roanoke Island and dispatched a letter to the Navy Department blaming Wise for the impending disaster.[14] Suffice it to say, as Rush Hawkins does in his monograph of the operation, "There was... a lack of cordial agreement between General Wise and Flag-Officer Lynch."[15]

The Attackers. These haphazard and belated Confederate efforts present a stark contrast to the strategic and visionary thinking of their Federal counterparts. In the fall of 1861, Brigadier General Ambrose

Burnside, sensitive to Major General George McClellan's previous resistance to drawing troops from the Army of the Potomac, suggested raising an amphibious or "coastal" division from the northeastern states.[16] Burnside planned:

> To organize in the Eastern states regiments near the sea-coast, composed as much as possible of men who knew more or less about steamers, sailing vessels, surf-boats, &c., and to arm and equip a sufficient number of vessels of light draught to carry this division of men, (which at that time it was intended should number about 10,000 men,) so that they could be moved quickly from one point on the coast to another. The object in arming these vessels with heavy guns was to enable them to overcome any slight opposition that they might meet with on the rivers or coast, without the necessity of waiting for assistance from the navy, which might not be at hand. All these vessels were to be well supplied with surf-boats, launches, and other means of landing troops. The vessels were to be of the lightest draught possible in order to navigate all the bays, harbors and rivers of the waters of the Chesapeake bay and of North Carolina.[17]

Burnside's organization was to be flexible, self-sufficient, responsive, joint, mobile, and light. Ivan Musicant terms it "a far-reaching idea, much ahead of its time."[18] Its potential was readily appreciated. McClellan, himself beginning to form the concept for an amphibious turning movement against Richmond, approved the proposal, and Secretary of the Navy Welles pledged the Navy's fullest cooperation.[19]

Burnside had no trouble raising 15,000 men, but acquiring the necessary ships was a problem. The Navy had already pressed into service nearly every craft capable of mounting a gun, forcing Burnside to assemble "a motley fleet" that by the beginning of 1862, had grown to more than 80 vessels.[20]

Annapolis, Maryland, was the staging area for what was

designated "Burnside's Expedition." Burnside organized his troops into three divisions under Brigadier Generals John Foster, Jesse Reno, and John Parke. All three brigadiers had been cadets with Burnside at West Point, and he called them "three of my most trusted friends."[21]

Burnside's naval component commander was Flag Officer Louis Goldsborough. Goldsborough was a career sailor if there ever was one. Commissioned as a midshipman at age seven, Goldsborough was the commander of the North Atlantic Blockading Squadron. Now, the foul Cape Hatteras weather and the ragtag fleet would test the seamanship of Goldsborough and his crews to the very extreme.[22]

Shelby Foote gives a vivid description of the Burnside Expedition's naval arm:

> In addition to twenty light-draft gunboats armed with cannon salvaged from the armories of various navy yards, there was a rickety lot of sixty-odd transports and supply ships, including tugs, ferries, converted barges, and flat-bottomed river steamers: a conglomeration, in short, of whatever could be scraped together by purchasing agents combing northern rivers and harbors for vessels rejected by agents who had come and gone before them. The only characteristic they shared was they all drew less than eight feet of water, the reported high-tide depth across the bar at Hatteras Inlet.[23]

This sad assortment of vessels caused a near-mutiny among the seasoned sailors that comprised much of Burnside's force, but Burnside quelled the grumbling by moving himself and his headquarters staff off of the fine new steamer, the *George Peabody*, that had been set aside for him, and on to the *Picket*, the smallest, most rickety vessel in the lot.[24]

With this crisis avoided, the Burnside Expedition steamed out of Annapolis the morning of January 9 for a rendezvous with its supply ships and gunboats at Fort Monroe the next day. On January 11, the fleet cleared Hampton Roads, and the skippers broke open their sealed orders instructing them to steer south. They also ran into some dangerously harsh weather that put Burnside's earlier show of confidence to a severe test. The little *Picket* was tossed about so roughly that it nearly foundered. As Burnside later recalled, "Men, furniture, and crockery below decks were thrown about in a most promiscuous manner. At times it seemed the waves, which appeared mountain high, would ingulf [sic] us, but the little vessel would ride them and stagger forward in her course." Indeed, the fleet weathered the storm, and on the morning of January 12 arrived off Hatteras Inlet, the entrance to Pamlico Sound. There, another surprise awaited Burnside.[25]

Burnside had amassed his fleet based on having been told that the water in Hatteras Inlet was eight feet deep. Upon arrival, however, Burnside "discovered to our sorrow" that, in reality, it was only six feet deep. This difference could have barred quite a few vessels from participating in the action. Here, however, Burnside was served quite well by the "goodly number of mechanics... familiar with the coasting trade" who comprised so much of his expedition.[26]

The plan these innovative sailors developed was to send several of the larger ships full-speed-ahead to ground on the bar. There, they were held in place with tugs and anchors while the racing current washed sand from underneath them. It was a slow, painstaking process, but it worked. Eventually, a broad, eight-foot channel had been cut, and by February 4 the fleet was safely assembled in the sound. That same day, Burnside, after a conference with Goldsborough, issued his final instructions to his brigadiers. There would, however, be one more delay. Once inside the sound, the fleet was again beset by rough weather, but finally the sun came out and on February 7, the Burnside Expedition was ready to attack.[27]

The Battle. Captain Lynch knew that he was no match for the vastly superior Federal fleet. Thus, instead of attacking, he decided to try to lure the enemy into a trap. The Confederates had not done much in the way of fortifying Roanoke Island, but they had been able to drive some piles to obstruct the channel. Lynch thought that if he could coax the Federals into these obstructions, their maneuverability would be lessened and the Mosquito Fleet might be able to do something. He also hoped that by causing the Federal fleet to hamstring itself on the obstructions, the Confederate batteries on Forts Blanchard and Huger on Roanoke Island's west coast, and the beached barge grandly styled Fort Forrest on the mainland could catch the enemy in a crossfire.[28]

Burnside and Goldsborough, however, had more than enough resources to overwhelm this weak ruse. Their plan was for the 19-vessel "naval division," commanded by Commander Stephen Rowan, to lead, "dashing without delay," straight at the Mosquito Fleet. With this annoyance thus neutralized, the three brigades, each supported by their own gunboats and Navy launches, would go ashore at Ashby's Harbor, midway on the landward side of the island. Burnside had the benefit of excellent intelligence when he made this plan. A young runaway slave, who had recently escaped from a Roanoke Island plantation, had provided what Burnside felt was "most valuable information as to the nature of the shore of the island," including information about the excellent harbor at Ashby's Landing which Burnside chose for his landing site.[29]

Down the boggy center of the island, little more than a mile from the beaches on either side, ran a causeway. The Confederates had emplaced a three-gun battery, supported by infantry and flanked by what was considered to be impassable quicksand marshes, along this avenue. To the battery's front was an open field of deep mud partially covered by an abatis.[30] It was a killing zone to be sure, but there was no other route. Burnside told Foster to charge straight up the causeway, and Reno and Parke to move through the swamps on the flanks.[31]

At about 11:30 a.m., Rowan's gunboats opened fire on Fort Bartow, which along with Forts Blanchard and Huger, covered the channel along the west coast of Roanoke Island. As they pounded away at the fort's earthen walls, the ships hugged the shoreline so that the Confederates could bring to bear only three of their eight guns. Fort Bartow was hit particularly hard, at times being almost completely obscured by the smoke, sand, and debris thrown up by the Federal bombardment. Rowan's vessels benefited from their own accurate fire and continued maneuvering to escape serious damage.[32]

Lynch slowly retired the Mosquito Fleet as was his plan, but, in the process, he took a terrible pounding. The *Forrest* was hit and had to withdraw from the fight, and the *Curlew* was so badly damaged that Commander Thomas Hunter had to ground it lest it would sink. Unfortunately, Hunter did this directly in front of Fort Forrest, thus blocking the aim of the fort's gunners. More importantly, the Federals refused to be distracted by Lynch's feeble attempt at a ruse, so much so that Wise wrote, "the enemy did not take the time to brush [Lynch] away." Stating that "not a pound of powder or a loaded shell [was] remaining," Lynch broke off the engagement and withdrew, under the cover of darkness, to Elizabeth City. As Wise had feared, the meager Mosquito Fleet had not had any affect on the Federal attack.[33]

While the naval battle still waged, Burnside began disembarking his land force in a manner suggestive of the typical landing pattern of World War II. At about 3 p.m., large longboats were lowered, filled with troops, and towed by shallow-draught steamers toward the shore. Each steamer pulled 20 boats and was equipped with specially designed ladders that allowed the troops to climb down into the boats.[34] Hattaway and Jones describe the arrangement as "clever and revolutionary."[35] It is one of the reasons Musicant concludes that the Burnside Expedition's "amphibious aspects... were precursors to similar operations later in the war, and indeed, throughout the century of naval history that followed."[36]

As the steamers neared the shore, they would veer off sharply, "sending the string of landing craft shoreward with the motion of a cracking whip." The towlines were then cut and oarsmen would row the boats in the rest of the way and ground them on the shore. In less than an hour, 4,000 troops were ashore in brigade order. Burnside was pleased, writing that he "never witnessed a more beautiful sight than that presented by the approach of these vessels to the shore and the landing and forming of the troops."[37] By midnight, 10,000 men had landed and were setting up temporary camp in preparation for the morning assault.[38] All of this was accomplished under close cover of naval bombardment provided by Commander Rowan and the *Delaware*. When Rowan saw the troops were about to land, he lobbed nine-inch shells into the trees where Confederate defenders would likely be concealed behind the landing point.[39]

The land assault was launched at 7 a.m. Foster, with the 25th Massachusetts in the lead, closely followed by a boat-gun battery manned by Coast Guardsmen, advanced up the center. As expected, Foster's column met a murderous fire along the causeway. At about 11:30 a.m., the 25th Massachusetts had sustained enough casualties that it was ordered to fall back. It was replaced by the 10th Connecticut, which advanced within a quarter mile of the Confederate position. At that point, the 9th New York Zouaves, led by Colonel Rush Hawkins, took the lead.[40] In the meantime, the flank brigades made much better progress than anticipated through the marshes. Burnside reported, "what seemed to be impassable ground… did not prove to be so for our troops."[41]

While Foster pressed the enemy from the front, Reno and Parke gained "advantageous positions" on the flanks and conducted a simultaneous assault.[42] A dispute would later result between Reno and Foster's men as to who reached the Confederate battery first, but the honors properly go to Reno. Amid these multiple threats, the Confederate line broke, and the defense of Roanoke Island was shattered. Among the casualties was Captain O. Jennings Wise, the son of General Wise.[43]

Results. Roanoke Island was the Federals' first major land victory east of the Alleghenies.[44] It was rapid and total. In the words of Allan Nevins, the Federals "went through the Confederate defenses like a battering ram through pasteboard."[45] The key to the successful attack was Reno's ability to flank the Confederates through the swamp, but naval gunfire contributed as well. Burnside and Goldsborough had planned that the ships would not resume fire unless the land force requested it against specific targets. When the Navy did fire, it was able to use the heavy musket smoke as a reference point. Musicant says that this coordination represented an "arrangement well in advance of its time."[46]

The Federals captured nearly the entire 2,500-man defense. The Confederates lost 23 killed and 58 wounded. Federal losses were 37 killed and 214 wounded.[47] The defeat set off a wave of recrimination in the South, especially in Richmond because of the loss of Wise's son. The Confederate Congress investigated the situation and found Secretary of War Benjamin to blame. Benjamin offered no defense to the charges, although Clifford Dowdey argues that the true responsibility lay with the faulty policies of President Davis.[48] Indeed, Davis, privately if not publicly, seems to have recognized the abilities of Benjamin. Succumbing to the public outcry, Davis removed Benjamin as Secretary of War—only to then reassign him as Secretary of State.[49]

In reality, there was plenty of blame to go around. Wise was an amateur general. The Confederate Navy was weak and too small. The War Department was unable to react even with ample warning of the Federal threat and Roanoke Island's vulnerability. The Confederate departmental system of command facilitated the narrow and local focus of commanders like Huger.[50] One thing was sure: the loss of Roanoke Island "shook the Southern *people* into startled awareness that the United States had settled down to real war—and was winning it!"[51] Beyond that, Roanoke Island provided valuable lessons learned for joint amphibious operations.

Far-reaching Lessons Learned. Perhaps what is so remarkable about the success of the Burnside Expedition is that it occurred well before the era of joint task forces and joint doctrine. Scott Stuckey notes that "in the absence of unified command or meaningful joint doctrine, the conception and execution of joint operations [in the Civil War] totally depended on ad hoc actions by the responsible commanders, and therefore upon their personal chemistry and communications."[52] In these areas, the Burnside Expedition was exemplary.

In fact, unity of effort and a sense of cooperation permeated the Burnside Expedition. There is Secretary of the Navy Welles's pledging the Navy's full cooperation with an Army-developed and led operation. There is Burnside's sensitivity to the concerns of the sailors, and his choice to forego the more seaworthy *Peabody* for the *Picket* in order to preserve morale and set the example. In addition, there is Burnside and Goldsborough meeting on the eve of the attack to finalize the details; the detailed planning and close cooperation required to provide naval gunfire in support of an advancing land force; their shared purpose of taking the fight directly to the enemy. All of this was accomplished because of the two commanders' willingness to work together. Indeed, Bern Anderson says that the Roanoke Island "operation was an excellent example of the coordination that could be achieved by competent commanders."[53]

Contrast this teamwork with the inefficiencies of the Confederate effort. Wise had a record of being uncooperative with fellow commanders, and he continued this pattern by speaking disparagingly of his naval component. For his part, Lynch tried to blame Wise for the defense's failure before the battle was even joined. In addition, a Confederate ship obstructed the line of fire of a Confederate fort. Thus, on the Confederate side, there was nothing of the "personal chemistry and communications" displayed by the Federals. True, this was not the sole reason for the Confederate defeat—the defenders were decidedly outgunned—but the lack of unity of effort just as certainly did not help the Confederate cause.

Burnside and Goldsborough overcame the lack of unity of command by achieving unity of effort. They likewise overcame the lack of doctrine by innovative thinking. Examples in this area include the measures taken to increase the depth of the channel in Hatteras Inlet, the use of troop ladders to move men from the larger vessels to the landing craft, rehearsals for loading and unloading landing boats, the use of steamers to tow a serial of landing craft close to shore, and the techniques for preventing fratricide and coordinating naval gunfire.

Modern complex operations often present the same unity of command and doctrinal challenges that faced the Burnside Expedition. The Burnside Expedition shows that these difficulties can be overcome by unity of effort and innovative thinking. It is an excellent case study for students of joint operations. It was also the beginning of a powerful and potentially decisive new dimension to the Federal threat to the Confederate coast.

NEW BERN: EXPANDED LOGISTICAL IMPACT OF THE COASTAL WAR

With Roanoke Island securely in Federal hands, the Burnside Expedition had the opportunity to greatly expand the logistical impact of the coastal war. Heretofore, the Federal attacks had primarily affected Confederate seagoing operations. By moving up the Neuse River from Pamlico Sound, Burnside could now seize New Bern, a location Richard Sauers considers so strategic that its capture "might throw the entire defenses of North Carolina into confusion."[1] Sauers's assessment rests on the fact that New Bern was not only North Carolina's second largest port, but also the site of an important railroad. From New Bern, the Atlantic & North Carolina Railroad ran to a vital junction at Goldsboro. At Goldsboro, the line intersected with the Wilmington & Weldon Railroad, which carried supplies to Richmond and points north. In addition to threatening these railroads, New Bern could be used as a jumping-off point for an attack on Beaufort Harbor and Fort Macon.[2] New Bern represented a significant expansion and improvement of the Federal logistical strategy to defeat the Confederacy. Archer Jones writes, "Capturing southern ports, which, like New Bern, had high value because of their vital rail connections, provided a sure means of implementing a blockade that so far had captured very few of the ships which attempted to use southern ports."[3]

The Defenders. With the fall of Roanoke Island, Confederate forces at New Bern bolstered their defenses and prepared for a Federal attack. Captain Lynch had withdrawn the Mosquito Fleet to Elizabeth City, but on February 10, Commander Rowan led 13 Federal gunboats with

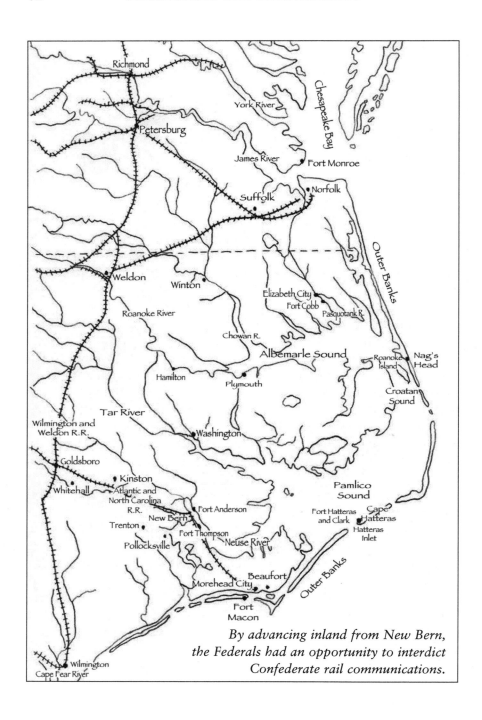

By advancing inland from New Bern, the Federals had an opportunity to interdict Confederate rail communications.

marines on board up the Pasquotank River to pursue Lynch. In an hour-long battle, Rowan sunk two Confederate ships, and Lynch destroyed three others to prevent their capture. This defeat left the Confederates with no armed warships that could challenge the attackers.[4]

By the second week of March 1862, however, a line of log and earth breastworks had been established downriver from New Bern. The key to the defense was Fort Thompson, which mounted 13 heavy guns. Ten of these were trained on the Neuse River, leaving just three to cover the land approaches. The Confederates had also obstructed the Neuse with floating mines—"torpedoes" in the lexicon of the day—and piles and sunken vessels. From Fort Thompson the line extended west for about two and a half miles, where it was anchored with a two-gun battery on the edge of a swamp along Brice Creek—terrain that Burnside described as "almost impassable ground."[5]

The line was manned by some 4,500 green North Carolina troops, including seven infantry regiments, two dismounted cavalry companies, and some artillery, all under the command of Brigadier General Lawrence Branch. Branch was a former newspaper editor and North Carolina congressman. He was a patriot to be sure, but one devoid of military training.[6]

Branch's defenses had one notable weak point in the center where the position was bisected by railroad tracks built on a causeway. From these tracks, there was a break of some 150 yards as the defenses skipped northward before resuming along the path of a small creek and continuing to the west. An old brick kiln was located near the railroad, and a small battalion of ill-trained and poorly armed militiamen occupied the position. They did not, however, adequately cover the gap.[7]

The Attack. With the destruction of the Confederate fleet at Elizabeth City, the Federal Navy enjoyed complete supremacy over the inland waters. Thus, Burnside had no fears for the safety of Roanoke Island. He left just one brigade there to garrison the island and devoted the remainder of his force to the New Bern operation.[8]

On February 26, Burnside ordered his troops at Roanoke Island to prepare to embark for New Bern, and within four days all were loaded on board. On March 11, Burnside set sail with 11,000 men to a rendezvous with 13 warships commanded by Rowan, who had become the ranking naval officer once Goldsborough was recalled to Hampton Roads because of the attack by the ironclad *Virginia*. By the next day, the entire command was anchored off Slocum's Creek, about 14 miles from New Bern, and night orders were issued for the landing.[9]

Early on March 13, the Federals began disembarking without opposition, as the Confederates expected that the main attack would come by water.[10] By 1:00 p.m., the landing was complete, and the Federals advanced to within two miles of the Confederate defensive line and bivouacked for the night. A hard rain had begun to fall, and Burnside, who would later orchestrate the infamous "Mud March" after his defeat at Fredericksburg, recalled that this was "one of the most disagreeable and difficult marches that I witnessed during the war."[11] One of Burnside's soldiers complained that the rain turned the road into "the muddiest mud ever invented; being knee-deep and of a black, unctuous, slippery character."[12]

Among the consequences of the weather was that the poor condition of the roads prevented any artillery from being brought forward except for some light naval howitzers. It also made it impossible to move any reserve ammunition. When Burnside gave the order to attack the next morning, his men would go into battle with only the 40 rounds they carried in their cartridge boxes.[13]

Burnside's plan of attack had Foster on the right, Reno on the left, and Parke in the center, ready to attack frontally or to shift to whichever flank proved advantageous. In the meantime, Rowan's fleet would support the attack by shelling Fort Thompson. Conspicuously absent was the careful fire control exhibited by Burnside and Goldsborough at Roanoke Island. Instead, Rowan fired rather indiscriminately, killing both Confederates and Foster's men alike. Rowan would later justify his generous fires, stating, "I know the persuasive effect of a 9-inch shell and thought it better to kill a Union man or two than to lose the effect of my moral suasion."[14] In spite of Rowan's enthusiastic contribution, Foster's attack ground to a standstill amid stiff Confederate resistance.

By this time, however, the 21st Massachusetts, on the right of Reno's line, had stumbled into the break in the Confederate defenses near the old brick kiln. Reno personally led a four-company assault on the position that scattered the Confederate defenders there. The 35th North Carolina, occupying the entrenchments adjacent to the brickyard, was hit on the right flank and also fell back in disorder.

Reno's success, however, was short-lived, as other Confederate regiments held firm, and soon the 21st Massachusetts was caught in a crossfire from both sides of the railroad. With the Federal momentum thus checked, Branch committed the 26th and 33rd North Carolina and regained the lost ground.

However, the brickyard defense was still vulnerable, and Parke called on Colonel Isaac Rodman's 4th Rhode Island Regiment to continue the fight. Rodman led his men and the 8th Connecticut in a charge that swept through the brickyard and threatened the Confederate left wing. Outflanked and low on ammunition, Branch ordered a retreat over the Trent River Bridge to New Bern. The retreat quickly degenerated into flight, with one Confederate officer recalling that "Every man struck out for the bridge as fast as his legs would carry him, and the additional spur from bombs crashing through the timber put them to top speed for a three mile sprint."[15]

Results. The combination of the timely arrival of a westbound train at New Bern and the fact that Burnside's men had to cross the river in boats to press the pursuit facilitated the Confederate escape. Still, the Confederates lost 64 killed, 101 wounded, and 413 missing, of which Branch concluded about 200 were "prisoners and the remainder at home." The Federals lost 90 killed and 380 wounded. Once he put some distance between himself and the Federals, Branch rallied his men at Kinston.[16]

In the wake of a string of successful Federal coastal operations at places like Hatteras Inlet, Port Royal, and Roanoke Island, the Confederates had by and large withdrawn to the interior. Given their limited resources, they may have had no choice, but the loss of New Bern seems to have shown the dangers of this strategy. The Federals were now able to project power from the coast into the interior. This capability brought an entirely new dimension to the Federal threat. Furthermore, with the loss of New Bern, Beaufort and Fort Macon had become isolated and were in serious danger.[17]

FORT MACON: FINAL VICTORY
OF THE BURNSIDE EXPEDITION

Fort Macon, North Carolina, was an attractive target for Burnside. Not only did it guard the water approach to the port of Beaufort, but it also protected Morehead City, the terminus of the Atlantic & North Carolina Railroad. Furthermore, if Burnside could control Fort Macon, he could free himself from reliance on Hatteras Island and its weather-related problems. The Navy would also benefit, because the North Atlantic Blockading Squadron could use the harbor as a coaling station, thus allowing for a more effective cordon of Wilmington and other nearby points of entry.[1]

The Defenders. Fort Macon was seized for the South without firing a shot on April 14, 1861, by a combined force of Captain Josiah Pender and his 54-man militia company, the "Beaufort Home Guards," comprised of some citizens from Beaufort and Morehead City, and a group of cadets from the A.M. Institute in Carolina City. This action was before North Carolina had even seceded from the Union, so Pender sent his news to South Carolina Governor Francis Pickens instead of North Carolina Governor John Ellis, noting, "We intend that North Carolina shall occupy a true instead of a false position, though it be done by revolution." After President Lincoln issued his call for 75,000 volunteers in response to Fort Sumter, Ellis sent the Goldsboro Rifles to seize Fort Macon, unaware that Pender had already completed the task. Additional troops arrived on April 17 and began the process of preparing the fort for war.[2] North Carolina ultimately seceded on May 20.

On October 5, Colonel Moses White arrived to take charge of Fort Macon's defenses. White was a 25-year-old West Point graduate from Mississippi who had a reputation for being a desperate fighter. Fort Macon's previous commanders had all been men from civilian walks of life with no formal military training. White's background in ordnance and artillery would help shore up the fort's weaknesses.[3]

Fort Macon was garrisoned by five companies that totaled about 450 officers and men. It contained 54 cannon, but only 12 were long-range rifled guns. Furthermore, there were no mortars to help defend against a land assault, and there was only enough powder available for three days of sustained fire. To help delay the expected Federal assault, White had dispatched a raiding party inland to destroy the 180-foot railroad bridge over the Newport River. The men accomplished this task and also burned a turpentine distillery, a hotel that had been used as a hospital, and the barracks near Carolina City, but they inexplicably failed to destroy the Beaufort Road Bridge over the Newport. However, they did tear up the terminus of the Atlantic & North Carolina Railroad at Carolina City and took several of the rails back to Fort Macon to strengthen the fort's interior.[4]

The Approach and the Siege Preparations. Burnside selected Brigadier General John Parke's brigade to reduce Fort Macon, and on March 19, the 4th Rhode Island and 8th Connecticut Regiments began embarking on steamers for the short trip to Slocum's Creek, where they landed the next day. The 5th Rhode Island took a more arduous route, marching twelve miles along the railroad. The two commands linked up at Havelock, where Parke learned that the Beaufort Road Bridge was still intact. Parke seized this bridge and began rebuilding the railroad bridge the Confederates had earlier destroyed. He continued his march and reached Carolina City on March 22. From there, he sent a surrender demand to Colonel White on March 23. White declined, and Parke began siege operations.[5]

Because of the absence of Confederate land defenses, Parke was able to quietly take possession of Beaufort on March 26. There he began preparing for siege operations by bringing forward his heavy cannons by railroad. He was initially slowed by the Confederate destruction of the Newport River railroad bridge, but repairs were soon made, and by March 29 Parke had landed his forces on Bogue Banks.[6]

These developments caused morale to sag within Fort Macon. The small Confederate force could see that many of their homes and families had fallen under Federal occupation, but the soldiers were powerless to do anything about it. The men began trying to communicate with their loved ones by floating small toy boats containing messages across the harbor. White unwittingly increased the anxiety by stating he would not hesitate to shell the town if Parke used it to shelter his siege batteries. White was successful in deterring Parke from taking such action, but in the process he alienated both the townspeople and his soldiers. Fort Macon State Park Ranger and Park Historian Paul Branch concluded that, as a result, "An undercurrent of discontent began to manifest itself in the local men of the garrison."[7]

Some of White's men began not just to desert, but to actively help the enemy conduct reconnaissance. The most visible indicator of White's growing command problem was the "Bread Incident." White had an abundance of flour on hand, and instead of issuing it unbaked as had previously been done, he ordered it to be baked before distribution. One of the soldiers had been a baker before the war, and at first all concerned thought the baked bread would be a welcome change of diet. Unfortunately, the baker, after repeated attempts, was unable to produce any edible loaves. The men began to grumble for a return to the basic issue of flour, but White stubbornly insisted on continuing his experiment. Even the company commanders agreed with the men and gave White a petition to cease his efforts to provide baked bread. White refused, and on the morning of April 8, the company commanders sent him an ultimatum stating unless the flour issue was restored by 9:00 a.m., they would storm the commissary. At first White protested, threatening to arrest the officers and place a guard on the commissary. When White soon realized that he could find no one among the disgruntled garrison to serve as his guard force, he relented and ordered the flour ration resumed. However, the "Bread Incident" was the last straw for eight more local men who deserted.[8]

Those who remained at Fort Macon were determined to save it. On the night of April 9, White successfully exfiltrated an officer and seven men by boat. This group was able to reach Confederate lines and request reinforcements to advance against Parke's siege lines. The request traveled all the way to General Robert E. Lee, who was then serving as President Davis's military advisor. Unfortunately, there were no reinforcements available, but even from Richmond, Lee could ascertain the inevitable fate of Fort Macon. He noted, "Indeed, from the account given me, I very much doubt whether even tolerable resistance would be made if the fort were attacked, and you are authorized, if it be possible, to withdraw the garrison and secure such of the public property as can be brought off, if you think it advisable." Of course, by then, such an evacuation was not possible.[9]

Parke, however, had no such shortages. He steadily ferried 21 companies of infantry and artillery—some 1,500 men—to Bogue Banks at Hoop Pole Creek and established siege positions. He reconnoitered his positions on April 11 and dug permanent positions into the sand dunes the next day. Parke was now in protected positions about 1,200 yards from Fort Macon, and Confederate cannon and a company-sized attack were unable to dislodge the Federals. The cover and concealment provided by the sand dunes, the numerical inferiority of the defenders, the inadequacy of the Confederate powder, and the absence of mortars greatly limited Fort Macon's ability to interrupt the Federal activities. Even improvised mortars, 32-pounders jacked up at a 40- degree angle, failed to have any real effect. Without serious impediment, Parke continued his preparations, spending the next week and a half constructing emplacements for three batteries of siege guns.[10]

On April 23, Burnside arrived by ship and anchored off Harker's Island. He issued White another surrender demand, which was refused, but the two did agree to meet the next day for further discussion. This meeting was inconclusive, and on April 25, the Federals opened fire.[11]

The Bombardment Begins. The Federal batteries began to shell Fort Macon at 5:30 a.m., and the fort began to return fire at 6:00 a.m. At first, the Confederates made a good showing of themselves. They hit two of the four gunboats that had begun firing at about 9:00 a.m., and in less than an hour and a half the ships left the fight. The Federals also were largely unsuccessful in getting their floating batteries in position because of wind and choppy seas. That left the three land batteries to carry the load, but the Confederates had found their range and had blown away much of the protecting embankments of one battery. Its gun crews were thus exposed and were forced to cease their work and take cover. The other two batteries kept firing, but heavy smoke so obscured the fort that the gunners could not see sufficiently to get accurate fires.

This initial Confederate success changed, however, when Federal signal officers on top of Beaufort's Atlantic Hotel began using their vantage point to adjust fires. Thanks to this spotting, Burnside's Chief Ordnance Officer, Lieutenant Daniel Flagler, estimated that some five-eighths of the shells were now landing in the fort. Branch calls this "the turning point of the battle." With accurate Federal fire now regularly pounding the fort, the Confederates were forced to leave their guns and run for cover. By mid-afternoon, it was clear that the Confederate defense had culminated. The fort's rate of fire continually slowed, and by 4:00 p.m., most of its guns were silent. To make matters worse, Colonel White—always in frail health—had eventually grown so weak that he had to retire to his quarters to regain his strength. Sickness, in fact, plagued many of the defenders. Of the garrison's 403 assigned men, only 263 were present for duty at the morning's roll call. The rest were sick. With White incapacitated, Captain Henry Guion assumed command.[12]

Guion called a council of officers to assess the situation and they confirmed that the defense was in bad shape. Many of the fort's most important guns had been knocked out, and enemy fire had forced many batteries out of position. Only seven men had been killed, but the rest were near the point of exhaustion, especially those who were already sick. Perhaps of greatest concern was the probability that the increasingly accurate Federal fire would eventually find the 10,000 pounds of gunpowder in the southwest magazine. The adjacent wall was already cracking under the bombardment, and a magazine detonation would catastrophically destroy the fort and its occupants.[13]

Guion and his council concluded that the fort could not hold out, and they went to White's quarters where the decision was made to surrender. At about 4:30 p.m., the Confederates raised a white flag. With that, the Federals halted their bombardment, and the two sides met under a flag of truce to discuss terms. The Confederates had hoped for the same terms originally offered by Burnside on April 23, which were that the garrison be paroled and allowed to return home until properly exchanged, but now Parke was demanding unconditional surrender. After much discussion and an inability to agree, the two sides decided to suspend hostilities for the night until Burnside could be consulted. When Burnside and Parke met early in the morning on April 26, they agreed to offer the Confederates the original terms which allowed for parole. This message was delivered to the fort about daylight, and White agreed to surrender. At 10:10 a.m., the Confederate flag over Fort Macon was lowered. Twelve minutes later the Federal flag was raised in its place.[14]

With the capture of Fort Macon, Burnside gained much more than just the 396 prisoners and assorted supplies, cannon, horses, and small arms. With Beaufort Harbor in Federal hands, Burnside now had an Atlantic port to receive supplies rather than having to rely on the weather-hampered Hatteras Inlet.[15] Burnside was now in a position to strike even deeper. Confederate apologist E.A. Pollard confesses that, "So far the Burnside expedition had been a train of success. The Confederate position at Norfolk had been flanked; complete possession had been gained of Albemarle and Pamlico Sound; and now, by the fall of Fort Macon, the enemy had the entire coast of North Carolina."[16] Burnside began requesting the cavalry, railroad equipment, and other necessary transportation he would need to use the railroads to move his force into the interior. There he could threaten communications between Virginia and the rest of the South.[17] In fact, the entire Confederacy between Richmond and Charleston was now open to invasion.[18]

End of the Expedition. Events in Virginia, however, would soon interrupt Burnside's rampage. In late June, Burnside was preparing to move on Goldsboro when he received an abrupt order from President Lincoln telling him, "I think you had better go, with any reinforcements you can spare, to General McClellan [on the Virginia Peninsula]."[19] Burnside had originally hoped to cooperate with McClellan as a flanking force, but during the Seven Days Battles, McClellan's Army of the Potomac had been hammered back from the outskirts of Richmond by Lee's Army of Northern Virginia. On July 6, "much to [his] sorrow," Burnside and 7,000 of his men sailed from

North Carolina to go to McClellan's direct aid.[20]

North Carolina had always been relatively unimportant compared to the other Federal offensives going on in the spring of 1862, and when events elsewhere did not go as planned, it became a convenient source of reinforcements. A force of about 8,000 Federals remained in eastern North Carolina, but the major Federal offensive there had lost its punch. Years of raids and counterraids would follow, with neither side gaining a decisive advantage.[21]

Burnside nostalgically reminisced that, "The Burnside expedition has passed into history; its record we can be proud of. No body of troops ever had more difficulties to overcome in the same space of time. Its perils were both by land and water. Defeat never befell it. No gun was lost by it. Its experience was a succession of honorable victories."[22] Peter Chaitin offers a less sentimental but more practical conclusion, noting, "if Burnside's campaign in North Carolina had failed to achieve all its objectives, it had provided the Federal forces with a thorough rehearsal in joint Army-Navy operations, a rehearsal that would prove valuable during the bolder and bloodier coastal offensives that lay ahead."[23]

The
Peninsula
Campaign

THE PENINSULA CAMPAIGN:
A FAILURE IN COOPERATION

Planning for the campaign that caused a halt to the Burnside Expedition began in late 1861, when Major General George McClellan met Colonel Rush Hawkins of the 9th New York. Hawkins was making a report to the cabinet about his part in the recent success at Hatteras Inlet, where he had exercised tactical command of the Army forces. When the meeting ended, McClellan called Hawkins aside and began to ask him questions. However, Hawkins soon learned that McClellan's interest was not in Hatteras Inlet at all, but in the area around Norfolk and Hampton Roads, Virginia.

Hawkins was eager to respond. As a matter of fact, he had already advised Major General John Wool, commander of the Federal garrison at Fort Monroe, that the Army ought to conduct an amphibious landing at the tip of the Virginia Peninsula and move towards Richmond from the east. Hawkins drew McClellan a rough sketch of the terrain that indicated the road networks and showed how gunboats could be used to provide both transportation and flank protection for an invading army using the York and James Rivers.

McClellan listened enthusiastically. What Hawkins was suggesting coincided with McClellan's own desire to avoid a frontal assault against General Joe Johnston's entrenched Confederates around Manassas and Centreville. McClellan pocketed Hawkins's map and began to develop a plan.[1] This idea would evolve into the Peninsula Campaign, a promising amphibious offensive that failed in part because of a lack of unity between the Army and the Navy. Nonetheless, the Peninsula Campaign would secure Norfolk for the Federals, an acquisition which would profoundly affect the coastal war.

Plans for an Amphibious Turning Movement. McClellan was concerned that at Manassas Johnston occupied a "strong central position" protected by "a strong line of defense enabling him to remain on the defensive, with a small force on one flank, while he concentrates everything on the other." To counter this advantage, McClellan proposed moving a force of 100,000 men by water from Annapolis, Maryland, through the Chesapeake Bay to the mouth of the Rappahanock River. There, they would land at the small hamlet of Urbanna, which lay about 60 road miles northeast of Richmond.[2]

McClellan hoped this Urbanna Plan "would probably cut off [Major General John] Magruder in the Peninsula, and enable us to occupy Richmond before it could be strongly re-enforced. Should we fail in that, we could, with the cooperation of the Navy, cross the James and throw ourselves in the rear of Richmond, thus forcing the enemy to come out and attack us," because "his position would be untenable with us on the southern bank of the river." The threat to Richmond would force Johnston into a decisive engagement outside of his prepared positions on a battlefield selected by the Federals.[3] The whole idea of the maneuver was to get to Johnston's rear, force him to conduct a hasty retreat, and then make him fight on terms favorable to McClellan in order to defend Richmond.

Johnston, however, was not willing to cooperate with such a scheme. He was beginning to feel very vulnerable in his position at Manassas, especially since the coming spring weather would dry the roads and make it possible for McClellan to attack with superior numbers. Johnston had no intention of waiting around long enough for this to happen. On March 7, he ordered all of his troops east of the Blue Ridge Mountains, some 42,000 effectives, to withdraw to the Rappahannock River, nearly half the distance to Richmond. Only Major General Stonewall Jackson's 5,400 men would remain in the Shenandoah Valley to threaten the right flank of any Federal advance.[4]

Johnston's move completely negated the very basis of the Urbanna Plan. Instead of turning the Confederates and getting between them and Richmond, McClellan now faced an enemy who had occupied the very area from which he proposed to begin his operation.

By this time, however, McClellan was committed to an amphibious campaign. He had previously noted that if Urbanna did not offer a suitable landing site, he could also use Mob Jack Bay or Fort Monroe, and then advance up the region between the James and York Rivers, known locally as "the Peninsula." Such an approach would allow him to use either river as a line of communication.[5] Under the present circumstances, however, such a maneuver did not offer the opportunity to cut off the Confederates as the Urbanna Plan would have. The campaign now would require a slow, toilsome march ending in a toe-to-toe fight at Richmond.[6]

The *Monitor* and the *Virginia*. This change was not the only new development that stood in the way of McClellan's offensive. Ironclad vessels had been introduced by the French in the Crimean War, but the tradition-bound U.S. Navy had not shown much interest. Now, the Confederates were well on their way to building one of their own from the remains of the *Merrimack*, once a 3,500-ton, 40-gun U.S. steam frigate that the Federals had burned and scuttled when they abandoned Norfolk's Gosport Navy Yard on April 20, 1861. Confederate engineers had raised the hulk, found it to be in good shape—except for the upper works, which had been destroyed by the fire—and were now converting it into an ironclad.[7]

Confederate Secretary of the Navy Stephen Mallory was an innovative thinker, albeit one who had few naval resources at his disposal. To offset this Confederate disadvantage, he developed the idea to equip the *Merrimack* with armor and use it to break the ever-tightening Federal blockade. With Mallory's backing, naval constructor John Luke Porter and Lieutenant John Mercer Brooke designed an ironclad ram which "made obsolete the navies of the world."[8]

Workers cut the hull down to the berth deck and built a casemate with slanting sides and ports for ten guns. The casemate walls contained 24 inches of oak and pine timber, with four inches of armor plating. An open grating covered the top of the casemate in order to admit light and air to the gun deck.

Brooke armed the ironclad with two 6.4-inch and two 7-inch Brooke rifles, and six 9-inch Dalhgren smoothbores. In addition, the casemate had a 36-degree slope and was covered down to two feet below the waterline with overlapping plates of 2-inch armor. An armored pilothouse was forward, and protruding from her bow was a fearsome looking 4-foot iron ram.[9]

The major shortcomings of the *Merrimack*'s conversion was a draught of 22 feet and inadequate engines from the scuttled warship.[10] This and her great size severely limited her maneuverability, but such a beast could still wreak havoc with any Federal flotilla. To counter this threat, the Federal Navy had proposed an attack on Norfolk to seize the Gosport Navy Yard before the Confederates could complete the *Merrimack*.[11] However, in an early example of the lack of unity of effort that would come to plague the Peninsula Campaign, the Federal Army did not support this operation, and the ironclad project continued without opposition. Now, this pre-emptive opportunity was gone.

On March 8, the *Merrimack*, since rechristened the *Virginia*, sailed down the Elizabeth River into Hampton Roads on what was supposed to be a trial run. Her guns had not yet been fired, and workmen swarmed over her superstructure, making last minute adjustments. She had a 300-man crew, largely recruited from the Army, and she was under the command of Commodore Franklin Buchanan. Buchanan was a seasoned and respected sailor from the "old Navy." Among his accomplishments, he was known as the "Father of Annapolis," because he had been instrumental in the founding of the U.S. Naval Academy and had served as its first super-intendent.

However, as the *Virginia* entered Hampton Roads, this "trial run" became something much more. Across the water, Buchanan saw five of the Federal blockade ships lying at anchor. The *Minnesota*, the *Roanoke*, and the *St. Lawrence* lay off of Fort Monroe, and the *Congress* and the *Cumberland* lay off of Newport News. Buchanan was faced with an opportunity he could not resist.

First, the *Virginia* went after the 50-gun *Congress* and the 30-gun *Cumberland*, making short work of them both. As the *Virginia* came within range, the *Congress* gave her a well-aimed broadside that slammed against the sloping armor with no effect. The *Virginia* continued her advance, impervious to additional salvos from the *Congress*, as well as shots now coming from Brigadier General Joseph Mansfield's coastal batteries. When Buchanan was as close as he wanted, he opened the *Virginia*'s ports and delivered a starboard broadside against the *Congress*. Then, he rammed the *Cumberland*, leaving a hole one of her officers said was large enough to accommodate "a horse and cart." When the *Virginia* swung clear, her iron ram-beak broke off in the *Cumberland*, and the Union ship began to fill with water. Called upon to surrender, her captain replied, "Never! I'll sink alongside." The *Cumberland* continued to fire as long as her guns remained above water but inevitably sank, leaving her mainmast flag still flying defiantly above the surface after the ship herself had struck bottom.

In the meantime, the wounded *Congress* had slipped her cable and run aground trying to escape. The *Virginia's* deeper draught forced her to remain at a 200-yard distance, but she nonetheless mercilessly raked the helpless *Congress* from end to end. With the captain dead, one of the *Congress'* lieutenants ran up the flag of surrender. Mansfield's coastal batteries continued to fire even as the *Virginia* approached the surrendered *Congress* to take on prisoners. When one of Mansfield's lieutenants protested that since the *Congress* had struck her flag the Confederates had the right to take possession of it unmolested, Mansfield replied, "I know the damned ship has surrendered, but *we* haven't." Confederates and Federals alike were wounded by Mansfield's artillery, including both Buchanan on the *Virginia* and his brother, who had remained with the Union, on the *Congress*. In retaliation, the *Virginia* dropped back and set the wooden *Congress* on fire with red-hot cannonballs.

By now, the other three frigates from Fort Monroe had entered the fray, and the *Virginia* singled out the *Minnesota*, forcing it to run aground. The tide, however, was beginning to ebb, and Executive Officer Lieutenant Catesby ap Roger Jones broke off the *Virginia's* attack against the *Minnesota* and withdrew toward the deeper waters of the Elizabeth River. The *Congress* burned into the night, creating an eerie glow until the fire reached the magazine and the frigate exploded. The Federal squadron awaited the next day with apprehension, but by then the odds would be a little more equal.[12]

Having been spurred into action by alarming reports of Confederate agents attempting to buy the latest in European ironclads, Congress met in a special session on July 4, 1861, to consider Secretary of the Navy Welles's plan for an initial ironclad program. Significantly, this event occurred seven days before Mallory had authorized work to begin on the Confederate ironclad. The result was the creation of a board of three naval officers tasked to consider various proposals for a new ironclad. By the first week of September, the board had received 16 different ideas and awarded a contract based on a design submitted by Swedish-American inventor John Ericsson.[13]

By this time, however, the Confederates had gained a three-month head start on actual construction. Nonetheless, the tireless Ericsson built the *Monitor* in less than 100 days, just in time to check the *Virginia's* rampage. The *Monitor* had a 172-foot-long, flat hull with no more than a foot or two of freeboard. The heavy oak beams of her raft deck supported a strake of seven-inch oak, which was then plated with an inch of iron. In the midship section, a revolving iron turret rose 9 feet above the deck and mounted two 11-inch Dahlgren guns that could throw a 165-pound solid shot one mile every 7 minutes. Aft of the turret was the smoke pipe, and forward was a stubby iron pilothouse. This claustrophobic structure of less than twelve square feet housed the pilot, helmsman, and commanding officer during battle. The most significant advantage the *Monitor* had over the *Virginia* was her twelve-foot draught and high maneuverability. She had a 60-man crew who had all volunteered directly from the Navy, which contrasted with the *Virginia's* largely ex-Army crew. Her captain was Lieutenant John Worden, a 28-year Navy veteran recently released from seven months in a Confederate prison. Nine days after she was commissioned, the *Monitor* was towed from New York to the Chesapeake by tug, and steamed past the Virginia capes late in the afternoon of March 8.[14] The fact that the Union's first ironclad arrived at the scene on the very same day that the Confederacy's first ironclad went into action must be considered one of the most remarkable coincidences of the war, although Union intelligence had been generally aware of the *Virginia's* development.

On the morning of March 9, the two ironclads presented an almost comical picture as they approached each other in what would become history's first duel between armored ships. Bruce Catton wrote that the *Virginia* looked like "a barn gone adrift and submerged to the eves."[15] The *Monitor's* appearance was commonly described as "a cheesebox on a raft" or "a tin can on a shingle."

Some members of the Monitor's 60-man crew are shown here relaxing on the deck. Photograph courtesy of the Library of Congress.

With Buchanan wounded, command of the *Virginia* fell to Lieutenant Jones. When the fight was joined, taking full advantage of her greater maneuverability, the *Monitor* scored several hits on the *Virginia*. John Wood, one of the lieutenants serving on the *Virginia*, reported that "The *Monitor* was firing every seven or eight minutes, and nearly every shot struck."[16] The pounding cracked the *Virginia's* railroad iron armor, but failed to penetrate the two-foot pitch pine and oak backing. The two combatants continued to duel indecisively for two hours, and then both ships withdrew for what amounted to a half-hour intermission.

In the second two-hour engagement, the *Virginia* made an attempt to ram the *Monitor*, but with the loss of her ram-beak from the previous day's fighting, this proved ineffective. Then, Jones tried to take advantage of the numerical advantage of his crew and made several attempts to board the *Monitor*. The Union ship evaded all efforts. Lieutenant John Eggleston, commander of the *Virginia's* starboard guns, confessed that "after two hours' incessant firing I find that I can do [the *Monitor*] as much damage by snapping my thumb at her every two minutes and a half." Worden took a moment to examine his ship and concluded, "The *Merrimac* could not sink us if we let her pound us for a month."[17]

Finally, Jones brought the *Virginia* to within ten yards of the *Monitor* and struck her pilothouse at point-blank range with a nine-inch shell. At the very moment of impact, Lieutenant Worden was peering out of the narrow pilothouse vision slit. The shell exploded right in his face, throwing a shower of iron splinters and gunpowder that destroyed his left eye. Worden screamed, "I am blind!" and commanded his helmsman to sheer off. Lieutenant Samuel Dana Greene, the executive officer, assumed command and maneuvered to re-engage the *Virginia*. However, after firing just a few rounds, the *Monitor* developed a problem with one of the pendulum shutters used to close the ports when the guns were run in for reloading. Greene broke contact and steered for the Middle Ground Shoal.

Aboard the *Virginia*, Jones could tell the *Monitor* was damaged, but the *Virginia*, too, had wounds to lick. She was leaking from the bow, her smokestack was shot away, and she could barely keep steam in her boilers. Chief engineer Ashton Ramsay reported, "Our ship was working worse and worse." Added to that, the men were exhausted, but the decisive consideration was that the tide had begun to ebb. Jones would have to either withdraw now or remain in Hampton Roads overnight. He decided to withdraw across Hampton Roads to Norfolk.[18]

Tactically, the battle had been a draw. In fact, neither ship suffered a single fatality. Strategically, however, it must be counted as a Federal victory, because although the *Virginia* was still a threat, anxiety over its potential to single-handedly destroy the Federal fleet had abated. The blockade would stand, and at least one obstacle to the success of McClellan's Peninsula Campaign had been lessened.[19]

The Peninsula Campaign. With the *Virginia's* threat neutralized, the embarkation of McClellan's Army began on March 17, with McClellan personally departing on April 1. The total tonnage moved was impressive. When McClellan arrived at Fort Monroe on April 2, some 58,000 men comprising 5 infantry divisions and some cavalry, as well as about 100 guns, were already disembarked and ready to go. A total of 90,000 men would eventually make the move. Along with these came nearly 15,000 horses and mules, more than 1,100 wagons, 44 batteries, rolls of telegraph wire, timbers for pontoons, medicine, and countless other supplies. The transfer was fully effected on April 5. During the process, the only losses suffered were eight mules that drowned when a barge floundered.[20]

To accomplish this feat, John Tucker, the general transportation agent of the War Department, had assembled a picturesque flotilla of more than 400 transports including ocean liners, bay and harbor steamers, tugs, barges, and schooners of almost every size, shape, and description.[21] Such a colossal move was without precedent, leading one British observer to liken it to "the stride of a giant."[22]

Once McClellan reached the Peninsula, however, things began to slow considerably. His original intention was to take Yorktown immediately with the help of the Navy.[23] When he arrived at Fort Monroe, he met with his naval counterpart, Flag Officer Louis Goldsborough, to finalize the plan. By McClellan's account, Goldsborough told him he could neither protect the James as a line of supply nor provide vessels to help reduce the batteries at Yorktown and Gloucester by either bombardment or threatening their rear.[24] McClellan reported that Goldsborough "could only aid in the final attack after our land batteries had essentially silenced [the Confederate] fire."[25]

Part of the reason for Goldsborough's conclusion was his belief that his main effort was to protect the Federal force from the *Virginia*, and this left him with only seven wooden gunboats to support other Army operations. These were adequate for furnishing escort and fire support for landing, but were by no means up to challenging shore batteries. In fact, their guns could not even elevate sufficiently to reach the batteries on Yorktown's bluffs.[26]

Bruce Catton's research yields a different account of the meeting between McClellan and Goldsborough. According to Catton, instead of discussing a bombardment of Yorktown, McClellan asked for the Navy's help in reducing the Confederate fort at Gloucester on the north side of the river. Between Gloucester and Yorktown, the York is a mere 1,000 yards wide, so the twin Confederate forts effectively sealed the mouth of the river.[27]

By Catton's account, McClellan briefed Goldsborough that he wanted to land troops on the banks of the Severn River, a few miles north of Gloucester, and then assault the city from its rear. Success here would ideally lead to the surrender of Yorktown, but at the very least would allow gunboats to advance up the York.

Goldsborough assigned the seven wooden gunboats for the Severn River operation, and on April 4 McClellan told his First Corps commander Brigadier General Irwin McDowell, who had still not left Alexandria, that his corps would be used to attack Gloucester. It was not until after issuing this order that McClellan learned that McDowell's corps had been retained for the defense of Washington because of Major General Stonewall Jackson's successful campaign in the Shenandoah Valley.[28] There would be no First Corps attack on Gloucester.

Thus, the final operation had nothing of the joint Army-Navy flair originally envisioned. Whether you prefer McClellan's recollection that Goldsborough could not help or Catton's conclusion that McClellan changed his plan and then felt stymied by the loss of McDowell, the result was the same. There was no naval bombardment, and there was no Severn River operation. The campaign then proceeded with a very uncomplicated maneuver in which one Union column marched up the Peninsula on the right towards Yorktown, while another marched on the left towards Williamsburg.[29]

This left column was the Fourth Corps commanded by Brigadier General Erasmus Keyes. Its aim was to turn the Confederate flank and push on to Halfway House between Yorktown and Williamsburg. Once Keyes gained control of the road network around the Halfway House area, Confederate Major General John Magruder would be forced to withdraw from Yorktown.[30] This hopeful plan quickly went awry when, late in the afternoon of April 5, Keyes's advance element came under fire from artillery and entrenched infantry at Lee's Mill, where the maps indicated only a harmless depot. At dusk, Keyes's force collapsed in an unorganized halt among the wooded swamps east of the Warwick. Based on this contact, Keyes reported that,

"Magruder is in a strongly fortified position behind Warwick River, the fords to which had been destroyed by dams, and the approaches to which are through dense forests, swamps, and marshes. No part of his line as far as discovered can be taken by assault without an enormous waste of life."[31]

Keyes's report motivated McClellan to cease maneuver and initiate siege operations, which lasted until May 3 when, as at Manassas, the Confederates abandoned Yorktown and withdrew up the Peninsula on their own terms. With the decision to evacuate Yorktown, General Johnston had the opportunity to pursue the strategy he had favored all along—retreat rapidly to the immediate vicinity of Richmond and thereby negate the possibility of the Federals' outmaneuvering him through their command of the waterways. Thus, Johnston felt a strong desire to put as much distance between the Confederate Army and Yorktown as possible.

Johnston withdrew along two roads that came together eleven miles past Yorktown and two miles short of Williamsburg. Major General James Longstreet fought a sharp delaying action at Williamsburg to buy time for Johnston's withdrawal, and then quietly withdrew his own force under the cover of darkness. As dawn broke on May 6, Federal pickets crept forward only to find the Confederate defenses empty.

In the context of the larger Peninsula Campaign, Johnston's delaying action allowed General Robert E. Lee, then serving as President Davis's military advisor, to effect a "re-concentration" of forces that would ultimately turn the tables on McClellan's offensive. However, of more immediate concern to the coastal war, Johnston's withdrawal up the Peninsula forced the Confederates to abandon Norfolk. On May 10, a force under Major General John Wool landed at Willoughby's Point and accepted the surrender of the city.[32] This left the *Virginia* without a home port. Her draught of 22 feet was too deep for her to withdraw up the James, and finally, on May 11, she was abandoned and blown up.

The Loss of Norfolk. Goldsborough dispatched Lieutenant Thomas Selfridge to Sewell's Point, and Commander A. Ludlow Case to Craney Island to ascertain the situations there. Both men found that the Confederates had departed, and the Federals assumed control of these strategic points. The *Susquehanna, Seminole, Dakota,* and *San Jacinto* all advanced to Norfolk and dropped their anchors. All the fleeing Confederates could do was set fire to some buildings.

This loss of Norfolk represented the end of any hopes the Confederacy had for home construction of a deep-sea navy.[33] Instead, Norfolk became the headquarters for the Federal Navy. David Porter concluded, "The re-occupation of Norfolk Navy Yard was a great convenience to the North Atlantic squadron, which had been obliged to send most of its vessels to Philadelphia and New York for repairs, and now the operations up the James River could be carried on more effectively."[34]

When the Federals regained the Navy Yard at Norfolk, they not only deprived the Confederacy of an important resource, they also greatly improved the logistical support base of the Atlantic blockade.
Photograph courtesy of the Library of Congress.

Goldsborough did attempt to project his force up the James in an operation that culminated with the battle of Drewry's Bluff. Ninety feet high, Drewry's Bluff stood on the south bank of the James River less than eight miles from Richmond. There, the river bends sharply to the east for a short distance and then turns again to the south. The first step for the Confederates was to improve the natural obstacle created by this bend in the river. To do this, they sank several stone-laden hulks and drove piles at critical points to narrow the channel. Now, any Federal gunboats making the turn would have to expose their flanks to the fort.

The Confederates then placed guns from the scuttled *Virginia*, along with other weapons, nearly 100 feet above the water level, knowing that the Federal gunboats would be unable to elevate their guns high enough to hit them. In all, the Confederates had four smoothbore and four rifled cannon trained on the river.

These defenses were tested on May 15, when Commander John Rodgers and a Federal squadron of five vessels—the ironclads *Monitor* and *Galena* as well as the wooden *Aroostook*, *Port Royal*, and *Naugatuck*—advanced on Drewry's Bluff. In a four-hour engagement, this picturesque Federal fleet proved no match for the defenders, with the astute Confederate artillery placement carrying the day. The *Galena* alone was hit 44 times. This fire was especially effective because the Confederates were able to deliver plunging fire down on the *Galena*, penetrating the ironclad's thin deck armor, while the Federal shells were unable to reach the Confederates high on the bluff. Because of this problem with elevation, the *Monitor* played virtually no role in the engagement. The defeat of the ironclads at Drewry's Bluff would serve as a caution to many in the Federal Navy. In particular, Admiral Samuel Du Pont would remember it as he contemplated his latter attack on Fort McAllister on the Ogeechee River, Georgia, in January–March 1863.

Part of the Federal failure at Drewry's Bluff can be traced to the continued difficulty in establishing true coordination between the land and naval forces. Against an unsupported naval attack, the accurate fire of the Confederate heavy guns on the bluff and effective sharp shooting from the riverbanks proved decisive. One Confederate officer, however, observed, "Had Commander Rogers been supported by a few brigades, landed at City Point or above on the south side, Richmond would have been evacuated."[35] For this reason, Douglas Southall Freeman notes that Drewry's Bluff "showed the possibility of joint operations on James River by the Federal Army and Navy" and led General Lee to believe that the Federals might later initiate an operation there similar to Yorktown.[36]

Although the Federal Navy recognized that a joint force was required, there would be no such cooperation. Goldsborough lamented, "Without the Army the Navy can make no real headway towards Richmond. This is as clear as the sun at noonday to the mind."[37] Indeed, the Navy had requested "a cooperating land force" for the Drewry's Bluff operation, but McClellan had wired the War Department that he was "not yet ready to cooperate with them." This was in spite of his previous promise that the "Navy will receive prompt support wherever and whenever required." The Federal forces on the Peninsula were still a long way from working jointly.

The Navy did provide assistance to McClellan when his retreating army came within range of its protective guns on the James, first at Malvern Hill and then at Harrison's Landing. And finally the ships returned the Army of the Potomac to northern Virginia in early August, once the campaign had been abandoned. Two years later, U.S. Grant would reprise it, reaching a decisive point south of Richmond, at Petersburg, though on a blood-soaked overland march rather than more easily via seaborne transit.

Despite the fact that the Drewry's Bluff operation and the Peninsula Campaign in general would be a Federal defeat, Norfolk would remain in Federal hands and provide the North Atlantic Blockading Squadron with an adequate base inside Confederate territory. To add even more to this momentum, the same day the Confederates evacuated Norfolk, they also evacuated Pensacola, giving the Gulf Coast Blockading Squadron a similar prize.[38]

The
Gulf
Campaign

SHIP ISLAND

NEW ORLEANS

PENSACOLA

GALVESTON

SHIP ISLAND: SETTING THE STAGE

In its August 6, 1861, report, the Navy Board had recommended the seizure of Ship Island, off the coast of Biloxi, Mississippi. The Federals already held one base in the Gulf—Key West, Florida—but Key West was not in a central location. It was 600 miles east of Mobile and 800 miles from New Orleans. Ship Island lay roughly halfway between these two major Confederate ports and would be exactly what the Federals needed. Buoyed by its success at Hatteras Inlet, the Navy Board turned its attention to Ship Island, its second operation designed to strengthen and improve the blockade, and thus began the Gulf Campaign.[1]

The selection of Ship Island indicated the outstanding strategic vision and foresight of the Navy Board. In its August 6 report, the Navy Board had recognized the importance of New Orleans, but considered direct operations against it at the time to require a prohibitively large force. Instead, the Board recommended that the capture of New Orleans be placed on the strategic back burner until "we are prepared to ascend the river with vessels of war sufficiently protected to contend with the forts." In the meantime, the Board suggested the Navy concentrate on "shutting [New Orleans] up, suspending its trade, and obstructing the freedom of its intercourse with the ocean and with the neighboring coasts, feeling assured that the moral effect of such a course will be quite as striking as that of its possession by the United States." Thus, instead of seizing New Orleans immediately, the Board recommended the capture of Ship Island.[2]

An Easy Prey. Ship Island was low and sandy, about seven miles long, less than a mile wide, and naturally barren save for a group of pine

110

trees at one end. In spite of its desolate appearance, it had much to recommend it as a Federal objective. Not only could it support blockade operations against Mobile and New Orleans, it could also be a fine jumping-off point for an assault against either location.[3]

These advantages were made even more attractive by the fact that Ship Island was an easy target. The Federal government had begun constructing Fort Massachusetts there in 1856 but never finished it. Indeed, a January 18, 1861, report to the Secretary of War listed Fort Massachusetts as "not prepared for much defense."[4] After Mississippi seceded, state forces seized Ship Island on January 20, 1861, and in July, the Confederate Navy landed a small force there. Toward the end of the month, Lieutenant Colonel Henry Allen arrived with three companies of the 4th Regiment of Louisiana Volunteers and did what he could, which was not much. Allen had his men build sandbag batteries, and Lieutenant Alexander Warley supplemented the fort's few small artillery pieces with an 8-inch naval gun and 32-pounder.

Duty on Ship Island was mildly uncomfortable, but overall fairly leisurely. On July 30, Allen was quoted in the Baton Rouge *Weekly Advocate* that "here we intend to stay and keep 'watch and ward' over this 'Isle of tranquil delight' in spite of mosquitoes, hot sun, bilge water, live Yankees and big ships." Nonetheless, some of Allen's men objected to the physical labor and one company mutinied. Allen quickly restored order and "marched the whole force, with loaded muskets, upon them, and quelled the mutiny without shedding a drop of blood." This internal threat quieted, Allen continued his work on his defenses and then settled into a routine characterized by discipline and drill. The daily regimen was strict. Alcohol was prohibited, and infractions of Allen's rules drew harsh punishments.[5]

In spite of this flurry of construction and façade of normalcy, there seems to be what Zed Burns calls, a "nonrecognition of the strategic importance of Ship Island to the Mississippi Coast and to the City of New Orleans by the Confederate authorities."[6] There were some halfhearted efforts to properly arm and fortify Ship Island, but no real progress was made.[7] Without the needed improvements, Ship Island was untenable.

On September 3, Colonel Johnson Duncan was ordered to take temporary command of Ship Island during a period when Allen was absent. Duncan was not impressed by Ship Island's fort and considered it nearly indefensible. He concluded the island should be evacuated and convinced his superior, Major General David Twiggs, headquartered at New Orleans, that this was the case. On September 13, Twiggs received orders from the Confederate government in Richmond to "take immediate measures to evacuate Ship Island, and cause the guns to be removed at once." That same day, Twiggs passed the order on to Duncan.[8]

The evacuation began on August 28 but was accelerated to completion on September 17 when Allen, now back in command, observed "two heavy frigates, two steamers, a brig, and two tenders" bearing down on what he once considered his "Isle of tranquil delight." Included in this armada was the five-gun *Massachusetts*, which had been stationed off of Ship Island for much of the summer. When the *Massachusetts's* commander Melancton Smith fired a few probing shots, he was surprised to see the Confederates set fire to their barracks and evacuate. Smith proceeded to occupy the island with men from the *Massachusetts, Preble,* and *Marion* and convert the slender prize into a naval supply depot.[9] He also found a note attached to the headquarters bulletin board that read:

> Fort Twiggs
> Ship Island
> September 17, 1861
>
> To: Commanding Officer of the USS *Massachusetts*
>
> By order of my government I have this day evacuated Ship Island. This my brave soldiers under my command do with much reluctance and regret. For three long months your good ship has been our constant companion.
>
> We have not exactly "lived and loved together," but we have been intimately acquainted, having exchanged cards on the 9th day of July last.

In leaving you today we beg you to accept our best wishes for your health and happiness while sojourning on this pleasant, hospitable shore.

That we may have another exchange of courtesies before the war closes, and that we may meet face to face in closer quarters, is the urgent prayer of very truly, Your obedient servant.

> H. S. Allen
> Lieutenant Colonel
> Commanding
> Ship Island[10]

Butler's Scheme. In the meantime, Major General Benjamin Butler had parlayed his minor role in the Hatteras Inlet success into a reputation as being somewhat of a strategist.[11] He used the opportunity to return to Massachusetts to raise troops for some future expedition. However, Butler's original idea for a follow-up to Hatteras Inlet in the North Carolina Sounds ultimately fell to Major General Ambrose Burnside for execution, and Butler's next plan to operate on the Eastern Shore of Virginia came to nothing.

Butler was an enterprising and self-promoting man who would not let such minor setbacks stand in his way. He had never thought the blockade was a good idea, feeling that instead of hurting the South, the blockade actually benefited it by making the Confederacy self-sufficient while greatly inflating the value of its primary export commodity, cotton. Rather than keep goods out of the South, Butler felt the proper strategy was to allow Northern merchants to flood the Southern market—especially with luxuries—and extract cotton and tobacco in payment. In Butler's mind, this trade would quickly depress the price of cotton, bankrupt the Confederate economy, fund the Federal war effort with customs duties and licenses, and fuel Northern industry.

While the Treasury Department saw some merit in Butler's scheme, it also saw the possibility of such an action provoking a European nation, such as England, to declare war on the Union. But if Butler's plan could not be fully implemented, the Secretary of the Treasury saw no harm in issuing licenses to ship goods to ports under Federal control or allowing agents to seize or buy cotton and tobacco within Federally occupied territory, as long as these shippers and agents were loyal to the United States and certified that the merchandise was not consigned to Confederate sympathizers. Beyond those concerns, where the cotton came from and where it went was the responsibility of local dealers and of no concern to the Federal government.

This policy was just the foot in the door that Butler needed. Butler was from Lowell, Massachusetts, where he owned half of a textile company. He knew New England mill towns were suffering from the blockade and by competition from English companies whose suppliers were able to run it. New England cloth manufacturers were eager to obtain cotton at almost any price, and the Deep South states bordering the Gulf of Mexico were the best source for the rough grade of raw cotton the buyers wanted. It was all coming together for Butler. He would seize a Confederate port on the Gulf, obtain cotton licenses for his agents, further his military reputation, shore up his political base back home, and all the while make a few dollars for himself.

With this new plan in mind, Butler set about recruiting, and by the end of November he sent the first contingent of his New England division to Ship Island. These 2,000 men were commanded by Brigadier General J. W. Phelps, who Butler instructed to fortify the island and, while waiting for the rest of the division, find a favorable point on the coast from which to ship cotton.[12]

But while Butler was preparing his commercial enterprise, Captain David Porter arrived in Washington on November 12 with a more militarily focused idea—reduce the forts below New Orleans with a mortar flotilla. Porter was convinced that the Navy could do the job alone, and soldiers from Ship Island could then move forward and garrison the captured forts. The plan was approved, and Rear Admiral David Farragut was tapped to command the West Gulf Blockading Squadron and the fleet for the New Orleans operation.[13]

Butler had been a troublesome personality back East, and many were glad to get him out of the limelight. Secretary of the Navy Welles recalled, "all would be relieved were this restless officer sent to Ship Island or the far

Southwest, where his energy, activity and impulsive force might be employed in desultory aquatic and shore duty in concert with the Navy."[14] Major General George McClellan's chief of staff and father-in-law Randolph Barnes Marcy saw Butler's assignment as a banishment, assessing, "I guess we have found a hole to bury this Yankee elephant in."[15]

Now, however, instead of being "put out to pasture," Butler's impending convergence on Ship Island made him the logical commander of the Army's contribution to the New Orleans operation. On February 23, he received orders to assume "command of the land forces destined to cooperate with the navy in the attack upon New Orleans.... Should the navy fail to reduce the works you will land your forces and siege-train, and endeavor to breach the works, silence their fire, and carry them by assault." The following day McClellan issued General Orders No. 20, which created a new "Department of the Gulf" to "comprise all the coast of the Gulf States as may be occupied by the forces under Major General B. F. Butler, U. S. Volunteers."[16]

The Federal Build Up. Federal forces began descending on Ship Island from a variety of locations. Farragut left Hampton Roads aboard his flagship *Hartford* on February 2 and reached Ship Island on February 20. The Army contingent also got in motion with Butler himself, setting sail on the steamer *Mississippi* on February 25 with 1,600 men and his wife. He reached Ship Island on March 23, and his additions brought the Army strength to 15,255. Porter had the toughest time. He worked feverishly to construct, assemble, equip, and man his mortar flotilla, and by the end of February, he rendezvoused at Key West. There he had to quell a small disciplinary problem with several of his merchant masters. With this incident behind him, Porter departed on March 6, still short two tugs, and reached Ship Island five days later. By March 18, the entire flotilla, including the two dilatory tugs, was in position.[17]

As Farragut assembled his ships, he encountered several obstacles. The first was that his fleet rapidly consumed most of the coal on Ship Island. To make matters worse, Captain James Alden brought word that the supply holds at Key West were out of coal. As a stopgap measure, Farragut borrowed 800 tons of coal from the advance unit of Butler's command and then sent a request to the Naval Office for

10,000 tons a month. In the meantime, Welles assured Farragut that 3,000 tons were on the way.[18] As Du Pont had experienced in Mexico, Farragut was feeling firsthand the logistical pressures of maintaining a blockade of the vast Confederate coastline. It was a poignant reminder of why seizing strategic points, like Ship Island, was necessary.

But Farragut did not sit idle while waiting for his fleet to assemble. Just two days after his arrival, Farragut sent Captain Thomas Craven and the *Brooklyn* to Head of Passes, the junction of the four main channels of the Mississippi River 15 miles up from the Gulf, with orders to take "all the vessels blockading the mouths of the Mississippi that can enter," and "keep your position until further orders from me." Farragut wanted telegraph wires to New Orleans cut, pilots captured and sent to Ship Island, and all blockade running stopped.[19]

A Warning Unheeded. In hindsight, Shelby Foote would write that the "seizure of Ship Island had exposed the [Confederate] nation's tender underbelly to assault."[20] Zed Burns would agree, noting, "It seems probable that had Ship Island been held and heavily fortified [by the Confederates], as well as the eastern end of Cat Island, Confederate control of the Mississippi Sound, as well as the coastal area from New Orleans to Pensacola, would have been more successful."[21] However, at the time, the Federal build-up caused remarkably little concern among the Confederate high command, including Secretary of War and native Louisianan Judah Benjamin. Like most locals, the Confederate leadership felt that the strong Forts Jackson and St. Philip would negate any attack on New Orleans from the south. If the city was to be attacked, the Confederates reasoned, it would be by a land assault from the north.[22] The Confederates' false sense of security for New Orleans would soon come back to haunt them.

Continued Service. While Ship Island's greatest contribution to the Federal war effort came as the staging area for the capture of New Orleans, it continued to provide an assortment of other services. After all but two companies departed Ship Island to occupy New Orleans, a new contingent of troops from New England arrived under the command of Major General Nathaniel Banks. Then on January 12, 1863, seven companies of the 2nd Louisiana Native Guards, a regiment of black soldiers, arrived to help garrison the island. As problems developed between the white and black soldiers, Banks decided to withdraw the white companies, and the Louisiana Native Guards remained as the primary garrison of Ship Island for the duration of the war.[23]

Ship Island had been used as a prison and detention center almost as soon as Federal troops landed there, and it would continue in this capacity. Butler sent the first detainees there from New Orleans in June 1862.[24] Common offenses involved pro-Confederate or anti-Federal statements and conduct. For example, Fidel Keller, a New Orleans bookseller, placed a skeleton labeled "Chickahominy" (a Virginia battlefield area that had cost many Federal casualties) in his store window and received a two year sentence to the Ship Island prison for having brought "the authority of the United States and our army into contempt." Ann Larue dressed up in Confederate colors to distribute handbills announcing that McClellan had been captured. In addition, a woman laughed when the funeral cortege of a Federal officer passed her residence, and another wore a Confederate flag on her person. John Andrew was accused of making a cross from the bones of a dead Federal officer. All these offenders landed in prison on Ship Island.[25]

Butler was also able to use Ship Island as part of his original cotton speculation scheme. Even before reaching New Orleans, he captured about $5,000 worth of cotton and turpentine, which he sent north from Ship Island aboard a government ship. After the capture of New Orleans things got even worse, with Porter complaining Butler was conducting illicit trade "for which he charges license, which goes God knows where."[26]

Even more important than these activities was the Federal build-up of troops preparatory for the attack on New Orleans. Federal troop strength on Ship Island peaked in April 1862 with more than 15,000 men.[27] Still, Confederate authorities such as Major General Mansfield Lovell, the man charged with New Orleans' defense, viewed such activity askance. Lovell wrote Richmond in late February, "I regard Butler's Ship Island expedition as a harmless menace so far as New Orleans is concerned. A black Republican dynasty will never give an old Breckinridge Democrat like Butler command of any expedition which they had any idea would result in such a glorious success as the capture of New Orleans." Time would prove Lovell dangerously wrong.

NEW ORLEANS:
THE PRICE OF UNPREPAREDNESS

If the Confederates were somewhat complacent about the threat from Ship Island, the Federals clearly considered its capture a preliminary step toward attacking New Orleans. New Orleans, by far the South's biggest city with a population of 168,000, was a lucrative target. Lieutenant General Winfield Scott was so confident in the importance of New Orleans that he considered it decisive to Federal victory. He told President Lincoln the Federals must "fight all the battles that were necessary, take all the positions we could find and garrison them, fight a battle at New Orleans and win it, and thus end the war."[1] Likewise, the Navy Board's John Barnard felt "failure [of an operation against New Orleans] would be a terrible blow; its success would bring us almost to the close of the war."[2]

New Orleans' importance lay in its status as a port, a shipbuilding center, and as a key city on the Mississippi River. Its wealth lay in cotton. In 1860, its port receipts exceeded $185 million, of which cotton accounted for 60 percent. That year New Orleans handled 2,000,000 bales of cotton. As a point of comparison, the Confederate government itself would never hold title to more than 400,000 bales.[3] If cotton was indeed King, then New Orleans was a key member of its court.

New Orleans was also one of the South's most important ship-building centers, and by 1861, every shipyard in New Orleans was busy building, converting, or repairing some type of warlike vessel. It was a largely decentralized effort with few of the ships actually earmarked for the fledgling Confederate Navy, but three ironclads were under construction. The *Manassas* was a private enterprise built to be a profit-making privateer. The *Louisiana* and *Mississippi* were being built under separate contracts authorized by Confederate Secretary of the Navy Stephen Mallory.[4]

The construction was in most cases a confused and competing effort that did not efficiently use the scarce Confederate resources that had been made even more limited by the Federal blockade. By sealing the mouth of the Mississippi, the Federals forced the New Orleans shipbuilders to bring the iron and machinery they needed from Virginia and the eastern Confederacy by rail. The rickety Southern railroads were inadequate to transport such loads efficiently. For example, construction of the *Mississippi* was held up while a Richmond firm shipped the propeller shaft across the Confederacy to New Orleans. Because of this delay, the *Mississippi* was still under construction when it was needed for New Orleans' defense.[5] Nonetheless, New Orleans was a hubbub of shipbuilding activity, and rumors of Confederate ironclads in New Orleans raised concerns in the Federal Navy office.

Initial Defense. Louisiana's convention did not meet to consider secession until January 23, 1861, but on January 8 the aggressive Governor Thomas Overton ordered the state militia to seize the Federal arsenal at Baton Rouge and the key Forts Jackson and St. Philip, which guarded the Mississippi approaches 75 miles south of New Orleans. Fort St. Philip was a citadel built by the Spanish in the 1790s and expanded two decades later. Fort Jackson was a more modern and powerful structure built in a pentagonal design. On January 10, the forts were in Louisiana hands, and on January 26, Louisiana voted itself out of the Union.[6]

The man first in charge of New Orleans' defenses was Major General David Twiggs, who arrived in New Orleans on May 31 as commander of Department No. 1, consisting of Louisiana and the southern parts of Mississippi and Alabama. Twiggs was hardly a popular choice for commander. The people of New Orleans would have much preferred native son Pierre Gustave Toutant Beauregard or even Braxton Bragg. Even when Twiggs was in his prime, Winfield Scott had considered him one of his worst officers in Mexico.[7] Now, although Twiggs was the Confederacy's ranking general at the time of his appointment, he was 71 years old, physically infirm, and often unable to leave his quarters.

Still, Twiggs was loyal to the cause, and he began organizing his defenses. By the summer he had 5,000 men camped around New Orleans, 4,000 being trained at Camp Moore, just north of the town of Tangipahoa, and new companies still forming. Significantly, and perhaps reflecting the relative lack of concern for New Orleans, 8,000 Louisiana soldiers were in service outside the state.[8]

Faulty Assumption. At this early point in the war, the Confederacy was most concerned with an attack on New Orleans from the south. On January 10, Louisiana Senators Judah Benjamin and John Slidell sent messages to New Orleans warning that "Secret attempts continue to be made to garrison Southern ports. We think there is special reason to fear surprise from the Gulf Squadron." Likewise the governor was warned, "The danger is not from St. Louis, but from the sea."[9] Commodore George Hollins, the man Secretary Mallory had dispatched to New Orleans on July 31 to tend to its naval defenses, shared this opinion.[10] These assessments were in fact consistent with the Federal strategy. Indeed, Scott's original Anaconda Plan had envisioned an amphibious attack on New Orleans from the Gulf.[11]

By the time of Hollins's arrival, however, a competing point of view had gained ascendancy in the Confederacy. Faith in Forts Jackson and St. Philip, as well as the broad inland bayous and a string of fortifications known as the New Orleans' Chalmette defense line, led observers like local resident George Cable to believe, "Nothing afloat could pass the forts. Nothing that walked could get through the swamps."[12] Instead, Federal ironclad construction upriver at places like Cincinnati, Carondelet (near St. Louis), and Mound City, caused many to think the real threat would be from the north. Twiggs shared this view, and he developed a plan to convert six large floating docks into floating batteries that he would have towed to a point upriver "where the channel is narrow and [could] be made an impassable barrier to the vessels of the enemy."[13] On August 24, Secretary of War Leroy Walker approved Twiggs's project. As for the southern approach, Twiggs anticipated the Federal Navy would use only wooden warships there and considered Forts Jackson and St. Philip to be capable of defending against such a limited threat.[14]

Pope's Run. Indeed, in the first naval encounter, the Confederates had reason to believe the Federal Navy was not really very powerful at all. As progress toward building the Confederate ironclads proceeded at a frustratingly slow pace, the aggressive Hollins finally lost his patience. On October 9, he commandeered the *Manassas*, running its crew of privateersmen and its part owner off the vessel. This acquisition gave Hollins a total of six lightly armed riverboats and an untested ram. He now planned to use these assets to strike the enemy with everything he had; an undertaking that would be made easier by the fact that the Federal commander, Captain John Pope, had not bothered to position a single picket boat as a guard.[15]

In the early morning hours of October 12, Hollins attacked the remarkably complacent Federal ships. Pope was thoroughly surprised, and by 8:00 a.m. he signaled his vessels below the bar "to get underway." One of his commanders misinterpreted the message to be an order to "abandon ship," and Pope's planned orderly withdrawal devolved into an unorganized rush for safety. Secretary of the Navy Welles derisively dubbed the fiasco "Pope's Run," and Admiral David Porter would later opine, "Put this matter in any light you may, it is the most ridiculous affair that ever took place in the American Navy."[16] But while the Confederate "victory" embarrassed the Federals and boosted Confederate morale, it did no permanent damage other than to Pope's career. The purely tactical contest did nothing to further the security of New Orleans or stem the growing Federal advantage.[17] In fact, Porter hypothesizes that it may even have caused the Confederates "to underrate the Northern Navy."[18]

Farragut Assumes Command. Until recently, Twiggs and others may have been justified in thinking that wooden ships were no match for heavy fortifications, but events at Hatteras Inlet and Port Royal had changed things. Twiggs may have missed this lesson, but Assistant Secretary of the Navy Gustavus Fox and then Commander David Porter had not. If Du Pont could defeat forts at Port Royal, Porter saw no reason that it could not also be done on the lower Mississippi, and Porter thought he should be the man to give it a try. It all made sense to Fox, who had likewise begun thinking of a plan to attack New Orleans from the south.[19]

After first seeing Fox, Porter obtained an audience with Welles and briefed him on a plan to precede the attack on New Orleans with a 48-hour bombardment of Forts Jackson and St. Philip with 13-inch mortar shells. By mounting these mortars on modified schooners, Porter explained, there would be no need for a large cooperating land force. With the Navy providing most of the firepower, the only support required from the Army would be a few thousand soldiers to garrison the captured forts and occupy the city. Welles was convinced, and together with Porter he obtained President Lincoln's approval. For his part, Lincoln was glad to see the Navy moving after the Pope's Run debacle, chiding Welles, "Now, Mr. Secretary, the navy has been hunting pet rabbits long enough; suppose you send them after skunks."[20]

But Porter was only a commander, far too junior to lead such an expedition. Instead, Welles dispatched Porter to meet with Captain David Farragut, Porter's foster brother, to determine Farragut's views on the New Orleans plan. Farragut had a positive opinion, and on January 9, 1862, Secretary Welles gave him command of the newly constituted West Gulf Blockading Squadron, stretching from western Florida to the Rio Grande. Ivan Musicant calls the decision Welles's "most important [appointment] of the war, not only for the navy's sake, but for the Lincoln administration as well."[21]

Flag Officer William McKean, who had previously commanded the Gulf Blockading Squadron, became commander of the new East Gulf Blockading Squadron. Dividing the command meant that each man could now concentrate on a smaller area. It also gave Welles a cover for sending Farragut to the Gulf without telegraphing his plans for New Orleans. On March 19, the Senate confirmed Farragut's appointment to flag officer.[22]

While the Federal plans and command arrangements were solidifying, those of the Confederates were falling apart. By this time, the prevalent opinion in the Confederate high command had become that an attack would come from upriver. Thus, Secretary Mallory sent Hollins, his Mosquito Fleet, and the floating battery *New Orleans* north to join Major General Leonidas Polk in the Confederate defense of Columbus, Kentucky. The move left New Orleans without naval protection as the several Confederate shipbuilding projects still lay in varying stages of completion and transportation. Perhaps Mallory felt that the Army had seen to the necessary improvements at Forts Jackson and St. Philip, but coordination between the Navy and War Departments was so weak, he really had no way of knowing. If such work was being done, it should have fallen to Army commander Twiggs, but he was not doing it. In fact, on October 5, he had asked to be relieved of his command. Historian Chester Hearn describes the situation for the Confederates as one in which "confusion continued to propagate, and over the next five months it grew steadily worse."[23]

Lovell's Arrival. Even before Twiggs had tendered his resignation, the War Department had dispatched Mansfield Lovell to New Orleans to serve as Twiggs's assistant. Twiggs's departure changed that. When Lovell arrived in New Orleans on October 17, he learned he was now the new commander of Department No. 1 and had been promoted to major general. Prior to leaving Richmond, Lovell had spoken with both President Davis and Secretary of War Judah Benjamin and argued that the only way to properly defend New Orleans was to unify the land and naval commands. Davis disagreed and wrote Lovell on October 17:

> The fleet maintained at the port of New Orleans and its vicinity is not part of your command; and the purpose of which it is sent there, or removed from there, are communicated in orders and letters of a department with which you have no direct communication. It must... be obvious to you that you could not assume command of these officers and vessels coming with your geographical department, but not placed on duty with you, without serious detriment to discipline and probably injury to the public service.

Davis added that he encouraged Lovell to maintain "unrestrained intercourse and cordial fraternization" with the Navy.[24] Interestingly, Davis failed to send a similar note to Mallory or Hollins imploring them to cooperate with Lovell. What Clifford Dowdey calls a

"Southern-style farce of divided command" would continue to plague the defense of New Orleans.[25]

At first, Lovell appeared to display the energy the residents of New Orleans had hoped for. He set out on an inspection tour and "found matters generally so deficient and incomplete that I was unwilling to commit their condition to writing for fear of their falling into the wrong hands."[26] Among other things, Lovell found inferior ammunition, antiquated cannon, manpower shortages, unimpeded river approaches, unfinished lines, incompetent officers, and dilapidated fortifications.[27] It was an unpromising situation for the new commander.

Undaunted, Lovell worked diligently and made progress. By January 1862, he had replaced many of the unsuitable guns, expanding local foundries and establishing his own ammunition factory in the process. He laid track to connect New Orleans with the Pontchartrain and Mexican Gulf Railroad in order to speed up the movement of supplies and men. He also scavenged loose chain and anchors from across the South to strengthen the defensive log boom across the Mississippi. Lovell now had a barrier securely chained to both banks, held in place by 15 anchors weighing from 2,500 to 4,000 pounds and laid in 25 fathoms of water. Obviously proud, Lovell wrote, "This raft is a complete obstruction, and has enfilading fire from Fort Jackson and direct fire from Saint Philip."[28] By the end of December, Lovell had 3,500 effectives manning his entrenchments and another 6,000 well-armed volunteers in the city. Including his exterior lines, Lovell commanded a total force of about 15,000 men.[29]

But as fast as Lovell could improve things, the War Department seemed to unravel them. Part of this problem was the low priority New Orleans was receiving from Richmond. Medical supplies, clothing, rifles, and even some of the big naval guns were being siphoned off for service in Virginia, South Carolina, and Tennessee, because neither Davis nor Benjamin considered New Orleans in imminent danger of attack. Even after Lovell raised and trained a force of 10,000 infantry, Benjamin sent half of them to reinforce General Albert Sidney Johnston's Army of Mississippi at Corinth after the loss of Forts Henry and Donelson.[30] The Confederate concentration prior to the April 6 Battle of Shiloh would leave New Orleans bereft of troops at exactly the wrong time.

Lovell knew there was a threat much closer to home. He could see the Federal force unloading troops on Ship Island and with Hollins's Mosquito Fleet still upriver, Lovell had only two small naval vessels operating on Lake Pontchartrain to help defend New Orleans against a landing. Lovell took his concerns about the lack of naval cooperation to Benjamin, who promptly ordered Lovell to impress 14 specific ships into public service to form what became known as the River Defense Fleet. This ragtag assembly was not quite what Lovell had in mind when he requested gunboats, and the River Defense Fleet became an on-going headache for him.

Lovell's predicament almost resembled a tragic comedy. First, he offered the fleet to Hollins, but he wanted nothing to do with vessels belonging to the War Department. Even when Commander John Mitchell replaced Hollins on February 1, 1862, problems concerning unity of effort continued to plague the naval arm. Mitchell showed little inclination to assume command of all the various naval components, but even if he had, Captain John Stevenson of the River Defense Fleet claimed his men had entered the service "with the condition that [the River Defense Fleet] was to be independent of the Navy, and that it would not be governed by the regulations of the Navy, or be commanded by naval officers."[31] He said he would cooperate, but was under no obligation to follow orders from Mitchell, and he specifically refused to station his rams along the chain barrier.[32] Virgil Jones concludes, "Nowhere was there unison of effort. Authority was divided between the Louisiana and the Confederate governments, as well as between the Army and Navy and the self-governing river-steamboat captains."[33]

Like so many other aspects of the defense of New Orleans, the River Defense Fleet had become another distraction. Lovell had to divert scarce resources, including his attention, to man, arm, and clad it. The defense of New Orleans was becoming "a more confused—if not fatal—mess."[34]

On March 13, 1862, Major General Benjamin Butler arrived at Ship Island with the final installment of his 15,255 men. In the meantime, Farragut was building his fleet and preparing for the attack. The *Brooklyn* occupied Head of Passes, light-draught steamers moved up river to reconnoiter the forts, and Porter positioned his mortar schooners.[35] The Federals were obviously up to something, but Confederate defensive preparations hardly kept apace. Competing and incompetent shipbuilding efforts maintained a flurry of activity, but no real progress was made due to shortages in materials and money, strikes, poor leadership, and a myriad of other problems.[36] The River Defense Fleet was sapping Lovell's strength, and he predicted, "Unless some competent person, of education, system, and brains, is put over each division of this fleet, it will, in my judgment, prove an utter failure."[37] To make matters worse, George Randolph had replaced Benjamin as Secretary of War, with the inevitable small transitional annoyances surfacing as a result. As if all this was not enough, the swollen Mississippi River ripped away the raft and chain barrier that was designed to obstruct a naval advance. Lovell replaced it with a second raft, but it was just one more thing he had to worry about. In the midst of this impending chaos, Davis issued Lovell an order to impose martial law.[38]

Farragut was also experiencing some difficulties. He was having trouble getting his fleet across the mud-filled bar, and by mid-March he had half his ships in the river and the other half still outside. Furthermore, continued rumors of Confederate ironclad production belied the true state of confused affairs and concerned Farragut about the vulnerability of his wooden ships. The admiral also had to contend with disloyal communications sent from Porter to the Navy Department, delays as vessels were lightened and then reoutfitted, and coal shortages.[39] As a result, it was not until April 8 that Farragut laid full strength in the river, and not until April 14 that he could report being "nearly all coaled."[40] Remarkably, with Richmond still insisting upon retaining Hollins and his Mosquito Fleet upriver, the Confederates had left Farragut unmolested to work through these difficulties.[41] Lovell himself seemed ambivalent. On April 15 he wrote a letter to Secretary Randolph stating, "No harm done. Twenty-seven vessels in sight from forts."[42] Like Emperor Nero, the Confederate command fiddled while New Orleans was about to burn.

Porter's "Bummers." The vessels Lovell had observed were part of Porter's mortar flotilla. On April 16, Porter towed three schooners to a marker 3,000 yards from Fort Jackson and lobbed a few shells to test the range. The next day, all 21 of Porter's vessels, derisively called "bummers" by the "real" sailors in the fleet, were in anchor in carefully determined positions. Then on April 18 at 9:00 a.m., Porter began his huge bombardment. For ten straight hours, each schooner fired a round every ten minutes for a total of over 2,000 shells. At nightfall, Porter ceased firing and rowed forward to reconnoiter. He "convinced [himself] that the fort itself was in flames," but also realized he would have to slow the pace of the next day's bombardment to conserve his ammunition as well as to save his men from exhaustion.[43] Porter knew now that his prediction of reducing the forts in two days was a miscalculation.

Still, Farragut let Porter continue his efforts until the morning of April 20, when Farragut summoned his officers to his flagship to announce his new plan. Farragut was convinced that mortars alone would not cause the forts to surrender, and now with Butler and 7,000 of his men across the bar, Farragut had other options.[44] He planned to destroy the chain barrier, run past the forts with his warships, and, once above the forts, land Butler's troops to seize them. Porter's mortars, much to their commander's chagrin, would remain in position.[45]

The first part of Farragut's plan began on the night of April 20, when a force under Captain Henry Bell departed on a mission to break the chain. The Confederates tried to disrupt the operation by launching a fire raft, but Bell and his men were ultimately successful in clearing the obstacle.[46] For the present, Farragut allowed Porter to continue his bombardment, but by April 23 the promised results had not yet come. When Porter asked for still more time, Farragut replied, "Look here, David. We'll demonstrate the practical value of mortar work." Farragut then ordered his signal officer to wave a red pennant every time a shell landed inside of Fort Jackson, and a white one for every shell that missed its target. The results spoke for themselves, as time after time the white flag was unfurled. Farragut summarized the results saying, "There's the score. I guess we'll go up the river tonight."[47] Intending to bar his way, the Confederates had positioned eleven vessels and some tugs along the Mississippi above the chain barrier.[48]

Farragut's Attack. Throughout the evening Farragut finalized his preparations, showing his characteristic energy, "hands-on" approach to leadership, and attention to detail. He had his sailors remove extra spars, rigging, boats, and all but a few sails. Heavy iron cable chains were draped on the outside of the vessels like chain mail armor to provide additional protection to the engines and boilers. Vulnerable boilers were protected by bags of ashes, clothing, sand, or anything else that was readily available. Weight was redistributed aboard the ships so they would draw less water aft than forward. This measure would ensure that if a ship was grounded while heading upstream, the bow would strike bottom first, and the swift current would be unable to turn the ship around. Hulls were coated with oil and mud to help conceal them from enemy observation, while decks were whitewashed to help gunners find their tools at night.[49] When all was ready, Farragut began his attack shortly after midnight on April 24.

The fleet took fire from both forts and the Confederate ram *Manassas*, but the passage was never really in doubt. Farragut had organized his ships into three divisions for the run. Singly or in small groups, they all made it except for the *Varuna*, which was sunk, and three gunboats from the rear division, which were forced to turn back. Farragut now sent word to Porter to demand the surrender of the forts, and to Butler to bring up the Army transports from Head of the Passes. Farragut then pushed on toward New Orleans and anchored for the night 15 miles below the city.[50]

Before dawn on April 25, Farragut was up and moving toward New Orleans. The city was in panic, and Lovell had torched the levee and retreated. As Farragut pulled alongside the city, he hammered it with broadsides. Ivan Musicant describes the scene as being "the supreme moment of the war" thus far for the Union.[51] Then Farragut dispatched his marines to take possession of the Federal mint, post office, and customs house, and replace the Confederate flag with the Stars and Stripes on all public buildings. Captain Theodorus Bailey, commander of Farragut's Red Division, worked his way through an angry mob and demanded the city's surrender, but the mayor claimed to be under martial law and without authority. When Farragut threatened a bombardment, the mayor and Common Council declared New Orleans an open city.[52]

In the meantime, the forts had refused Porter's demand to surrender, so he resumed his bombardment. He made a second offer two days later but still the forts refused. Finally, as word drifted down river of New Orleans' fate, Confederate morale broke. At midnight on April 27, the troops mutinied, with half running off and the rest just sitting down. Brigadier General Johnson Duncan was left with no choice but to surrender. Commander Mitchell held out a little longer aboard the *Louisiana*, but he ultimately blew her up and surrendered the remnants of the naval command.[53]

On May 1, Butler and the Army came up from their landing at Quarantine and began a controversial occupation of New Orleans. Butler gained such a terrible reputation in New Orleans that for years after the war, the bottom of chamber pots bore his likeness. Throughout the South, he became known as "Beast Butler" for his oppressive occupation regime or "Spoons Butler" for his alleged pilfering of New Orleans' wealth. Most notorious was his general order that any Confederate women who insulted or showed contempt for a Federal soldier would be treated as a "woman of the town plying her avocation."

In addition, a debate would develop between Butler and Porter over their relative contributions to the victory. One objective observer, Rowena Reed, gives much credit to Butler, believing that without his force to isolate Forts Jackson and St. Philip and pacify the hostile New Orleans population, Farragut could have remained in New Orleans just a short time. Citing relatively minor damage to Fort Jackson, she concludes, "the Southerners could have held out indefinitely against any number of the strongest warships brought against them" and that it was "the Army's presence [that] made [the forts' and New Orleans'] eventual capture certain."[54] Spencer Tucker agrees that Farragut's "success resulted from the sure knowledge that, once he had run past the Confederate forts, Union troops would be able to land and cut the defenders off from New Orleans."[55]

Unrealized Strategic Significance. New Orleans was indeed a great triumph for the Union, placing one of the South's premier cities and the mouth of the Mississippi under Federal control. Still, New Orleans was a limited victory in that the strategic momentum was lost.[56] Like so many other times in the coastal campaign, there was not a detailed plan in place for what to do next.

As Farragut pondered this situation, one obvious target was the Confederate Mississippi River bastion at Vicksburg, about 400 miles above New Orleans. Using a plan similar to what had worked at New Orleans, Farragut attempted to subdue the city in May, but this time his bombardment was unsuccessful. Situated on high bluffs and bristling with batteries, Vicksburg was able to give as good as it got. Then, fearing the receding waters of the Mississippi might strand his oceangoing warships in the summer months, Farragut reluctantly decided to withdraw. He left six gunboats below Vicksburg and returned to New Orleans. Rowena Reed laments Farragut's delay and halfhearted attempt at Vicksburg, writing, "Had the Federal expedition moved up river in force immediately after the fall of New Orleans, without allowing the enemy time to recover from the initial confusion of defeat, the entire Mississippi would have been in Union control by the summer of 1862."[57]

Farragut made another attempt on June 28, running a three-mile gauntlet of Confederate fire at Vicksburg, and eventually linking up with Flag Officer Charles Davis's Mississippi River Flotilla above the city on July 1. The most scintillating event of the siege occurred in mid-July when the Confederate ironclad Arkansas churned out of the Yazoo River and blasted its way through the combined Union fleets. It then fought off a counterattack with the help of Vicksburg's guns. Farragut ran past the city's batteries again on the night of July 21–22, but was unable to destroy the Arkansas and became increasingly worried about the low water. Two days later he returned to New Orleans, leaving two gunboats at Baton Rouge to deter the Arkansas from venturing south. Farragut understood the problem. He reported to the Navy Department, "The Department will perceive from this report that the forts can be passed, and we have done it, and can do it again, as often as may be required of us. It will not, however, be an easy matter for us to do more than silence the batteries for a time, as long as the enemy has a large force behind the hills to prevent our landing and holding the place."[58] To do so would require a cooperating Army force of some 12,000 to 15,000 men according to Farragut's estimation. In fact, the Federals would not be able to wrest

Vicksburg from Confederate control until some 75,000 men commanded by Major General Ulysses Grant, with the help of a powerful fleet commanded by Porter, did so on July 4, 1863, after a lengthy campaign of maneuver and siege.[59]

In spite of this failure to follow the operation with a preplanned and decisive sequel, New Orleans was a great Federal victory. It denied the South a key shipbuilding facility and the potential ironclads that were so fearful to the Federal Navy. It was a huge blow to Confederate morale, which led Commander Porter to crow that the Southerners were now "broken backed."[60] Indeed, the Confederate diarist Mary Chesnut lamented, "New Orleans gone—and with it the Confederacy. Are we not cut in two?"[61] Although a little premature, Chesnut's observation still captured the magnitude of the situation. The Federal victory at New Orleans was a huge step toward isolating the Trans-Mississippi Confederacy and reopening the Mississippi River. It was the pivotal battle of the Gulf Campaign.

PENSACOLA: THE CONFEDERACY IS STRETCHED TOO THIN

With the best harbor in the Gulf of Mexico and a U.S. Navy Yard just seven miles down the bay from the city of Pensacola, Pensacola Bay was a strategic plum. The Navy Yard was of modest size and primarily a coaling and repair station, but since there were only three shipyards in the South—Norfolk, New Orleans, and this one—it was of key importance. To protect this valuable location, the entrance to the bay was guarded by Forts McRae (or McRee) and Barrancas on the land side, and by Fort Pickens on the tip of the 40-mile long Santa Rosa Island.[1]

On January 10, 1861, the day Florida seceded from the Union, Lieutenant Adam Slemmer spiked the guns at Fort Barrancas, blew up the ammunition at Fort McRae, and occupied Fort Pickens. Slemmer took this bold action in the absence of the fort's actual commander, the future Confederate general John Winder who was in Maryland on sick leave. In contrast to Slemmer's defiance, the aged Commodore James Armstrong surrendered the U.S. Navy Yard intact on April 12 to a force of about 350 militia from Florida and Alabama. Not a shot was fired, and Armstrong made no attempt to evacuate property to Fort Pickens. A court martial later determined him to be senile and criminally incompetent for his role in the surrender.[2] However, not everyone at the Navy Yard shared Armstrong's submissive attitude. Seaman William Conway refused the order to haul down the U.S. flag, and 30 seamen withdrew to Slemmer's garrison, giving the Federals a strength of 81 men at Fort Pickens.

Unusual Proceedings. Within two weeks of the surrender of the Navy Yard, U.S. Secretary of the Navy Isaac Tocey ordered the *Brooklyn* to deliver reinforcements to Fort Pickens. He also ordered two warships to Pensacola, but then things slowed down. Florida Senator Stephen Mallory, the future Confederate Secretary of the Navy, arranged a truce with President James Buchanan that promised the Confederates would not attack Fort Pickens if the en route troops were not landed. An uneasy freeze in the situation followed, just one of the many unresolved issues Buchanan left for Abraham Lincoln to handle upon assuming the presidency. Indeed, when Lincoln took office and his new Secretary of the Navy Gideon Welles learned of the situation at Fort Pickens, Welles gave the order in the middle of March for the troops to be landed. A confused mess of intrigue, bureaucratic wrangling, orders, and counterorders ensued that left even President Lincoln "astonished and perplexed," but eventually, on April 17— four days after the fall of Fort Sumter—a U.S. Navy squadron arrived to reinforce Fort Pickens, now one of the last Federal bastions in the South. The Confederates, without ammunition to service the guns they found at the Navy Yard, "stood in groups on the opposite shore watching the proceedings, but with no apparent intention of interfering for the present."[3]

The Federal Presence Strengthens. Slemmer now had 500 men at his disposal, and on April 18, Colonel Harvey Brown arrived to establish the headquarters of the newly created Department of Florida. On April 12, 15, and 18, the Confederates issued surrender demands, but each time the Federals refused.

Among the newly arrived Federal naval officers was Lieutenant David Porter on the *Powhatan*. Rather than surrender, the aggressive Porter wanted to force the harbor and engage the inner Confederate works, but the Army was still unloading its horses and supplies and dissuaded Porter from acting before it was ready. Porter then joined Captain H. A. Adams and the squadron off Pensacola, and the pair began strengthening the naval posture. By May 13, Adams notified the Confederate officials ashore that he was enforcing a blockade. Fort Pickens was resolutely in Federal hands, and the Federal Navy's presence denied the Confederates the use of Pensacola's harbor.[4]

Opposing the Federals was the Confederate Army of Pensacola, created on October 22 and consisting of some 8,100 troops from

Florida, Alabama, Georgia, and Mississippi. The Army went through a series of commanders including Braxton Bragg, A. H. Gladden, Samuel Jones, and finally Thomas Jones. While Bragg was in command, he launched an amphibious raid of 1,063 men on Santa Rosa Island on October 8–9. Landing undetected at 2:00 a.m., the Confederates routed about 250 men of the 6th New York Zouaves, but Brown sent a counterattack force from Fort Pickens, about a mile from the Zouave camp, and forced the Confederates to withdraw. The misadventure cost the Confederates 87 casualties, compared to 67 for the Federals.[5]

The Federals were much bolder. On September 2, Brown sent a raiding party to destroy the Navy Yard's dry dock, which he believed the Confederates were going to sink to block the channel opposite of Fort McRae. On September 14, a crew from the *Colorado* burned the Confederate privateer *Judah* after a hand-to-hand fight with her crew. It was in retaliation for this action that Bragg launched his Santa Rosa raid. On November 22 and 23, the *Niagara* and *Richmond* joined with Fort Pickens to shell the Confederate steamer *Time* as she entered the harbor, and also delivered a bombardment that almost destroyed Fort McRae. On January 1, 1862, Fort Pickens again bombarded Forts McRae and Barrancas.[6]

The Confederates Get Spooked. In the midst of this Federal initiative and relative Confederate passivity at Pensacola, Admiral David Farragut captured New Orleans on April 25, 1862. Farragut then had to decide on his next move, and one place he was considering was Mobile. In early May, he dispatched Porter to lob a few mortar shells into the forts guarding the entrance to Mobile Bay and await the arrival of Farragut's main squadron.

Porter's practice shots had an unintended consequence. The Confederates at Pensacola, already feeling vulnerable, decided to evacuate. This move appeared to be a preplanned action, as the Confederates removed their sick, set fire to "every combustible from the navy yard to Fort McRee," and withdrew north to reinforce Bragg, who had taken command of a corps in General Albert Sidney Johnston's Army of Mississippi. Bragg had sensed early on that defending Pensacola was beyond the Confederacy's capabilities, arguing that Confederate "means and resources" were "too much scattered" and that "strategic points only should be held." It was a conclusion similar to the one General Lee had reached on the Atlantic coast after the Federal success at Port Royal Sound. Even President Davis conceded, "I acknowledge the error of my attempt to defend all the frontier, seaboard and inland." Instead, he planned on "abandoning the seaboard in order to defend the Tennessee line which is vital to our safety."[7] On March 13, the Confederate Army of Pensacola ceased to exist.[8]

The Federal Navy ferried troops from Fort Pickens to the mainland and secured the Navy Yard. Although greatly damaged, the facility was still a sheltered harbor with serviceable wharves that represented a great improvement over Ship Island. Combined with the reoccupation of Norfolk, the Federal Navy now had adequate bases for both its Atlantic and Gulf squadrons. In August, Farragut established his fleet headquarters at Pensacola, and the location became the Gulf Blockading Squadron's most important supply depot. Not only did Farragut have a spacious anchorage there, he could keep a close watch on developments at Mobile Bay, just 30 miles away.[9]

But the easy capture of Pensacola Bay disguised a serious flaw in the Gulf Campaign. The campaign had started out as a well-arranged operation with the seizure of Ship Island serving as a base for the larger New Orleans offensive. After that, in the absence of a preplanned sequel, things slowed drastically. Farragut's follow-on attempt at Vicksburg was an uncoordinated one in which he successfully ran the batteries, but then stood idle and impotent waiting for troops that never came. Pensacola had been a Federal victory for sure, but one that the Confederates lost rather than the Federals won. In the meantime, blockade runners were bringing vital supplies to the Confederacy via Galveston and Mobile.[10]

GALVESTON:
A FEDERAL SETBACK

Admiral David Farragut chafed during the subsequent period of idleness after he had been stymied at Vicksburg. He was a man of action whose temperament lay toward battle rather than administration of a blockade. Farragut would have liked to move against Mobile Bay, but that would require Army troops he did not have.[1] Instead, he devoted his attention to closing off the Texas coast.

There, Farragut's principle target was Galveston, the "Island City" on the Gulf of Mexico that the Federals had begun blockading in July 1861. Although remote from the heartland of the Confederacy, Galveston had become the home of a sophisticated manufacturing and service business specializing in the shipping trade. Before the war, two-thirds of all the cotton exported from Texas had passed through Galveston. With the loss of New Orleans, Galveston and Mobile Bay were the last major ports open to blockade runners on the Gulf, and ships like the *Denbigh* made regular runs between Galveston and Cuba.[2]

The Capture of Galveston. Nonetheless, when Brigadier General Paul Octave Hebert assumed command of the Confederate Department of Texas in 1861, he quickly determined Galveston to be too exposed to be successfully defended. Thus, the Confederates offered just token resistance on October 4, 1862, when Commander William Renshaw moved his squadron into Galveston harbor and demanded the city surrender. Colonel Joseph Cook, the Confederate commander in the city, agreed but only on the condition of a four-day truce, during which key military supplies and personnel were evacuated to Fort Hébert on the mainland.[3] Those citizens who remained in the city

136

were either Union sympathizers or were willing to act as if they were. Accordingly, the mayor reportedly expressed pleasure in the city passing back into Federal hands, and one occupier noted, "Not a single sentry had to be detailed to keep the crowd back" during the landing. The surprisingly cordial reception from the people of Galveston motivated Renshaw to initially occupy the city only during the daytime, and he instructed his marines to retreat to the safety of the ships each night.[4]

Renshaw's squadron included the flagship *Westfield, Harriet Lane, Owasco, Clifton,* and the mortar schooner *Henry James.* To assist in the occupation, the little gunboats *Corypheus* and *Sachem* arrived from New Orleans along with three companies from the 42nd Massachusetts Infantry led by Colonel Isaac Burrell, which did not reach Galveston until December 24.[5] Renshaw had hoped for a larger contingent from the Army. Indeed, Farragut had written Navy officials in Washington, "All we want is a few soldiers to hold the places, and we will soon have the whole coast."[6] However, Major General Benjamin Butler, notorious for resisting to cooperate with the Navy—especially if it meant weakening his own command—would release only this token force of 260 men.[7]

This small band of soldiers did what they could to secure the immediate area around the waterfront docks at the end of Kuhn's Wharf. There stood a large three-story storehouse that Burrell ordered his men to reinforce with sacks of plaster and a barricade. He also had his men pull up all but one of the planks from a section of wharf near the shore and use the lumber to create another barricade. Burrell's strategy was that the single plank would limit the number of Confederates that could attack down the wharf. In spite of such detail in this area, Burrell left the bridge that linked Galveston Island with the mainland unguarded, a bridge over which any land attack would have to come across. Army transports with field artillery arrived, but the guns were not landed.[8] It was by all accounts a lightly defended position.

Magruder's Attack. When Major General John Magruder assumed command of the Confederate military forces in Texas in late November 1862, he made retaking Galveston—which he considered the key to the survival of the Confederacy in the west—a priority. He wrote Lieutenant General Edmund Kirby Smith, "In my judgment, Texas is virtually the Trans-Mississippi Department, and the railroads of Galveston and Houston are virtually Texas. For whoever is the master of the railroads of Galveston and Houston is virtually master of Texas, and this is not the case with any other part of Texas."[9]

Magruder envisioned a joint Army-Navy operation in which Confederate land forces would attack the Federal troops while Confederate ships prevented the Federal Navy from interfering. The problem was that Magruder had no naval forces whatsoever assigned to his command, a land force of only a few small artillery companies, and a mere handful of local militia units. Many of Magruder's subordinates questioned the feasibility of attacking amidst such deficiencies, but one officer told Magruder, "General, I think the best plan is to resolve to retake [Galveston]. And then canvass the difficulties."[10] Buoyed by such optimism, Magruder moved forward with his plans.

To handle the naval end of things, Magruder was fortunate to have the industrious and brave Leon Smith to build and command the Confederate flotilla. Smith was an experienced steamboat captain who called himself "Major" or "Commodore," depending on the occasion. Although there were no suitable Confederate naval vessels available, there were plenty of large steamers that had been used to transport cotton between Galveston and Houston. Smith procured two of these, the *Bayou City* and *Neptune*, and began converting them into "cottonclads" by protecting their vulnerable points with two and three layers of cotton bales.

Captain Armand Weir, commander of Company B of Cook's 1st Texas Heavy Artillery, offered some of his guns to outfit the cottonclads, and Magruder placed Weir in charge of a 32-pounder rifled gun on the *Bayou City*. Captain L. C. Harby and Lieutenant Harvey Clark commanded two 24-pounder howitzers on the *Neptune*. For soldiers, Magruder turned to the Sibley Brigade that was recruiting and regrouping near Houston in preparation for an impending relocation to Louisiana. Magruder was able to persuade the commander to provide about 300 soldiers from the brigade. Magruder then equipped them with Enfield rifles or double-barreled shotguns and assigned the soldiers to the cottonclads to serve as sharp-shooters and boarders. These makeshift warships were accompanied by the armed tenders *John F. Carr* and *Lucy Gwin*.[11]

Renshaw had long suspected some Confederate attack was in the works. In fact, in the first week of November he had warned his men of a possible attack "by boats drawing very little water, and they may come upon us without coming through the channel; and their object will be to board us."[12] Nonetheless, the Federals were seemingly caught off guard when Magruder attacked in the predawn hours of January 1, 1863. Magruder had hauled more than 20 pieces of artillery, including an 8-inch Dahlgren mounted on a railway car, across the unguarded Houston & Galveston Railroad bridge that linked Galveston Island and the mainland. Magruder had hoped to have his guns in position by midnight, but the seven to nine mile movement took longer than anticipated, and all the guns did not arrive until 4:00 a.m. Once he did arrive, Magruder spread his artillery out along the waterfront for about two and a half miles, placing some in the second stories of buildings to improve their fields of fire. Shortly after 4:00 a.m., Magruder personally fired the first gun at the *Owasco* to signal the Confederate attack. Having performed this task, Magruder announced, "Now, boys, I have done my best as a private, I will go and attend to that of General" and moved to his headquarters at a large house ten miles from the waterfront.[13]

Rather than attack frontally down the single plank of Kuhn's Wharf, Magruder's plan called for his men to wade through the shallow waters on each side, climb ladders at the end of the wharf, and attack the Federals from the rear. The plan failed when the ladders the Confederates carried proved to be too short to reach the top of the wharf, and the wet and dejected Confederates were forced to wade back to shore under heavy fire. By now it was daylight, and the Federal ships had pinpointed the Confederate artillery positions and were delivering a deadly fire. It looked as if the Confederate attack was a disaster, and Magruder was beginning to consider ordering a general retreat when Leon Smith and his cottonclads arrived and completely changed the tide of the battle.[14]

In accordance with the original plan, Smith had been in place at midnight but had not attacked because of Magruder's delay in moving the artillery. Magruder had told Smith the land forces would initiate the attack, and Smith had grown tired of waiting and turned around and headed up Galveston Bay. By the time the Confederate attack actually began shortly after 4:00 a.m., Smith was far away and now had to make a dash to the sound of the guns. Once he got in range of the Federal ships, Smith began firing, but as Captain Wier fired the fourth shot from his big 32-pounder aboard the *Bayou City*, the gun exploded, killing Wier and wounding several of the crew. Smith was undeterred by the loss of his big long-range gun. He knew all along that his best hope for success lay in a close fight. As Smith explained to one sharpshooter, "Our only chance is to get along side before they hit us."[15]

The first Federal ship Smith encountered was the *Harriet Lane*, whose large paddle wheels on each side made her vulnerable to the type of ramming attack Smith envisioned. First, the *Bayou City* made a run at the *Harriet Lane*'s port paddle wheel but skidded off with little effect. Then, the *Neptune* rammed the *Harriet Lane*'s starboard side. The *Neptune* hit the *Harriet Lane* firmly but missed the paddle wheel. In fact, the *Neptune* received the worse of the encounter and began to sink. Her captain, however, was an experienced Galveston Bay skipper who skillfully navigated her to a nearby reef. This maneuver allowed the *Neptune* to sink in such a fashion that her decks remained sufficiently above water for her sharpshooters to continue engaging the *Harriet Lane*.[16]

In the meantime, the *Bayou City* turned and rammed the *Harriet Lane* again. The ships became hopelessly entangled in the collision, and Confederate troops aboard the *Bayou City* rushed the Federal ship and took it by storm. The *Harriet Lane*'s captain, Commander Jonathan Wainwright, and the first officer, Lieutenant Commander Edward Lea, were both killed. Unbeknownst to Lea, his father, Albert Lea, was then serving as a volunteer on Magruder's staff. During the battle, the senior Lea had been posted on one of the tall buildings to observe the status of the attack, and he saw the *Harriet Lane* disabled. Only after the battle did Lea reveal to Magruder that his son was aboard the *Harriet Lane*. Lea reached his son before he died, but could offer him no help to save his life.[17]

The Confederates then arranged a truce and called for Renshaw to surrender, but he refused. Instead, he ordered Lieutenant Commander Richard Law, captain of the *Clifton*, to withdraw the remaining Federal vessels from the harbor and escape. In the

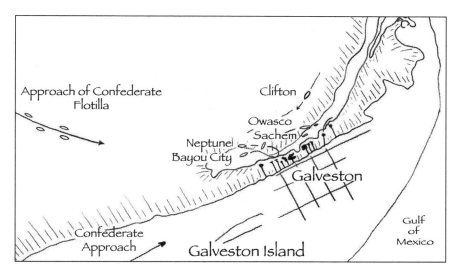

In a bold joint army-navy attack, Magruder succeeded in recapturing Galveston, but he also benefited from lax Federal security.

meantime, Renshaw would scuttle the *Westfield*, which had run aground in the Bolivar Channel. Disaster struck when fire reached the *Westfield's* magazine before Renshaw and his crew could clear the ship, and all aboard were killed. Law, however, succeeded under a hail of Confederate fire in saving the remainder of the Federal fleet. The blockade of Galveston had been lifted.[18]

Results. The daring Confederate attack was a stunning victory. In addition to destroying two Federal ships, the Confederates killed or captured 414 Federals. The Confederates lost the *Neptune*, along with 26 dead and 117 wounded. It had been a poor showing for the Federals. Assistant Secretary of the Navy Gustavus Fox complained, "It is too cowardly to place on paper. Poor Wainwright did well. Renshaw—bah! He is dead. The others ran."[19] Admiral David Porter records that "many officers consider the retreat from before the harbor a disgraceful affair."[20]

Farragut moved quickly to re-establish the blockade off Galveston, dispatching Captain Henry Bell with the *Brooklyn* and six gunboats to retake the position. Bell's force was not completely in place on January 11 when Confederate Commander Raphael Semmes arrived with the *Alabama*. Semmes had learned from Northern newspapers that Major General Nathaniel Banks was about to set sail with a force of 20,000 men for the Gulf of Mexico, and Semmes deduced Galveston was a likely destination for Banks's expedition. There, Semmes decided to try to wreak havoc among the transports as they lay at anchor outside the bar.[21]

Semmes did not know that the Confederates had retaken Galveston ten days earlier and was surprised when, instead of a fleet of Federal ships, he saw just five blockade ships lobbing shells at the city. Semmes stopped his ship some twelve miles offshore, and the Federal squadron commander, Captain Bell, dispatched the *Hatteras* to investigate the unidentified vessel. The *Hatteras* was a former Delaware River excursion side-wheeler with only four 32-pounders and a 20-pounder rifle. It was no match for the formidable *Alabama*, which boasted two 300-horsepower engines, six 32-pounders, a 100-pound rifled Blakely, and a smoothbore 8-incher. The battle lasted just 13 minutes. After sinking the *Hatteras*, Semmes departed for the West Indies, but Bell thought the *Alabama* might still be lurking nearby and paused to re-evaluate his plan of attack. The Confederates used this respite to build up their fortifications surrounding Galveston. By the end of the month, Farragut was forced to give up any plans to recapture Galveston.[22]

The battle was a proud moment for Semmes, as it was a unique victory over a Federal warship. Porter, however, laments it as a lost opportunity in which Bell violated the maxim to "never send a boy on a man's errand." Had Bell dispatched two gunboats instead of just the *Hatteras*, Porter believes the *Alabama* "would probably have fallen into our hands and her wild career would have ended then and there."[23]

Farragut wrote in his diary, "Our disaster at Galveston has thrown us back and done more injury to the Navy than all events of the war."[24] Federal commanders all along the Gulf were thrown into a panic, and Farragut was beset by frantic requests for reinforcements from Pensacola and Ship Island. Farragut tried to go to Texas to shore things up, but his flagship grounded on the Mississippi River bar, so he returned to New Orleans.[25]

The failure at Galveston showed just how frazzled the Federal campaign in the Gulf had become. Instead of a juggernaut gaining steam with each successive victory, the Gulf Campaign was now haphazard and uncoordinated. As a result, Galveston was the only major port the Confederates recaptured during the war, and it remained in Confederate hands until it surrendered June 2, 1865.

In fact, both the Atlantic and Gulf Campaigns had reached their culminating points. The Atlantic Campaign suffered from weakening Army-Navy cooperation and a disparity in the capabilities of the two services to cover a large geographic area. The Gulf Campaign was also plagued by a paucity of planning that resulted in "only the opening phases of the campaign [being] a success."[26] As a consequence, the remaining battles of the coastal war would present much tougher challenges for the Federals.

Tougher Challenges

CHARLESTON

MOBILE BAY

FORT FISHER

CHARLESTON: TOO STRONG FROM THE SEA

Charleston, the very font of secession and the home of Fort Sumter, where the Civil War's opening salvos were fired, had long been a thorn in the Federals' side. Assistant Secretary of the Navy Gustavus Fox wrote, "The fall of Charleston is the fall of Satan's Kingdom."[1] As such, it was as much a political objective as a military one, and due to the fact that by the summer of 1863 it and Wilmington, North Carolina were the only remaining major ports of entry open for Atlantic blockade runners, it was a practical target as well. The result of the Federal effort to capture Charleston was a siege that became the longest campaign of the war.[2] Still, Charleston held on, succumbing only to the impending approach of Major General William Sherman in the dying days of the Confederacy.

Tough Defenses and Early Failures. Admiral Samuel Du Pont knew that Charleston could only be taken by a joint sea and land effort, and after Port Royal he had urged the Army to move on Charleston, but the Army had refused. Army cooperation was even less likely now. Major General David Hunter had just 10,000 troops at Hilton Head, much fewer than the job would require, and reinforcements were unlikely given the competing priorities of Gettysburg and Vicksburg. At first the Federals tried to shut down Charleston on the cheap by blocking the harbor with a "Stone Fleet" of hulks filled with rocks and scuttled to obstruct the main channel. However, powerful tides and storms soon washed these halfhearted efforts away.[3] A more promising attempt was made possible on May 16, 1862, when Robert Smalls, a 23-year-old slave employed by the Confederates as the pilot of the *Planter,* escaped with his vessel and brought news that the Confederates had abandoned

146

their positions guarding the seaward approaches to James Island. This development left Charleston vulnerable to an attack from the rear across the island. Du Pont immediately saw the opportunity for a coup de main joint operation to seize Charleston, and on June 2 he landed two of Hunter's divisions, backed by considerable naval support, on James Island. However, instead of pushing forward against the meager Confederate resistance, Hunter convinced himself he was grossly outnumbered. He left Brigadier General Henry Benham in command and directed him not to attack until ordered. For two weeks the Federals idled away their advantage while the Confederates reinforced the island. When Benham finally disobeyed his orders and attacked on June 16, he was badly defeated near the town of Secessionville. Fearing a Confederate counterattack, Hunter ordered James Island be evacuated and sacked Benham.

Du Pont was disgusted by this missed opportunity, complaining to Fox, "Oh those Soldiers I put them nearly on *top* of the house in Charleston, but I did not push them into the windows and they came back."[4] Still, the Secessionville debacle only served to reinforce Du Pont's opinion that an Army force, if competently led, was critical to any operation against Charleston.

Some saw promise in Admiral Farragut's daring run past the forts at New Orleans. Secretary Welles and others reasoned that if Du Pont similarly ran past Fort Sumter, the Confederates would be forced to withdraw. Du Pont, however, felt otherwise, believing that Welles had woefully underestimated the might of Charleston's defenses. Charleston had been steadily strengthened, and by 1862 a combination of land-based artillery, torpedoes, submersible vessels, obstructions, and prepared positions had made it the Confederate city best able to withstand an assault from the sea. By 1863, these formidable defenses had been expanded into a three-tiered defensive system. The end result was that the "only thing that awaited the attacking force once they passed Fort Sumter was additional fortifications."[5]

The outer layer consisted of fortifications that covered the mouth of the harbor and the channel from the barrier islands and Fort Sumter. These included Fort Wagner and Battery Greg on Morris Island to the left of the harbor entrance. Fort Sumter was immediately ahead guarding the main harbor entrance, while Sullivan's Island and its Fort Moultrie and Batteries Bee and Beauregard stood on the left of the main entrance. Battery Greg, Fort Sumter, and Fort Moultrie combined to deliver three-sided fire on any vessel that reached the harbor mouth.

Behind this tier was a second layer of artillery batteries in the inner harbor sighted to engage any Federal ships that might break

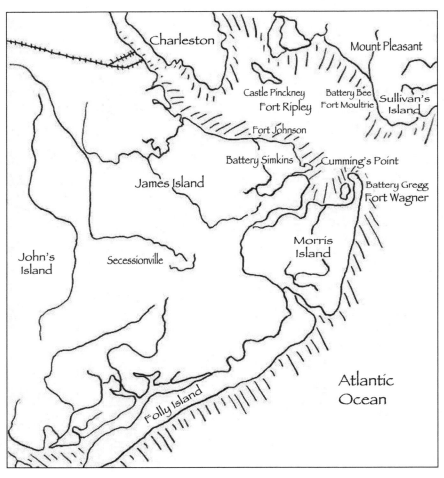

As the Confederates lost territory elsewhere, they were able to focus their efforts on places like Charleston where they developed a formidable defense in depth.

through. These included Fort Jackson and Battery Glover on James Island, Fort Ripley and Castle Pinckney in the harbor itself, and the White Point Battery (Battery Ramsay) in Charleston. Finally, a series of land forts protected the flanks, barring a repeat of the strategy the British had used to seize Charleston during the American Revolution.[6]

Even nature seemed to conspire against the attacker. Fast currents and a shallow bar with irregular breaks were made even more difficult after the Confederates had removed the buoys marking the channels. As it was, the wide and deep Main Ship Channel was the only safe approach.[7] The result was that Charleston Harbor was a "bag" or "cul de sac," according to Du Pont's apt description. Once a naval force entered it, there was no clear channel that could be used to run past the fortifications as there had been at New Orleans.[8]

Secretary Welles believed that these stout defenses could be matched by ironclads including the *New Ironsides*, the Navy's most powerful monitor. Du Pont was skeptical, but he agreed to try if Welles could provide the necessary quantities. "The limit of my wants in the need of ironclads," Du Pont wrote Welles, "is the capacity of the [Navy] Department to supply them." Ultimately, Du Pont received all but one of the Navy's new ironclads, making his fleet at Charleston the first integration of the revolutionary monitor technology into the Navy's larger organization. Still, Du Pont's requests for more and more resources and his continued delay in attacking caused Lincoln and Welles to liken him to the overly cautious George McClellan, a man Lincoln complained was infected by "the slows."

The root of the problem was a clash in philosophies. Du Pont thought the solution to Charleston lay in a joint operation with a robust Army component. Welles, on the other hand, favored an all-Navy solution he felt was made possible by the new miracle weapon, the monitor.[9] Reconciling these disparate positions proved problematic.

Indeed, there was a serious rift developing with Lincoln, Welles, and Fox on one side, and Du Pont on the other. The civilian leadership was pushing Du Pont into an operation of which he had serious reservations and felt unprepared. In a series of meetings in Washington in October 1862, Du Pont reiterated his position that a joint operation was necessary, and that no amount of ships or even ironclads could take Charleston alone. Lincoln and the Navy Department leadership, however, had already made up their minds. After providing his informed counsel, Du Pont accepted the realities of the civil-military relationship and returned to Charleston.[10]

Fort McAllister. Having made his case to his superiors to no avail, Du Pont resolved to conduct a limited test, and he selected Fort McAllister on the Ogeechee River in Georgia as a target. The results seemed to support Du Pont's reluctance. On January 27, 1863, Du Pont sent the ironclad *Montauk*, the gunboats *Seneca*, *Wissahickon*, and *Dawn*, and the mortar schooner *C. P. Williams* to attack Fort McAllister. Sunken obstacles that appeared to be torpedoes blocked the *Montauk's*

Confederate guns from Fort McAllister were able to turn back Du Pont's ironclads in a way that confirmed his reluctance to attack Charleston. Photograph courtesy of the Library of Congress.

advance, so the ironclad blasted the fort at a distance for four hours with no noticeable effect. The Confederate fire was accurate, striking the *Montauk* 14 times but inflicting no damage.

The next day, Du Pont learned from a runaway slave the position of the torpedoes that had blocked the previous attack. Armed with this new intelligence, the Federals tried again on February 1. The *Montauk* advanced within 600 yards of the fort, and both sides unleashed accurate fire for four hours. The *Montauk* was hit 48 times but retired without serious damage. Fort McAllister was also still sound. Of the experiment Du Pont lamented, "If one ironclad cannot take eight guns, how are five to take 147 guns in Charleston Harbor?"[11]

Fort McAllister confirmed what Du Pont had already concluded from the Confederate repulse of the ironclads *Monitor* and *Galena* before Drewry's Bluff in the Peninsula Campaign. It "was a very ill-advised and incorrect operation to expose those gunboats before the Army could take the forts in the rear," Du Pont opined.[12] In his mind, the situation at Fort McAllister was no different.

Du Pont's Naval Attack. Du Pont launched attacks on Fort McAllister again on February 28 and March 3 with more disappointing results. His monitors could withstand the fort's punishment, but their slow rate of fire limited their ability to inflict serious damage to shore fortifications in a short span of time. This inefficiency of fire would plague Federal attempts on Charleston throughout the war.[13]

In the meantime, the Confederates did not remain passive. On January 31, Flag Officer Duncan Ingraham used the cover of the morning fog to attack ten unarmored Federal vessels of the blockading squadron just off the harbor. Ingraham inflicted much damage and caused enough panic that General Pierre Gustave Toutant Beauregard, the Confederate commander at Charleston, indulged himself in the hyperbole of declaring that the blockade had been lifted. Of more lasting concern, however, was the regular threat posed by Confederate torpedoes, which one Federal naval officer said the Confederates had "strewn about like autumn leaves."[14] A torpedo badly damaged the *Montauk* in the February 28 attack on Fort McAllister, and the *Weehawken* and the *Patapsco* would eventually be sunk by them.[15]

All of this activity resulted in the Confederates being well prepared when Du Pont made his all-out attack on Charleston at 12:10 p.m. on April 7. Du Pont's plan was to run past Morris Island without returning fire, steam into the harbor, and open fire on Fort Sumter at close range. After Fort Sumter had been reduced, Du Pont would then concentrate on the Morris Island forts. This plan ran afoul when Du Pont's lead vessel encountered obstacles strung across the channel from Fort Sumter northeastward to Fort Moultrie. The ensuing delay foiled Du Pont's plan of running past the point where Confederate fire was the most concentrated. Now, at about 3:00 p.m., Du Pont's fleet was under fire from nearly 100 Confederate guns and mortars. About 15 minutes later, Du Pont ordered his ships to return fire. For about two hours, Confederates and Federals exchanged fire at ranges between 550 and 800 yards. The Confederate guns were especially accurate, delivering some 400 hits and heavily damaging

Morris Island was one of many Confederate positions the Federals had to capture on their way to Charleston.
Photograph courtesy of the Library of Congress.

several monitors. The volume of fire was extremely lopsided, with the Confederates firing 2,229 rounds compared to just 139 for the Federals. Du Pont broke off the action at dusk, writing his wife, "We have failed as I felt sure we would." The Confederate forts had held.[16]

Du Pont now declared that Charleston could not be taken by a naval attack alone. He was especially fearful that the Confederates might sink and then salvage one of his ironclads, so he withdrew all his monitors except the *New Ironsides* to Port Royal. In Washington, Du Pont's prudence was perceived as defeatism. Welles bowed to calls for Du Pont's removal and named Rear Admiral Andrew Foote as the replacement commander, but Foote died on the way to his new post. Reluctantly, Welles turned to Rear Admiral John Dahlgren, an acknowledged ordnance expert but a man with little experience at sea. On July 6, Dahlgren assumed command of the South Atlantic Blockading Squadron.[17]

Fort Wagner. From July to September, Dahlgren kept up a bombardment of the Charleston defenses, but this time the Navy would not be alone. On June 12, Major General Quincy Adams Gillmore had assumed command of the Department of the South and brought with him the excellent reputation he had earned by using long-range rifled artillery to pound Fort Pulaski into capitulation. Now, he aimed to replicate this success against Forts Wagner and Sumter.

On July 10, Gillmore crossed nearly 3,000 troops to the south end of Morris Island and advanced to within a half mile of Fort Wagner. In the meantime, Dahlgren's ironclads dueled with Fort Wagner for nearly twelve hours. Gillmore's men dug trenches to shelter Parrott guns that could range both forts, but there things stalemated. Over the next two months, the Federals launched at least 25 separate attacks to try to capture the rest of Morris Island without success.[18]

The Federals also kept Fort Sumter under fire. On August 17, Gillmore and Dahlgren began a week-long bombardment. On August 23 and again on September 1, Dahlgren attacked Fort Sumter with his ironclads. Throughout it all, the fort held.[19]

Next, Gillmore turned his attention to Charleston itself. On August 21, he sent Beauregard a demand for the evacuation of Fort Sumter and Morris Island within four hours. If Beauregard failed to comply,

Gillmore promised to open fire on Charleston. Gillmore responded to the Confederate intransigence by opening fire at 1:30 a.m. on August 22. Shells from the "Swamp Angel," a 200-pounder Parrott, caused fires and panic in the waterfront district but little more.[20]

Other attacks continued. On September 7, Dahlgren mounted a major ironclad assault on Fort Sumter. Thinking the position had been partially evacuated, over the next two days he sent 400 sailors and marines on more than 30 boats to attack Morris Island. Gillmore had planned an Army operation as well, but by this time interservice rivalries had again surfaced, and any cooperation between Gillmore and Dahlgren floundered. The Confederates were ready for the purely Navy show and took more than 100 Federal prisoners.[21]

By now, all the ironclads were in need of extensive repairs at Port Royal and active operations ceased for several weeks. When they resumed, both Federal ships and troops continued to harass the forts. The Confederates responded by shifting heavy guns from Fort Sumter to the more powerful Forts Moultrie and Jackson, and continued to plague the Federals with torpedoes and submersibles.

The most famous of these innovations was the *H. L. Hunley*, a 40-foot long, 3.5- foot wide, and 4-foot deep cigar-shaped submarine. The *Hunley* was designed for a crew of nine: one man to steer and the other eight to power the vessel by hand-turning a crankshaft that moved the propeller. In spite of sinking twice and drowning 13 men, including its builder Horace L. Hunley, the *Hunley* received a third crew of volunteers. On the night of February 17, 1864, this crew approached the 1,934-ton screw sloop *Housatonic*. The *Housatonic* spotted the *Hunley* and engaged her with small arms and tried to escape, but it was too late. The *Hunley* exploded its 130-pound spar torpedo, and the *Housatonic* became the first ship in the history of naval warfare to be sunk by a submarine. The blast, however, likely damaged the *Hunley* as well, and she sunk while returning to shore.[22]

In the end, the Federal Navy Department decided Charleston was not worth the risk of losing its lone ironclad squadron. The capture of Charleston would have to wait for Major General William Sherman and the Carolinas Campaign that followed his March to the Sea. On February 17–18, 1865, the Confederates evacuated and Charleston succumbed to Federal occupation.

Mobile Bay: Damn the Torpedoes

The last two holdouts among the Confederacy's major open ports were Wilmington, North Carolina, and Mobile Bay, Alabama. The Federals wanted to shut down both in order to halt the slow trickle of European supplies that was keeping General Robert E. Lee's Army of Northern Virginia alive. Wilmington had survived because the Cape Fear River's two entrances made it difficult to blockade and because it was guarded by the mighty Fort Fisher. Mobile Bay, on the other hand, had been victim to higher Federal priorities elsewhere. Vicksburg, Charleston, and the Red River Campaign all had served to distract attention and resources from Mobile Bay.[1] Finally, in January 1864, Admiral David Farragut arrived off Mobile Bay to begin assembling the ships and men he would need to settle the matter.

The Importance of Mobile. Blockading in the Gulf of Mexico was extremely difficult. There were some 600 miles between Pensacola and the Rio Grande, not counting the Mississippi River Delta. Behind the coast lay a complex network of inland waterways that allowed shallow-draught schooners to find exits and inlets not covered by blockaders. By this point in the war, Mobile was by far the most important Gulf port used by the Confederate blockade runners. It had been second only to New Orleans as the South's largest cotton-exporting port before the war, and now blockade runners plied their trade between Mobile and Bermuda, Nassau, and Cuba.

Enhancing Mobile's status as a commercial center was its access to the Confederate interior. Thirty miles above the city, the Alabama and Tombigbee Rivers joined to form the Mobile River. Additionally, the Mobile & Ohio Railroad, the longest railroad in the Confederacy,

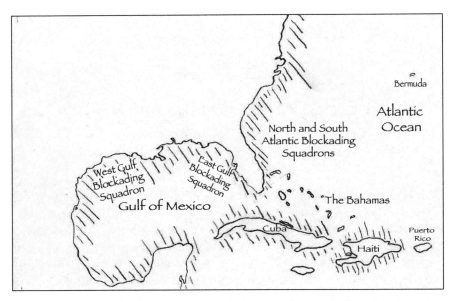

Blockade runners had several convenient ports from which to bring cargoes into and out of the Confederacy.

ran from Mobile all the way to Columbus, Kentucky.[2]

Moreover, Mobile Bay and its port were vital to the Southern war-making effort. Alabama was second only to Richmond's Tredegar Iron Works as the Confederacy's center for manufacturing iron and rolling heavy iron plate. About 130 miles north of Mobile along the Alabama River was Bassett's yard in Selma, where three ironclads were under construction. In all, eight were being built on the Alabama and Tombigbee Rivers, but only one, the *Tennessee*, would be completed in time to see action. The desire to halt further ironclad production made Mobile an even more important target for the Federals.[3]

The Defenders. Mobile Bay would prove to be a difficult target, because although the bay stretched some 30 miles inland, its entrance was only three miles wide. There, Fort Gaines guarded the western side from Dauphin Island. Stretching eastward from the fort, the defenders had placed a series of sunken pilings that reduced the bay's entrance by over half. From the far edge of the pilings, shallow water and three lines of torpedoes further narrowed the channel. Each line was staggered behind the one in front of it to prevent a boat of any size from slipping through. Brigadier General Gabriel Rains, who had pioneered the use of land mines during the Peninsula Campaign and had also helped protect Charleston with torpedoes, had been instrumental in laying out the system for Mobile.[4]

On the eastern edge of the minefield was a thin opening stretching some 200 yards to Mobile Point that provided a passageway for blockade runners. However, the powerful Fort Morgan, a massive pentagon-shaped, three-tiered structure with 47 guns, covered this route. Completing the defenses, a much smaller Fort Powell blocked Grant's Pass, a narrow intercoastal passage north of Dauphin Island via the Mississippi Sound.[5] Behind these forts were the ironclad *Tennessee* and three wooden gunboats under the able command of Admiral Franklin Buchanan. Buchanan had commanded the *Virginia* and, like Farragut, was a seasoned and aggressive fighter. His gunboats were of little consequence, but the *Tennessee* was a force to be reckoned with. She had six inches of armor on her casemate, five inches on her sides, and two inches on her deck. She had six Brooke rifles, but she was inadequately powered for her weight and therefore hard to maneuver. It was on the *Tennessee* that Buchanan pinned his hopes, and Farragut knew it. He wrote his son, "Buchanan has a vessel which he says is superior to the *Merrimack* with which he intends to attack us.... So we are to have no child's play."[6]

A respected and veteran seaman, Admiral Franklin Buchanan considered the ironclad Tennessee *to be critical to Mobile's defense.*
Photograph courtesy of the Library of Congress.

The Federal Navy. The Federals knew the Confederates could mount a spirited defense against wooden vessels, so in January, Assistant Secretary of the Navy Gustavas Fox had asked Farragut how many ironclads he thought he would need to blast his way into Mobile Bay. Farragut replied, "Just as many as you can spare; two would answer me well, more would do better."[7] By July, the Navy had four monitors on the way to Farragut. The *Manhattan* and the *Tecumseh* were large and improved vessels, mounting a pair of 15-inch Dahlgren guns behind 11 inches of turret armor. They were the most powerful warships then in existence. Complementing them were the *Chickasaw* and the *Winnebago*, twin-turret, quadruple-screwed river monitors with batteries of four 11-inch guns. The *Tecumseh* was the last to arrive, reaching Farragut on August 4, just in time for the battle. In addition, Farragut had 14 wooden ships and an initial army contingent of 2,000 troops.[8]

The Battle is Joined. On August 3, Brigadier General Gordon Granger landed his brigade at the west end of Dauphin Island, in the rear of Fort Gaines. Farragut had hoped to simultaneously begin the naval engagement, but the *Tecumseh's* late arrival had made that impossible. As Granger moved to invest Fort Gaines the next day, Farragut retired to his cabin and wrote, "I am going into Mobile in the morning if God is my leader, as I hope He is, and in Him I place my trust. If He thinks it is the place for me to die, I am ready to submit to His will."[9]

Farragut had good reason to be somewhat fatalistic. His plan was as dangerous as it was bold. The four monitors would take the lead with their shallow draught permitting them to hug the shore and avoid the mines, while their low profiles and armor plating would protect them from Fort Morgan's guns. The wooden ships would follow, echeloned slightly to the left of the monitors to use them as a shield. As a further caution, Farragut would lash each of his smaller gunboats to the port side of one of his larger vessels. This measure would not only protect the smaller ships from Fort Morgan; if the larger vessel's engines were disabled, the gunboat could act as a tug to pull the damaged ship to safety. Once the pairs had passed out of range of Fort Morgan, the connecting cables would be cut, and each vessel would operate independently.[10]

A master of detail, Farragut used a fleet of little wooden blocks shaped like ships to fine-tune his plan. He experimented with various configurations of the models on a table upon which the points of a compass had been drawn. In the end, Farragut felt he had determined the best position of his vessels relative to each other in entering the bay.[11]

Farragut was exactly the man for a hazardous undertaking such as Mobile Bay. Secretary Welles considered Farragut to be "better fitted to lead an expedition through danger and difficulty than to command an extensive blockade; is a good officer in a great emergency, will more willingly take risks in order to obtain great results than any other officer in high position in either Navy or Army."[12] Throughout the night of August 4, the meticulous Farragut made his final preparations. Any unnecessary spars and rigging were removed to facilitate speed and maneuverability. As at New Orleans, chain garlands were hung over the ships' starboard sides, and sandbags were piled "from stern to stern, and from the berth to the spar deck" for added protection.[13] At dawn on August 5, the Federal fleet drew up in battle formation.

Farragut gave the order to get under way with the monitors leading and the wooden ships behind. He had originally planned to lead with his own flagship, but his officers had convinced him that the admiral should not be so exposed. Reluctantly, and, later to his regret, Farragut acquiesced and assigned the *Brooklyn* to lead. Even having made this decision, Farragut wrote, "This I believe to be an error, for apart from the fact that exposure is one of the penalties of rank in the Navy, it will always be the aim of the enemy to destroy the flagship."[14]

Shortly after 6:30, the *Tecumseh* fired a ranging shot, and the fleet pressed forward, closing its order as it advanced. Virgil Jones hypothesizes that, "Perhaps never had there been such a disparity of strength between two hostile fleets about to engage in battle."[15] On the Federal side there were 30 vessels, of which four were ironclads, with a total of 252 guns and crews totaling 3,000 men. The Confederate fleet had a single ironclad and three hastily built gunboats, all told mounting 22 guns and 473 men. Undaunted by this disparity, Buchanan told his men, "Now men, the enemy is coming, and I want you to do your duty; and you shall not have it to say when you leave this vessel that you were not near enough to the enemy, for I shall meet them, and then you can fight them alongside of their own ships; and if I fall, lay me on the side and go on with the fight, and never mind me—but whip and sink the Yankees or fight until you sink yourselves, but do not surrender."[16]

Fort Morgan opened fire at 7:10, with the fleet a half-mile away. The *Brooklyn*, at the head of the Federal wooden ships, returned fire. "Soon after this," Farragut deadpanned, "the action became lively."[17]

Buchanan brought the *Tennessee* and the three small ships out from behind Mobile Point and lined them up just behind the minefield, executing the classic naval maneuver of crossing Farragut's T and sending a raking fire down the long axis of the Federal line. By this time, the *Brooklyn*, with her superior speed, had drawn even with the rear of the monitors. At this rate, Farragut would be faced with the dangerous situation that a wooden ship would end up leading the attack.

Just then the *Brooklyn* spotted "a row of suspicious looking buoys… directly under our bows." Unsure what to do, Captain James Alden ordered the ship to back engines to clear the hazard, a maneuver that compressed Farragut's entire fleet and exposed it to a murderous fire from Fort Morgan. To make matters worse, the *Tecumseh*, located at the head of the formation, struck a torpedo and went down swiftly. "Sunk by a torpedo!" bemoaned Captain Alden. "Assassination in its worst form! A glorious though terrible end for our noble friends, the intrepid pioneers of that death-strewn path. Immortal fame is theirs; peace to their names."[18]

Remarkably spry for a 63 year old, Farragut had climbed the rigging of his flagship *Hartford's* mainmast to ascertain the situation. A sailor scurried up behind him to tie a rope around Farragut to prevent him from falling. At first the admiral protested against the precaution, but eventually he consented and secured himself. Farragut knew the battle had reached its crisis point, and he knew what he had to do. "I shall lead," he said famously. "Damn the torpedoes! Full speed ahead."[19]

With that, the *Hartford*, with the *Metacomet* lashed alongside, turned sharply to port and sped past the *Brooklyn* directly across the minefield into Mobile Bay. Buchanan continued his raking fire, but from the moment the Federal fleet made its turn, its starboard batteries unloaded on Fort Morgan, driving the Confederate gunners to shelter. However, once the stronger lead ships passed, Fort Morgan was able to return fire against the weaker ones in the rear. The last tandem, the *Oneida* and the *Galena,* were hit badly but limped on.

The main threat now was the *Tennessee*. The Federals delivered repeated broadsides, but these efforts barely dented the ironclad. A mile into the bay, Farragut gave the order to cut the smaller ships loose and commanded, "Gunboats chase enemy gunboats." The small Confederate ships were quickly neutralized, but Buchanan readied the *Tennessee* for one last run. With only six hours of coal left, Buchanan knew he had to act. He headed straight for the Federal fleet that had anchored four miles beyond Fort Morgan.

Farragut, who had ordered his men to begin eating breakfast, was in a state of disbelief. "I did not think Old Buck was such a fool," he said, and then commanded, "Destroy the enemy's principal ship by ramming her." The *Monongahela* obeyed the order and struck the *Tennessee* a glancing blow. The *Tennessee* stood her ground but was soon swarmed by the *Manhattan*, and then the *Lackawanna*, and finally the *Hartford*. In the midst of the chaos, the *Lackawanna* accidentally rammed the *Hartford*, momentarily endangering Farragut himself. By now, the *Tennessee* was barely hanging on. Her flagstaff had been shot away, and most of her smokestack was gone. Several port covers were damaged, and her gun primers repeatedly failed. Now, the *Chickasaw* pulled into position and delivered a terrible fire. With his characteristic understatement, Farragut recorded that the *Tennessee* "was at this time sore beset."[20] Buchanan, himself suffering from a compound fracture in his leg, turned to the commander of the *Tennessee*, Commander James Johnston, and said, "Well, Johnston, if you cannot do any further damage you had better surrender." Johnston took one last look from the gun deck, saw the *Ossippe* fast approaching, and decided to lower the Confederate colors and hoist a white flag.[21]

The naval battle had lasted but a couple of hours. Of the 3,000 Federals engaged, there were 319 casualties, including 93 who drowned when the *Tecumseh* sank. The percentage of Confederate naval personnel lost was much higher. Out of 470 Confederates engaged, 312 were lost.[22]

The forts did not hold out much longer, with the Confederates abandoning tiny Fort Powell that night and blowing it up as they departed. Fort Gaines mustered a faint-hearted show of resistance and then surrendered the next day on August 8. Granger netted 818 prisoners there and then moved his entire force of about 5,500 against the 400 Confederates at Fort Morgan, where Brigadier General Richard Page vowed, "I am prepared to sacrifice life and will only surrender when I have no means of defense."[23] In reality, Page's brave words were about all the defense the Confederates could muster. On August 17, the Federals received a siege train from New Orleans, and on August 22, they began a heavy land and naval bombardment. At the same time, Granger pushed his trenches to within assaulting distance of the fort. The Confederates raised a white flag the next morning and formally surrendered at 2:30 p.m. Losses on both sides were negligible. From all three forts, the Federals captured 1,464 prisoners and 104 pieces of artillery.[24]

Results. Farragut considered Mobile Bay, "one of the hardest-earned victories of my life." The Federals had lost 172 men killed and another 170 wounded. The *Brooklyn* had been struck 59 times. Farragut described his own flagship, the *Hartford*, as "greatly cut up."[25] Nonetheless, when Secretary Welles brought news of the hard-fought victory to President Lincoln, he was disappointed by the president's apparent lack of enthusiasm. After three years and four months of fighting, blockade running on the Gulf of Mexico had now virtually ceased to exist. Wilmington remained the Confederacy's last significant open port. Welles considered this a magnificent accomplishment, but he lamented in his diary, "It is not appreciated as it should be."[26] Without access to the sea, the city of Mobile was of no strategic importance and withered on the vine. It was finally occupied by Federal forces on April 12, 1865.

Like Lincoln, Lieutenant General Ulysses Grant found it hard to get too excited about the victory at Mobile Bay. He had planned for his spring 1864 campaign to include a drive against Mobile that would help support Major General William Sherman's Atlanta Campaign. Instead, however, Major General Nathaniel Banks had followed political motivations and marched up the cotton-rich but strategically unimportant Red River Valley. By early April, Banks's campaign was a failure and Grant's hope for a supporting operation in the rear of General Joseph Johnston's Army of Tennessee was lost.[27] When Mobile finally fell, Grant was unimpressed. In his *Memoirs* he explained, "I had tried for more than two years to have an expedition sent against Mobile when its possession by us would have been of great advantage. It finally cost lives to take it when its possession was of no importance."[28]

Perhaps the greatest significance of Farragut's success was political. When combined with Sherman's capture of Atlanta in September, Mobile Bay provided the Federals with twin victories that indicated the overall war effort was succeeding. Up to that point, there was a real possibility that war weariness would cost Lincoln the 1864 election. Had that been the case, the Civil War would have likely ended in some negotiated settlement. Instead, the momentum gained by battlefield victories and Lincoln's re-election ensured the ultimate defeat of the Confederacy.

FORT FISHER: THE FINAL CHAPTER

With Farragut's victory at Mobile Bay, the entire Gulf Coast east of the Mississippi was closed to Confederate shipping and blockade runners. Wilmington, North Carolina, was the only seaport still open to supply the slowly strangling Confederacy with the imported arms and equipment it needed.[1] General Robert E. Lee warned that if Wilmington was not held, he "could not maintain his army."[2]

Blockading the port had proved difficult because the Federals had to watch two separate inlets into the Cape Fear River, separated by 25 miles of shoals and creating an arc 50 miles long. Throughout the course of the war, about 100 blockade runners had sailed in and out of Wilmington.[3] Now, their cargoes were more important than ever. In the last nine weeks of 1864 and the first two weeks of 1865, blockade runners had brought 69,000 rifles, 43 cannon, more than 4 tons of meat, 500,000 pair of shoes, about a ton of saltpeter, and three quarters of a ton of lead into Wilmington.[4]

Defending this key port was Fort Fisher. Located 18 miles south of Wilmington, the fort straddled Confederate Point, a long, tapering peninsula between the Cape Fear River and the Atlantic Ocean. The Federals would launch two massive assaults, one in December 1864 and the second in January 1865, to try to capture Fort Fisher. Major General Benjamin Butler and Rear Admiral David Porter both commanded the December 1864 attempt. It would end in failure, principally because of Butler's negative influence and the two commanders' failure to work together. For the second attempt, Major General Alfred Terry replaced Butler. The difference was striking. The Army and the Navy forces achieved remarkable unity of effort, and the fort surrendered. With that, the coastal war was over.

The Defenders. In the aftermath of the Federal successes at Roanoke Island and New Bern, Colonel William Lamb was assigned to command Fort Fisher on July 4, 1862. Upon his arrival, he found a humble collection of earthworks containing 6 artillery batteries mounting 17 guns. Lamb concluded, "The frigate *Minnesota* could have destroyed the works and driven us out in a few hours."[5] Lamb had much more than this in mind. What he envisioned was a massive fortress able to protect blockade runners coming in and out of the adjacent New Inlet, imposing enough to deter an attempt to close the Cape Fear, and formidable enough to withstand an assault. He "determined at once to build a work of such magnitude that it could withstand the heaviest fire of any gun in the American Navy."[6]

Over the next two years, Lamb worked to fulfill his vision, transforming Fort Fisher into the largest seacoast fortification in the Confederacy. Lamb was an ardent student of fortifications. In December 1861, he purchased a book on the Crimean War that apparently went into great detail concerning fort architecture, and his plans were greatly influenced by the Malakoff Tower, a Russian earthwork stronghold that protected Sevastopol in 1854.[7] The end result of Lamb's labors was a fort built in the shape of an upside down L, which stretched nearly half a mile across Confederate Point from the river to the Atlantic, and then wound more than a mile down the beach.

The land face section was a bumpy line of 15 huge earthen mounds called "traverses," which were approximately 30 feet high and 25 feet thick. These were hollow inside in order to shelter the garrison during bombardment. Between the traverses were heavy artillery pieces mounted in elevated "gun chambers" and surrounded by sandbags. By late 1864, the fort's land face boasted 20 heavy seacoast artillery pieces, mostly large Columbiads, and was supported by 3 mortars and several field pieces. For almost half a mile north of the land face, trees and bushes had been removed to provide a clear field of fire. Nine-foot-high sharpened logs formed a palisade fence parallel to the land face from the river to the ocean. To the north of the fence was an electronically detonated minefield.

At the angle of the L, where the land face and sea face intersected, Lamb had built a massive Northeast Bastion with sloping sod walls that were 43 feet high. Adjacent to the Northeast Bastion was the Pulpit Battery, Lamb's combat headquarters. From this position, Lamb could see the enemy fleet miles away.

From the Northeast Bastion, the sea face line of traverses ran along the beach. Midway down was the pride of Lamb's arsenal—a colossal 150-pounder Armstrong rifled cannon with long enough range to keep the blockaders away. Ammunition, however, was in short supply, so Lamb husbanded his limited rounds for battle.

At the southern end of the sea face, a full mile from the Northeast Bastion, was a massive 60-foot-high artillery emplacement known as Mound Battery. It was a huge fortification, which housed two heavy seacoast artillery pieces and was visible for miles from the sea. Finally, Lamb protected the rear of his fort with Battery Buchanan on the tip of the peninsula.

Fort Fisher's thick earthen walls could absorb the impact of the largest artillery rounds of its day, and its bombproofs offered more than 14,500 square feet of protection and storage. Fort Fisher scholar Rod Gragg concluded, "Lamb had built one of history's greatest fortresses."[8]

Gragg also points out one of the fort's major weaknesses—a severe lack of personnel. Fort Fisher's permanent garrison numbered just 600.[9] Lamb himself noted another deficiency: Fort Fisher had been built to withstand a bombardment more so than an assault. The soldiers in the gun chambers had 100 feet of deadspace in front of their positions in which they could not see the enemy, so in order to repel an assault they had to leave their cover and fight from the open parapet.[10]

Opposite: Wilmington, the Confederacy's last open port, was protected by a set of massive fortifications built under the direction of Colonel William Lamb.

The Attackers. In the fall of 1864, Secretary of the Navy Welles confided in Admiral Farragut that the Navy had been advocating an amphibious assault on Fort Fisher since the winter of 1862, but the Army had refused. Welles felt that the new Federal General-in-Chief

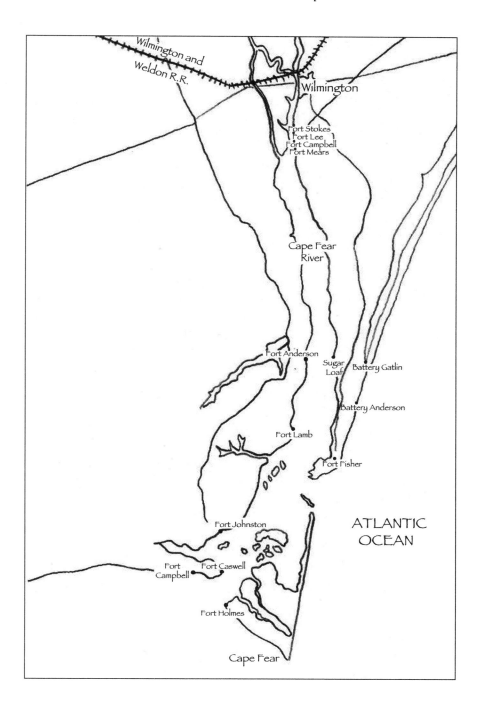

Wilmington and
Weldon R.R.

Wilmington

Fort Stokes
Fort Lee
Fort Campbell
Fort Mears

Cape Fear
River

Fort Anderson

Sugar
Loaf   Battery Gatlin

Battery Anderson

Fort Lamb

Fort Fisher

ATLANTIC
OCEAN

Fort Johnston

Fort   Fort Caswell
Campbell

Fort Holmes

Cape Fear

Lieutenant General Ulysses Grant would support such an attack, and Welles offered command of the naval forces to Farragut. Farragut declined the offer, citing worsening health, and David Porter was selected in his stead.

In spite of this optimism, Army support for the venture remained quite thin. Grant was reluctant to release any of his troops until he could replace his losses from the bloody fighting in Virginia, and he had strong concerns for the safety of Washington. Major General Henry Halleck, the Army chief of staff, agreed, feeling that the War Department already had "more irons than we can keep from burning." Furthermore, Halleck had never been a supporter of joint operations, and the recent failures at Charleston had confirmed his opinion. Nonetheless, Grant knew Lincoln favored the Wilmington operation, so Grant lent it his support.[11] For the land commander, he earmarked Major General Godfrey Weitzel, but to the annoyance of both Grant and Porter, Major General Benjamin Butler, whose command included North Carolina, chose to exercise his prerogative as department commander and personally lead the troops.[12]

Butler had learned of two recent ship explosions that fueled his imagination. In one, a British canal boat had blown up with 75 tons of powder in its hold, and in a more recent instance, a U.S. ordnance vessel had exploded at City Point, east of Richmond. Both blasts had destroyed nearby buildings and caused great loss of life. The always-conniving Butler surmised that a similar explosion could be used in an assault on Fort Fisher.[13]

Grant was skeptical, writing, "While I hope for the best [I] do not believe a particle in" the idea. Halleck was much more blunt, saying, "Butler's torpedo ship would have about as much effect on the forts as if he should—at them."[14] Porter, however, felt that Butler's idea was "an experiment at least worth trying" and increasingly became one of its proponents.[15] At one point he predicted, "The names of those connected with the expedition will be famous for all time to come."[16]

Thus, the plan proceeded. The ship selected was the *Louisiana*, an ancient, flat-bottomed, shallow-draught vessel assigned to blockade duty. It was disarmed, cut down, camouflaged to look like a blockade runner, loaded with 215 tons of gunpowder, and fitted with an elaborate ignition system. It was commanded by Commander

Alexander Rhind, who was well aware that he and his men were risking their very lives.[17]

The First Attack. Butler's expedition left Hampton Roads on December 13 and 14 with transports carrying two divisions totaling 6,500 men. Butler reached his appointed anchorage on December 15, but Porter, with his fleet of 57 ironclads, frigates, and gunboats, was nowhere in sight. It was not until the night of December 18 that Porter finally arrived. The delay had been caused by the powder ship's taking longer to load than expected, and then the fleet had to wait for high tide to leave Beaufort.[18]

According to Peter Chaitin, Butler and Porter "cordially disliked each other."[19] According to Scott Stuckey, they "despised each other."[20] Suffice to say, they were not on good terms, the trouble stemming from New Orleans. Butler had started it by tactlessly asserting, though with considerable justification, that Porter's mortar bombardment of the two forts below the city had made no contribution to their surrender because the defenders had given up the fight only after New Orleans fell.[21] To make matters worse, Porter was convinced that Butler was continuing the cotton speculation in North Carolina that he had pursued at Ship Island and New Orleans. Porter even accused Butler of trying to lure him into a scheme to run cotton through his own blockade.[22] In Porter's mind, Butler "was all jingle and feathers and [had a] staff as large as all outdoors."[23] Butler felt that Porter, "hates me as the devil hates holy water."[24]

Acting out the continuing friction, Porter and Butler now chose to communicate by dispatch rather than meeting face to face. Through intermediaries, Butler learned that Porter had just sent the powder ship toward shore for immediate detonation. Butler was shocked.

The whole time Butler had been waiting for Porter, the weather had been excellent, but now the wind was up and a gale seemed to be on the way. That would prevent the troops from landing and give the Confederates time to recover from the explosion. Butler advised detonating the *Louisiana* only when a landing could immediately follow, and that meant waiting to see if the weather would clear. Porter consented and dispatched a fast tug to recall the *Louisiana*.

The next morning, the weather had indeed worsened, and Butler took his transports to Beaufort to recoal, resupply, and ride out the storm. The storm lasted three days, which gave the Confederates time to bolster their defenses. By December 23, Lamb had some 1,400 troops in the fort, including reinforcements from two companies of the Tenth North Carolina Artillery and the Seventh Battalion of Junior Reserves, a unit of teenagers commonly called "The Seventeen-Year-Olds." That same day, Butler had sent a note to Porter telling him the Army would return to the rendezvous site the night of December 24 and that the naval bombardment and landing could take place Christmas morning.[25]

Porter, however, had other plans. He had decided to detonate the *Louisiana* at 1:00 a.m. on December 24 and begin the bombardment sometime during the day—without the Army. When Butler learned of this new development, he was furious. To him, it appeared as if Porter and the Navy were trying to steal all the glory. [26] Immediately, Butler ordered his headquarters ship to head for Fort Fisher, and he instructed the transports to follow as soon as they completed their recoaling. By then, however, the powder ship was already underway.

At 10:30 p.m. on December 23, the *Wilderness* had begun towing Commander Rhind and his crew of twelve volunteers aboard the *Louisiana* toward the shore. At 11:30, estimating they were 500 yards away from Fort Fisher, the Federals cut loose the towlines and the *Louisiana* fired her engines. When Rhind judged he was about 300 yards offshore of the Northeast Bastion, he killed his engines and dropped anchor. He set the ignition fuses to activate at 1:18 a.m., then rowed with his crew to the safety of the *Wilderness* and then rejoined the rest of Porter's fleet. In spite of his efforts, including a close call with a blockade runner named *Little Hattie*, Rhind never got the *Louisiana* closer than 600 yards to the fort. [27] It was not close enough.

1:18 came and went. So did 1:30 and 1:45. Then, at 1:46, the *Louisiana* exploded. Ensign John Gattan wrote that "Suddenly a bright flash was observed and a stream of flames ascended to a great height and spread out in an immense sheet of fire, illuminating for an instant the whole horizon." [28] In spite of this captivating visual spectacle, the explosion had no effect on the fort. Confederate commander Lamb matter of factly recorded in his diary, "A blockader got aground near the fort, set fire to herself, and blew up."[29]

Commander Rhind, who had risked his life in the adventure, was equally unimpressed. Watching from the deck of the *Wilderness*, he remarked, "There's a fizzle," and then he went below. [30] Fort Fisher was undamaged. In the words of Allan Nevins, the powder ship was "one of the most ludicrous fiascoes of the war." [31]

Porter appeared unfazed by the disappointment and pressed ahead with his naval attack. Expecting a gigantic explosion, he had ordered his vessels to remain twelve miles offshore, but now he moved them forward. By 11:30 a.m., he had deployed his fleet in a semicircle along the fort's seaface. The ships began their bombardment, and for five hours they unleashed their fury.[32]

Porter had 627 guns and was capable of firing 115 shells a minute. On the first day of the bombardment, he launched 10,000 heavy caliber rounds. The Confederates, necessarily conserving ammunition, replied with just 672.[33] Lamb describes the disparity in arms as follows:

> The *Minnesota, Colorado,* and *Wabash*, came grandly on, floating fortresses, each mounting more guns than all the batteries on the land, and the two first, combined, carrying more shot and shell than all the magazines in the fort contained. From the left salient to the mound Fort Fisher had 44 heavy guns, and not over 3600 shot and shell, exclusive of grape and shrapnel. The Armstrong gun had only one dozen rounds of fixed ammunition, and no other projectile could be used in its delicate grooves. [34]

Nonetheless, the massive Federal fire had little effect. Two Confederate guns were dismounted, one man was killed, 22 were wounded, and about half of the living quarters were damaged. Lamb concluded that "Never, since the invention of gunpowder, was there so much harmlessly expended as in the first day's attack on Fort Fisher." As for the Federals, 83 were killed and wounded, more than half of them in an explosion of five new 100-pounder Parrotts. [35]

At dusk, Butler arrived off Confederate Point with a few transports. Continuing their antics from the initial rendezvous, Butler and Porter did not meet face to face. At first, Porter even declined to meet with Butler's staff. Later he relented, but during the meeting with Major General Weitzel and Colonel Cyrus Comstock, Porter insisted that his bombardment had left the fort defenseless. He cited the limited return fire as evidence that the fort's guns had been rendered useless, and boasted that "There was not a blade of grass or a piece of stick in that fort that was not burned up." All the Army would have to do was walk inside the fort and claim possession. [36]

The Confederate defenders at Fort Fisher survived the uncoordinated and poorly planned first Federal attack.
Photograph courtesy of the Library of Congress, Prints & Photographs Division

Butler and his staff disagreed and were incensed at Porter's premature and unilateral initiation of the battle. They saw it as further proof that the Navy was trying to get all the glory for itself, and Butler felt that with surprise lost, a landing was now futile. He argued for an immediate return to Fort Monroe. Others agreed, but Comstock suggested going ashore anyway to reconnoiter and then decide what to do. Butler acquiesced, and a landing was planned for the next morning to test the Confederate defenses. Clearly, however, the spirit of Army-Navy joint action was gone. Writing in his diary, Comstock captured the predominant mood, grumbling, "Fine cooperation." [37]

At 10:30 a.m. on December 25, Porter renewed his bombardment, and three hours later Weitzel came ashore with about 2,000 soldiers. They landed unopposed north of Fort Fisher, but Porter's claims of rendering the fort defenseless were soon proved untrue. In fact, all 17 cannon on the landface were unharmed, and soon canister and mines were taking their toll of Weitzel's men. The Federals managed to capture a few Confederate pickets who reported that Major General Robert Hoke had arrived at Wilmington with 6,000 reinforcements and was marching to Fort Fisher. Weitzel no doubt recalled the slaughter of Federal soldiers in the repeated assaults against Fort Wagner at Charleston in July 1863. He did not like the similar potential he saw at Fort Fisher and decided to return to Butler and report the situation. [38]

Butler had been explicitly directed by Grant to entrench and besiege the fort if necessary, but the alleged threat from Hoke prompted Butler to decide to stop the attack. He ordered a hasty retreat, even though Brigadier General Newton Curtis had begun to enjoy some success after Weitzel had departed. Curtis begged Butler to reconsider, stating "the garrison has offered no resistance," but Butler only issued a second order to retreat. As other commanders began returning their forces to the landing site, Curtis stubbornly attacked, but Fort Fisher's defenses were too strong. By the time Curtis decided to withdraw, the surf had become too high to bring in the boats, and Butler sailed to Hampton Roads with Curtis and about 700 of his men still on the beach. All during the next day and into the morning of December 27, Porter kept up a steady fire to cover "those poor devils" until they could be evacuated. After that, the ships gradually withdrew to Beaufort. [39]

The two days of bombardment had totaled 21,000 rounds—the Civil War's heaviest naval shelling to date—but it had amounted to little damage to Fort Fisher.[40] Butler's land force had sustained just 16 casualties, including one death to drowning. Shelby Foote describes such small loss as "clearly indicative of something less than an all-out try at the fort's reduction." [41]

On December 28, Grant informed President Lincoln that "The Wilmington expedition has proven a gross and culpable failure. . . . Who is to blame I hope will be known." Grant assured Porter, "I will endeavor to be back again with an increased force and without the former commander." For Porter's part, he felt, "If this temporary failure succeeds in sending General Butler into private life, it is not to be regretted." Clearly, Porter had had his share of political generals, having previously suffered through Butler at New Orleans and Major General Nathaniel Banks during the Red River Campaign. Now he lamented, "Let the people see the folly of employing such generals as Butler and Banks. I have tried them both, and God save me from further connection with such generals." Butler's political connections had rescued him from failure many times, but now enough was enough. Although the Joint Congressional Committee on the Conduct of the War would eventually conclude that "The determination of General Butler not to attack Fort Fisher seems to have been fully justified by all the facts and circumstances then known or afterward ascertained," his military career was over. [42]

Interestingly, Lamb sided with Butler. He wrote that "Butler, with wise discretion, determined not to assault. There were not enough Federal troops landed to have stormed our palisade that Christmas night." [43] Lamb was confident he could withstand a frontal attack. What concerned him was an attack in his rear from between the Mound Battery and Battery Buchanan. In Lamb's mind, "Admiral Porter was as much to blame as General Butler for the repulse." [44]

In making this comment, Lamb does not explain exactly why he faults Porter, and he does not mention that it was Butler's own decision to land a force of the size and at the location that he did. Clearly, Butler had lost his zeal for the attack before he ever put troops ashore, and it did not take much to dissuade him from continuing the assault. Nonetheless, Lamb's comment does raise some correct criticism of Porter.

Porter showed no more desire to cooperate with Butler than vice versa. He acted unilaterally, parochially, and seemingly selfishly. In the words of Rod Gragg, both Porter and Butler had let "their longtime personal feud [spill] over into their professional lives, affecting their military judgment and undermining the expedition." [45] Porter would redeem himself during the next assault on Fort Fisher, but neither he nor Butler could be particularly proud of his performance during the first attempt.

Federal Adjustments. The first attack on Fort Fisher had failed because of a lack of Army-Navy cooperation, a massive but indiscriminate naval bombardment, and a tepid land assault. The second attack would correct these deficiencies.

Perhaps the most fateful change was Grant's choice of Major General Alfred Terry to replace Butler as the Army commander. Terry had participated in the first assault, so he had firsthand knowledge of what had gone wrong. Addressing one of these problems, Grant specifically instructed Terry to get along with Porter, telling him, "It is of the greatest importance that there should be a complete understanding and harmony of action between yourself and Admiral Porter. I want you to consult the admiral fully, and to let there be no misunderstanding in regard to the plan of cooperation in all its details." [46]

Grant need not have worried. Terry was the perfect man for the job, possessing the equanimity necessary to work closely with the temperamental Porter. He was "affable, modest, and capable," almost the polar opposite of Butler. For his part, Porter was extremely pleased with his new partner, eventually concluding Terry to be "my beau ideal of a soldier and a general."[47]

In addition to a spirit of tact and cooperation, Terry brought a sense of aggressiveness to the Army command. When Lincoln met Terry for the first time, the President asked, "Why have we not seen you before?" Terry replied that his duties had kept him at the front, a sharp departure from the politically minded Butler. Likewise, in contrast to Butler's lack of commitment, Terry told Porter that, once ashore, he intended to stay there until "Confederate Point" was "Federal Point" again—by right of exclusive occupation. [48]

As for Porter, there would be none of the "ragged gunnery" and "wild cannonading" that had resulted in massive expenditures but scant results in the first attack. Instead, Porter's gunners, under his personal direction, would display "sharpshooter accuracy" in providing close-in fires to the Army. [49]

Grant also was much more enthusiastic about the second attack.

With Major General William Sherman in the midst of his Carolinas Campaign, Grant knew that if Wilmington was in Federal hands, Sherman could advance toward Virginia without having to detour to the coast to capture the port or to hunt for provisions.[50] In addition to providing Terry the same units Butler had had, Grant ordered the aggressive Major General Phil Sheridan to be ready to reinforce Terry if necessary.[51] Porter was elated with Grant's suddenly heightened interest in Wilmington, writing him, "Thank you for so promptly trying to rectify the blunder so lately committed." [52]

Thus, the second attack on Fort Fisher would be all that the first one was not. Above all, it would be a vivid demonstration of the power of unity of effort in joint operations. While the Federal force comprising the second attack was modestly increased, the real difference was that Terry and Porter would cooperate where Butler and Porter had not. It would be the difference between success and failure.

Confederate Disappointments. After demonstrating his ineptitude for high command in the Tullahoma Campaign and at Chickamauga and Chattanooga, General Braxton Bragg had been recalled to Richmond to serve as President Davis's military advisor. Subsequently, Davis sent him to replace the popular Major General W.H.C. Whiting as commander of the Department of North Carolina. Whiting had been more to Lamb than just his commander; he had been a mentor and friend. Bragg would be nothing like Whiting, and his arrival was unwelcome. The *Richmond Examiner* editorialized, "Bragg has been sent to Wilmington. Goodbye Wilmington!"[53] A local citizen lamented, "Bragg the Unlucky is a Millstone which Mr. Davis persists in tying around our necks."[54]

Such misgivings were soon born out. Bragg refused to send Lamb reinforcements from Hoke's division, feeling that they were necessary to defend Wilmington, and that a second seaborne assault would not be coming soon. Frustrated by this turn of events, Whiting would soon join Lamb at Fort Fisher, saying, "Lamb, my boy, I have come to share your fate. You and your garrison are to be sacrificed." [55]

The Second Attack. On January 8, 1865, Terry and more than 8,000 troops, many of them veterans of Butler's abortive attempt, embarked from Bermuda Hundred on the James River for a second attack on Fort Fisher. During the first attack, Porter and Butler had had no personal contact whatsoever, but Terry's first act upon rendezvousing with the fleet was to meet Porter aboard the *Malvern*. The two commanders carefully planned the operation. On January 12, the Navy fleet and Army transports appeared off Confederate Point. At this time, Lamb's garrison consisted of just 800, at least 100 of whom were not fit for duty.[56]

Two hours before dawn on January 13, Porter committed all five of his ironclads at short range. His object was to draw fire from Fort Fisher that would disclose the location of the Confederate guns by their muzzle flashes. The ploy worked, and just after sunrise, Porter brought to bear his 627 guns against targets the lookouts had spotted.[57] This technique was the first indication of the precise and well-measured fire Porter would deliver in this attack—a marked improvement over the previous attempt.

Rear Admiral Porter and his staff aboard the Malvern. The second attack on Fort Fisher included a new spirit of cooperation between the Army and Navy, as well as a much more accurate bombardment from Porter.
Photograph courtesy of the Library of Congress, Prints & Photographs Division.

During the night of January 12 and the morning of January 13, about 700 reinforcements had made their way to Lamb, bringing his total to 1,500. In contrast, Terry had been landing since 8:00 a.m., and by 3:00 in the afternoon all 8,000 of his men were ashore. Each man carried three days' rations on his person, and the command had a six-day reserve of hard bread and a 300,000-round supply of ammunition. Terry had come to stay, and he punctuated the point by digging a stout defensive line across the peninsula. These works were manned on the river side by two brigades of United States Colored Troops under the command of Brigadier General Charles Paine, and on the ocean side by Colonel Joseph Abbott's 2nd Brigade of the First Division. The line was oriented to the north to guard against an attack by Hoke from Wilmington. Hoke, however, had gone on the defensive himself. [58]

Thus, Lamb was left alone to absorb the merciless naval bombardment. In the December attack, Porter had fired 20,271 projectiles weighing 1,275,000 pounds. This time his demand for more deliberate and accurate fire resulted in 19,682 rounds being fired, a few hundred less than before, but by using heavier weapons, the total weight was 1,652,638 pounds, a new record for a single naval engagement. Bragg finally acquiesced to Lamb's pleas for reinforcements and dispatched a scant 1,100 to Fort Fisher. Of these, only 350 made it to the fort, the rest being turned back by the fury of Porter's fire. [59]

Porter had instructed his men to aim not at the fort's flag but at individual guns.[60] The results were devastating. Lamb wrote:

> In the former bombardment the fire of the fleet had been diffuse, not calculated to effect any particular damage, and so wild that at least one-third of the missiles fell in the river beyond the fort or in the bordering marshes; but now the fire was concentrated, and the definite object of the fleet was the destruction of the land defenses by enfilade and direct fire. . . . All day and night on the 13th and 14th of January the navy continued its ceaseless torment; it was impossible to repair damages at night on the land-face. . . . At least two hundred had been

killed and wounded in the two days since the fighting began. Only three or four of my land guns were of any service. [61]

In the midst of this bombardment, Terry had led a probe of the Confederate defenses on the morning of January 14 and advanced to within 700 yards of the parapet. He decided to launch a full-scale assault the next day. That evening, he returned to Porter's flagship where the two planned the joint attack. [62]

Even amid this spirit of cooperation, Porter retained a measure of service pride. He suggested that a contingent of 1,600 sailors and 400 marines participate in the assault with Terry's soldiers. This naval force was to be commanded by Lieutenant Commander K.R. Breese. Its objective would be the Crescent Battery where the land and sea faces met. [63] Breese's men succeeded in landing without detection on January 15, and at 2:30 p.m., as the ships ceased firing, Breese launched his assault. Scott Stuckey describes the scheme as "a dubious proposition, consisting of sending sailors ignorant of infantry tactics and armed only with cutlasses and pistols against strong works."[64] As should have been expected, the tactic failed miserably, with Breese taking about 300 casualties before retreating—"ingloriously flying along the beach away from the fort" as one Federal soldier described it. [65]

The debacle, however, had an unintended benefit. The Confederates were convinced that this effort in the east was the main attack and were thus distracted when the true main attack, by a 3,300-man division commanded by Brigadier General Adelbert Ames, moved against the western salient. [66]

Ames's three brigades attacked one after another in the type of mass close-in assault that Lamb knew was one of Fort Fisher's vulnerabilities. At 2:00 p.m., a group of 60 sharpshooters from the 13th Indiana, armed with Sharps repeating rifles, and 40 men from Brigadier General Custis's brigade rushed forward and dug themselves in within 175 yards of the fort. With the sharpshooters covering the parapet, Custis advanced the rest of the brigade to a position 50 yards behind the sharpshooters. Colonel Galusha Pennypacker's brigade moved up behind Custis, and Colonel Louis Bell formed up his brigade 200 yards behind Pennypacker.

At 3:25 p.m., Curtis's brigade led the assault, with axmen hacking a breach in the palisade and the rest of the brigade gaining the parapet. Pennypacker moved up on Curtis's right, and Bell moved up on the right of Pennypacker. The assault became a desperate hand-to-hand fight from one traverse to the next. [67]

In the midst of this struggle, Porter demonstrated just how the accuracy of his fires had improved from the December attack. The *New Ironsides* and several smaller vessels used their rifled pivot guns to deliver precise fires to clear the Confederates out of each successive gun platform just ahead of the advancing Federal soldiers.[68] Rod Gragg writes that "The lethal hail of artillery shells fell with incredible precision, walking around the landface wall, clearing it of Confederate defenders, edging up to within yards of the Federal infantry . . ." [69]

Ames had sent more than 3,000 men into the fort, but it still had not fallen. He asked Terry for reinforcements. Terry turned to Colonel Comstock for advice, and Comstock advocated audacity. He recommended committing both Colonel Joseph Abbott's reserve brigade and Paine's division. Paine had already repulsed one attack from Hoke, but Terry decided to accept the risk of another. Both Abbott and Paine would attack Fort Fisher. [70]

The exhausted Confederates had little hope against Abbott's fresh troops. On Comstock's advice, Abbott's brigade was organized into 100 man teams which assaulted each traverse in turn. Losses in one team were immediately reinforced by another. Still, the Confederates refused to surrender, stubbornly expecting Bragg to order Hoke to counterattack at any moment. But such help would not come, and, after six hours of incredible fighting, Federal soldiers occupied Fort Fisher from the river to the ocean. [71]

Once the landface was in Federal control, the rest of Fort Fisher was doomed to fall. What resistance that remained was consolidated at Battery Buchanan. Against this objective, Abbott advanced with his brigade on one side and the 27th US Colored Troops under Colonel Albert Blackman on the other. At 10:00 p.m., the Confederates surrendered. The fighting had been horrific. One Federal sailor wrote, "If hell is what it is said to be then the interior of Fort Fisher is a fair comparison." Federal casualties were 955 for the Army and 383 for the Navy. The Confederates lost about 500 killed or wounded and well over 1,000 taken prisoner. Both Lamb and Whiting were wounded, the latter mortally. All three of Ames's brigade commanders were severely wounded, Bell mortally. Even after the fighting ended, casualties continued to be sustained. In an unfortunate tragedy, two celebrating sailors accidentally ignited the fort's main powder magazine. In the explosion, 104 Federals were killed or wounded. [72]

The coastal war was over. From Virginia south to Florida and west along the Gulf of Mexico to the Mississippi, not a single important port remained open to sustain the Confederacy. True, the Civil War would ultimately be decided by the great inland armies rather than in the smaller coastal battles, but the Federal victories on the coast, from their modest beginnings at Hatteras Inlet to the climatic struggle at Fort Fisher, had made valuable contributions.[73] Guiding these efforts had been the pioneering work of the Navy Board at the war's beginning.

THE COASTAL WAR AND THE
ELEMENTS OF OPERATIONAL DESIGN

What the Navy Board had brought to the coastal war was an exemplary display of the operational art—"the application of creative imagination by commanders and staffs ... to design strategies, campaigns, and major operations and organize and employ military forces."[1] The elements of operational design (formerly known as the facets of operational art) are termination, end states and objectives, effects, center of gravity, decisive points, direct versus indirect, lines of operations, operational reach, simultaneity and depth, timing and tempo, forces and functions, leverage, balance, anticipation, synergy, culmination, and arranging operations.[2] Although from a different era, these elements provide a useful framework for discussing the Navy Board and the coastal war.

Termination. Deciding on the national strategic end state and termination criteria enables the development of more detailed military strategies.[3] For the Federal side in the Civil War, the termination criterion revolved around the reestablishment of the Union under federal authority. To bring this eventuality about, the Federals would have to either militarily defeat the Confederacy or compel it to surrender. Thus, the Navy Board knew that the blockade would have to last for the duration of the war. This understanding affected the Board's planning, especially in the area of sustainment. The blockade would not terminate before the war did.

End States and Objectives. Once the termination criteria are established, operational design develops military strategic objectives which comprise the military end state conditions. This end state normally represents a point in time or circumstances beyond which the President no longer requires the military instrument of national power to achieve the remaining objectives of the national security end state. [4]

One clear adherent to this concept in the coastal campaign was Admiral Du Pont. For Du Pont, the most important strategic objective was to maintain and improve the integrity of the blockade. His experience in Mexico had shown him the dangers of deviating from this course. Thus, when Du Pont found himself under increasing pressure to attack Charleston, he considered it "impulsive nonsense," arguing that the port's capture would result in mere symbolic importance rather than making a genuine improvement in the strategic situation. [5]

Du Pont's assessment is very consistent with the "end states and objectives" element of operational design. Du Pont believed that improving the blockade was his most important mission, because it was this condition that would lead directly to the strategic goal of strangling the Confederacy. Thus, he considered seizing Charleston to be unimportant to the overall blockade campaign. Worse than that in Du Pont's mind, an operation aimed at Charleston would drain resources away from what was strategically important: tightening the blockade.[6] Although unable to make his point in Washington, Du Pont clearly understood that operational objectives must relate to the larger strategic objective.

Effects. An effect is the physical or behavioral state of a system that results from an action, a set of actions, or another effect. A set of desired effects contributes to the conditions necessary to achieve an associated military objective.[7] Effects in the coastal campaign include forcing the Confederates to abandon coastal territory and the reduction of blockade running.

The Federal successes on both the Atlantic and Gulf Coasts caused panic among the Confederates. In the Atlantic Campaign, Du Pont's victory at Port Royal sent Confederates fleeing from the coast, virtually abandoning it to the Federals. Porter wrote that "there seemed to be a stampede along the coast as soon as our naval vessels made appearance."[8] Du Pont agreed, observing that the string of successful Federal operations had the Confederates "flying about like moths around a lamp."[9] The easy seizures of Fernandina, Jacksonville, and St. Augustine were the result. In fact, Du Pont's Port Royal success caused the Confederates to completely reorganize their coastal defensive system, withdrawing to a few key areas such as Charleston.

Likewise, Farragut's success at New Orleans had the effect of weakening Confederate morale and sowing panic along the Gulf. A few practice shots at Mobile were all it took to convince the Confederates at Pensacola, some 30 miles away, to evacuate. Again the effect impacted broader Confederate strategy, causing President Davis to begin "abandoning the seaboard in order to defend the Tennessee line which is vital to our safety." [10]

Another effect of the coastal war was obviously a reduction in blockade running. Historians have long debated the overall effectiveness of the blockade, but David Surdam's analysis is among the most persuasive. Surdam concludes, "The Union Navy's control of the

Wreckage from a blockade runner near Sullivan's Island, South Carolina. While the Blockade was not decisive in breaking the Confederacy, it did greatly contribute to the Federal victory.
Photograph courtesy of the Library of Congress.

American waters had three main effects: denying the Confederacy the badly needed purchasing power that exporting its staple products would have generated; raising the costs, and reducing the volume of imported goods; and deranging intraregional trade."[11] While not alone decisive, these effects certainly contributed to the overall objective of defeating the Confederacy.

Center of gravity. The center of gravity is the source of moral or physical strength, power, and resistance that enables a belligerent to fight.[12] The great military theorist Carl von Clausewitz called it "the hub of all power and movement, on which everything depends." [13] One of the strategic centers of gravity for the Confederacy was foreign commerce. The South needed to secure weapons and other manufactured goods from Europe that its own limited industrial base could not produce. It also needed a market for its cotton in order to generate much needed income.

Clausewitz argues that the center of gravity is "the point at which all our energies should be directed."[14] The Federal blockade and the coastal campaigns that supported it clearly reflected this Clausewitzian understanding of the center of gravity.

Decisive points. Decisive points are the keys to attacking centers of gravity. They are geographic locations, key events, or critical factors or functions that give a marked advantage to whoever controls them.[15] The ten seaports that had rail or water connections with the Confederate interior—Norfolk, New Bern, Wilmington, Charleston, Savannah, Fernandina, Jacksonville, Pensacola, Mobile, and New Orleans—were the decisive points of the coastal campaign. Secretary of the Navy Welles showed a firm understanding of the concept of decisive points when he instructed the Navy Board, "It is imperative that two or more points should be taken possession of on the Atlantic Coast, and Fernandina and Port Royal are spoken of. Perhaps others will occur to the board. . . . Subsequently, similar points in the Gulf of Mexico will be considered."[16] The locations that the Navy Board went on to select accurately reflected the decisive points in the coastal war, and the Federal successes there marked progress in the overall attack on the Confederate center of gravity of foreign commerce.

Direct versus indirect. Ideally, the quickest path to victory is by directly attacking the enemy's centers of gravity. However, sometimes this means attacking into the enemy's strength. In these cases, it may be advisable to "seek an indirect approach until conditions are

The Blockade Board had wisely identified targets that affected both Confederate shipping and rail transportation. The Burnside Expedition greatly expanded the logistical impact of the Federal coastal operations by moving inland to interdict Southern railroads.

established that permit successful direct attacks."[17]

The Confederate operational center of gravity was General Robert E. Lee's Army of Northern Virginia. However, for much of the war, Lee's Army was too formidable for a direct Federal attack to succeed. In this regard, the coastal war played a critical indirect role by attacking Confederate logistics and thereby weakening Lee's Army.

Burnside's Expedition, especially the New Bern operation, is a good example. New Bern was not only North Carolina's second largest port, but also the site of an important railroad. From New Bern, the Atlantic & North Carolina Railroad ran to a vital junction at Goldsboro. At Goldsboro, the line intersected with the Wilmington & Weldon Railroad which carried supplies to Richmond and points north. By interdicting these rail operations in North Carolina, Burnside was indirectly attacking Lee's Army in Virginia.

Lines of operations. A line of operation describes the various actions on nodes and/or decisive points with an operational or strategic objective. Physical lines of operation in particular connect the force with its base of operations when positional reference to the enemy is a factor.[18]

At the beginning of the Civil War, the Federals controlled southern bases only at Fort Monroe, Virginia and Key West, Florida. These widely separated locations did not provide the physical lines of operation necessary to sustain the blockade. Du Pont was faced with the same prospect of having to lift the blockade for sustainment requirements as he had experienced in Mexico.

Thus, the Atlantic Campaign progressed in an organized pattern that facilitated physical lines of operation. The sequence of Hatteras Inlet, Port Royal Sound, Fernandina, Jacksonville, and Fort Pulaski made perfect sense. Each successive capture extended the Federal physical lines of operation deeper into the Confederacy. The Burnside Expedition's sequence of Roanoke Island, New Bern, and Fort Macon did the same thing.

Operational reach. Operational reach is the distance and duration over which a force can successfully employ military capabilities. The arrangement and successive positioning of advanced bases underwrites the progressive ability of the force to conduct rapid, continuous, and sustained operations throughout the operational area.[19] Welles's instructions for the Navy Board to study locations such as Fernandina and Port Royal on the Atlantic and others on the Gulf shows his understanding of the need to expand Federal operational reach beyond the meager possessions of Fort Monroe and Key West. The capture of decisive points along a physical line of operation demonstrates the Federals' progressive extension of their operational reach. The Burnside Expedition showed that joint operations could extend Federal operational reach into the Confederate interior by targeting rail communications, and Du Pont's successes at Fernandina, St. Augustine, Jacksonville, and Brunswick allowed him to project his reach into the inland waterways and establish an inside blockade.

However, operational reach is fundamentally linked to culmination.[20] As Du Pont continued to use his unchecked naval power to extend his operational reach along the South Carolina, Georgia, and Florida coasts, his more constrained Army partners began to feel they had exceeded the limits of their operational reach. Thus, Major General Hunter ordered the withdrawal of troops from Jacksonville, an act which forced the Navy to abandon both the town and the river and withdraw its gunboats to the mouth of the Saint Johns River. Issues of culmination halted the heretofore expanding Federal operational reach.

Simultaneity and depth. By simultaneously applying power against the enemy's key capabilities and sources of strength, the commander places more demands on enemy forces and functions than can be handled.[21] The Gulf Campaign achieved this element of operational design when it combined with Federal land operations to convince the Confederate commander at Pensacola, Braxton Bragg, to withdraw his forces north. Bragg knew the Confederacy was stretched too thin and could not handle the simultaneous Federal threats from the land in Tennessee and north Mississippi and from the Gulf. The simultaneous threats caused the Confederates to abandon the seaboard in order to defend Tennessee.

The concept of depth seeks to overwhelm the enemy not just in the obvious manner of space, but in the dimension of time as well. Operations in depth destroy enemy potential before its capabilities can be realized or employed.[22] Thus, the Federal seizure of New Orleans represented an operation in depth not just because it took the war to the Deep South long before Federal land forces could get there. By denying the Confederacy its most promising shipyard, Farragut also destroyed the fledgling Confederate ironclad fleet before it could develop into a threat. New Orleans is a fine example of an operation in depth that had both spatial and chronological dimensions.

Timing and tempo. Forces conduct operations at a tempo and point in time that best exploits friendly capabilities and inhibits the enemy. Commanders adjust the rate of military action in order to retain the initiative.[23] The fact that the Federals already had a Navy of 90 warships when the war began and the Confederate Navy would have to be built from scratch gave the Federals a huge advantage in exploiting tempo. Thus, operations such as New Orleans were in part driven by timing considerations to strike before the Confederates could complete their ironclad construction. In many cases, however, especially at the tactical level, this element was a shortcoming of Federal efforts in the coastal war.

The Army was particularly guilty of this error. During the Peninsula Campaign, McClellan gained an early advantage after his amphibious move, but he then slowed the pace of his operation and lost the initiative. At Secessionville, outside of Charleston, the Federal Army again had the initial upper hand, but delayed in attacking and allowed the Confederates to bring in reinforcements.

There is one excellent example, however, of a tactical decision concerning timing and tempo that turned the tide of a battle in the Federals' favor. When Farragut saw his battle plan falling apart at Mobile Bay, he knew time was the critical factor. His bold decision to "damn the torpedoes" maintained the initiative and saved the day for the Federals.

Forces and functions. Commanders design campaigns and operations to defeat either enemy forces or functions, or a combination of both.[24] The overall objective of the coastal war was a Confederate function—

the ability to run the blockade. To achieve this objective, the Federals attacked both Confederate forces and functions.

Early on in the coastal campaign, the Confederate forces were relatively easy targets. The meager defenses at places like Hatteras Inlet and Roanoke Island were little match for the Federals. However, as the Confederates realized the error of their initial strategy for defending the entire coast and began to concentrate their forces at a handful of strategic locations, the defenses stiffened. Fort Pulaski proved a tougher obstacle for the Federals to surmount than earlier objectives in the Atlantic Campaign, and Fort Macon held out longer than previous targets of the Burnside Expedition. Ultimately, the Confederate force at Charleston became an insurmountable obstacle for the Federal joint forces.

An alternative to attacking an enemy force is to attack its function. For example, the function of Forts Jackson and St. Philip was to guard the southern approaches to New Orleans. To attack the Confederate forces at those bastions would have been costly to Farragut, so he targeted the forts' functions instead. Rather than engaging the forts in a bloody slugfest, Farragut rendered them irrelevant by running past them and capturing New Orleans. With New Orleans in Federal hands, the mighty forts had lost their function and soon surrendered.

Leverage. Leverage is gaining, maintaining, and exploiting advantages in combat power.[25] The Federals enjoyed excellent resource advantages throughout the war, especially in the area of technology. The Federals leveraged their technology to change the very face of the war.

At Hatteras Inlet and Port Royal Sound, Stringham and Du Pont respectively leveraged the advantage that steam power gave ships over forts. Freed from the vagaries of winds and currents, ships could now fire while maneuvering to avoid land-based fire. This ability, along with superior ordnance, allowed the Federals to make short work of the Confederate defenses and reverse the old maxim that one gun on land was worth four on the water.

Fort Pulaski was another instance where the Federals leveraged technology, using long-range rifled artillery to breach masonry walls for the first time in history. Since the hallmark of the South's coastal defense network was masonry forts like Fort Pulaski, this was an unfortunate development for the Confederacy.

Both sides attempted to leverage the promising new ironclad technology. The Confederacy especially hoped to offset its numerical disadvantage with a few strategically placed ironclads such as the *Virginia* at Hampton Roads and the *Tennessee* at Mobile Bay. While these vessels prompted an element of fear among the Federals, they were hardly enough to counter the overwhelmingly superior Federal Navy. Unable to match the Federals conventionally, the Confederates resorted to an asymmetric response that leveraged torpedo technology.

As is always the case, the introduction of new technology in the midst of a war presents certain challenges. An excellent example is at Charleston where Secretary of the Navy Welles was confident that the new monitors would be decisive, but Admiral Du Pont felt they were unsuitable for attacking shore installations. Du Pont has been accused of being a dinosaur hopelessly mired in the outmoded wooden Navy while Welles is accused of falling victim to preconceptions of the new technology as a panacea. Their difference of opinion shows the difficulty of figuring out how exactly to leverage technological change. [26]

Balance. Balance is the maintenance of the force, its capabilities, and its operations in such a manner as to contribute to its responsiveness. [27] For the most part, the Federals executed a well-balanced coastal war, especially in the areas of facilities and vessels. The capture of key harbors such as Norfolk, Port Royal, and Pensacola gave the blockading ships the necessary facilities they needed to conduct repair operations and to take shelter during storms. Thus at Charleston, Dahlgren was able to withdraw his entire ironclad fleet to Port Royal for extensive repairs, and Pensacola was able to serve as the Gulf Blockading Squadron's supply depot.

The Department of the Navy also showed balance in its ability to orchestrate industrial production and delivery to meet the needs of its commanders. Thus, at New Orleans when Farragut asked for "Just as many [ironclads] as you can spare; two would answer me well, more would do better," the Department was able to provide him with four ironclads. Secretary Welles was even able to accommodate Du Pont at Charleston when he wrote, "The limit of my wants in the need of ironclads is the capacity of the [Navy] Department to supply them."

The campaign was less successful in meeting the modern doctrinal requirement to achieve the appropriate mix of forces.[28] Repeatedly at Jacksonville, Mobile Bay, Charleston, and Galveston, naval commanders were hamstrung by a shortage of their soldier counterparts. Indeed, entire operations such as New Orleans were planned to mitigate the requirement for a large Army force. At Hatteras Inlet, the coastal war began as a Navy dominated affair. Although it would end in a truly joint fashion at Fort Fisher, the ability to balance the Army and Navy contributions remained one of the campaign's greatest challenges.

Anticipation. The element of anticipation requires commanders to consider what might happen, to look for indicators that were likely to bring the possible event to pass, to remain alert for the unexpected, and to look for opportunities to exploit the situation.[29] The most fateful failure of the Federals in this area occurred at Galveston. Although Commander William Renshaw had long warned his men of a possible Confederate counterattack, very little was done to prepare for this eventuality. Contrary to the Navy's expectations, the Army provided a meager 260-man token force to assist in Galveston's defense. Thus, when Major General Magruder attacked, the Federals were overwhelmed relatively easily. Perhaps a more accurate assessment of Federal adherence to this particular element would be that the Federals possessed the necessary anticipation to expect the attack, but they lacked the necessary balance to send to Galveston a sufficient land force to prevent it.

Synergy. Especially in today's complex operational environment, the contributions of any individual or organization cannot be isolated from another. It is the commander's responsibility to integrate and synchronize the wide range of capabilities at his disposal.[30] Critical to obtaining this synergy is unity of effort: coordination through cooperation and common interests. [31]

One purpose of today's campaign plans is to arrange for strategic unity of effort. While the idea of the formal joint task force was unknown in the Civil War era, the importance of unity of effort was unmistakable in the coastal operations. Scott Stuckey observes, "Neither command arrangements nor doctrine for joint operations existed at the time [of the Civil War]. Successful joint operations, like much else, would have to be improvised by those on the scene."[32] Stuckey adds, "in the absence of unified command or meaningful joint doctrine, the conception and execution of joint operations totally depended on ad hoc actions by the responsible commanders, and therefore upon their personal chemistry and communications."[33] Command teams who were unable to achieve unity of effort, such as Wise and Lynch at Roanoke Island, McClellan and Goldsborough on the Virginia Peninsula, and Butler and Porter in the first battle of Fort Fisher, failed. Those who achieved unity of effort, such as Burnside and Goldsborough at Roanoke Island, Magruder and Smith at Galveston, and Terry and Porter in the second battle of Fort Fisher, succeeded. In all instances, personalities played a major role.

Fort Fisher is perhaps the best example of the difference that unity of effort can make. In the first battle, Porter and Butler's relationship was so marred by friction, mutual contempt, and parochialism that the two commanders had ceased to communicate directly with each other. Obviously, unity of effort under such circumstances was nearly impossible. The battle's results were predictable based on this violation of such a bedrock principle of war.

The common theme in all accounts of the second battle of Fort Fisher, however, is that it was as much a triumph of Army-Navy cooperation as the first one was a failure. Porter wrote to Secretary Welles that "Our [his and Terry's] cooperation has been most cordial; the result is victory, which will always be ours when the Army and Navy go hand in hand."[34] Peter Chaitin writes that Terry and Porter planned "every detail of the . . . attack in harmony."[35] Allan Nevins cites the "cooperation of a high degree . . . achieved between Porter and Terry [as] an important factor" in the attack's success.[36] Rod Gragg declares the second attack on Fort Fisher was "a model of army-navy cooperation."[37] Perhaps the last word should be given to the Confederate commander Lamb, who had noted the failures of both Butler and Porter in the first attack. In closing his narrative in *Battles and Leaders*, Lamb writes,

Had there been no fleet to assist the army at Fort Fisher the Federal infantry could not have dared assault it until the land defenses of the works were destroyed, not by any act of the besieging army, but by the concentrated fire, direct and enfilading, an immense fleet poured upon them without intermission, until torpedo wires were cut, palisades breached so that they actually afforded cover for assailants, and the slopes of the work were rendered practicable for assault. [38]

Fort Fisher stands as a testimony to the difference personality makes, the importance of unity of effort, and how far cooperation between the Federal Army and the Navy had advanced. Through unity of effort, the Federals achieved the synergy that had often eluded them during other coastal operations.

Culmination. In the offense, culmination is the point in time and space at which an attacker's combat power no longer exceeds that of the defender.[39] Both the Atlantic and Gulf Campaigns eventually reached their point of culmination because of exceeding the limits of their operational reach, strengthening Confederate defenses, insufficient resources, and poor planning.

The best example of a campaign culminating because of exceeding its operational reach is during the Atlantic Campaign when the Army felt that the Jacksonville operation took it beyond its limits. This ended Du Pont's progress along the coast and actually forced Jacksonville to be abandoned.

Charleston is an excellent example of how strengthening Confederate defenses caused culmination. As the Federals gobbled up more and more Confederate coastline, the Confederates were able to concentrate their forces at the few remaining critical locations. Charleston was one such strategic point, and the Confederates built a powerful defense there. Charleston's defenses were in fact so strong that they exceeded the offensive strength of the Federals. However, for the Confederates to take full advantage of having forced Federal offensive culmination, they would have had to be able to mount a counteroffensive of their own. The

Confederates were unable to do this, and a stalemate ensued until Sherman captured Charleston during his Carolinas Campaign.

At Galveston, the Gulf Campaign culminated for a lack of resources. Commander Renshaw of the Navy needed Army troops to secure his gains, but he did not receive them in sufficient numbers. This allowed a Confederate counterattack to recapture Galveston.

In the broadest scope, planning failures contributed to the culmination of both the Atlantic and Gulf Campaigns. The initial planning effort by the Navy Board was deliberate and detailed, but as the campaigns progressed, planning became much more haphazard. In September 1862, Du Pont pleaded with Assistant Secretary of the Navy Fox to not "go it half cocked about Charleston—it is a bigger job than Port Royal. . . . You & I planned the first . . . let us consult together again." [40] Instead of the careful planning of the Navy Board, Du Pont lamented that now the "desire of the President and others '*to strike a blow*' somewhere" was not accompanied by having "someone [who] would sit down and study how the blow was to be given."[41] The result, according to Du Pont, was that Charleston was a "chaotic conception" rather than the result of a military plan.[42] For Du Pont, the outcome was predictable.

Arranging operations. Commanders seek the best arrangement of operations to accomplish assigned tasks and missions. Key to this process are considerations of sustainment, phases, and sequels. The Navy Board ensured that the coastal campaigns were prosecuted well with regard to sustainment and phases, but in most cases the planners failed to develop appropriate sequels.

Du Pont knew from his experience in Mexico that sustainment considerations would be critical to the success of the blockade. This reality drove the Navy Board's planning process as it selected its targets. The first report's observation that "It seems to be indispensable that there should exist a convenient coal depot on the southern extremity of the line of Atlantic blockades . . . [and it] might be used not only as a coal depot for coal, but as a depot for provisions and common stores, as a harbor of refuge, and a general rendezvous, or headquarters, for that part of the coast" reflects this understanding.[43] The Navy Board also knew that capturing a port was meaningless unless the fort could then be held. Thus, even though the Navy alone was sufficient to capture Hatteras Inlet, Army forces came along to occupy the forts and secure the area for future operations.

The Board's understanding of phased operations is best reflected in the New Orleans operation. The Board knew that the nature of the Mississippi River Delta made this region particularly difficult to blockade, and that blockading the river would not close the port of New Orleans. Because the capture of New Orleans would require such a large naval and military force, the Board recommended delaying action against New Orleans until "we are prepared to ascend the river with vessels of war sufficiently protected to contend with the forts."[44] In the meantime, the Board recommended seizing Ship Island, which would serve as a jumping off point for any future attack. Ship Island became phase one of the larger operation against New Orleans.

The effective planning of sequels proved more problematic for the Federals. Sequels are "subsequent operations based on the possible outcomes of the current operation—victory, defeat, or stalemate."[45] Operations after both Port Royal and New Orleans suffered from not having well planned sequels.

Du Pont has been criticized by many historians for not moving on Charleston or Savannah or both immediately after his success at Port Royal. Indeed, at least one of his captains believed that Savannah "could have been taken by a regiment within forty-eight hours after the Port Royal affair I have not the least doubt."[46] However, in spite of this naval enthusiasm, Thomas Sherman's 13,000 man Army force probably would have been insufficient for the task. Additionally, with Savannah nearly 40 miles from Port Royal, and Charleston over 60 miles away, the lengthy overland move would have further sapped time and strength from Sherman. Lee had also anticipated such a move and contracted his line. On November 21, 1861, shortly after the fall of Port Royal, he wrote, "The guns from the less important points have been removed, and are strengthening those considered of greater consequence. The entrance to Cumberland Sound and Brunswick and the water approaches to Savannah and Charleston are the only points which it is proposed to defend."[47]

A more realistic sequel would have been to move to cut the Charleston and Savannah Railroad, which ran only 20 miles from

Port Royal. There was a belated and halfhearted attempt to disrupt the railroad in October 1862, but for the most part Du Pont, in spite of his suggestion that the Army's forces at Port Royal "should be largely increased and a regular campaign in the South be commenced," was plagued by timid Army counterparts who showed little interest in anything beyond routine blockade duties.[48] Part of the problem was that Army planners and commanders had their attention focused on Richmond and considered the joint operations on the South Carolina coast to be secondary efforts at best.[49] Bern Anderson writes that "the war might have taken an entirely different course if the Army had chosen to exploit its opportunities in that region."[50]

Likewise after New Orleans, Farragut had no planned sequel. The result was the abortive attempt at Vicksburg. Overall, this failure to plan sequels was probably the Navy Board's most glaring shortcoming.

Conclusion. Though planned independently of current joint doctrine, the Federal operations against the Confederate coast show why modern campaign planning has been codified as it has. The coastal operations can be viewed as a related series comprising a campaign. They represented the translation of national strategy into operational concepts, the work of a present-day campaign plan. For the most part, the campaigns adhered to the elements of operational design. In the elements of effects, center of gravity, decisive points, direct versus indirect, lines of operation, simultaneity and depth, and leverage, the campaigns were particularly strong. Eventually, the campaigns exceeded the limits of their operational reach, which contributed to their culmination. There were also issues with timing and tempo, balance, and anticipation. Synergy proved a special challenge as various commanders struggled to achieve unity of effort. The area where the campaigns suffered the most was in the planning of sequels as part of the element of arranging operations.

The coastal war was on the leading edge of US military evolution in the areas of campaign planning and joint operations. Taken as a whole, especially when one considers the absence of modern day joint doctrine and organization, the results were outstanding. Without knowing it, Captain Du Pont and his Navy Board were impressively expert at following the tenets of modern campaign planning.

NOTES

Introduction

[1] Archer Jones, *Civil War Command & Strategy*, (NY: The Free Press, 1992), 140–141.

[2] Joint Pub 3-0, *Operations*, (Washington, DC: Joint Chiefs of Staff, 17 Sept 2006), GL-8.

[3] Kevin Weddle, *Lincoln's Tragic Admiral: The Life of Samuel Francis Du Pont*, (Charlottesville: University of Virginia Press, 2005), 108.

[4] Joint Pub 5-0, *Joint Operational Planning*, (Washington, DC: Joint Chiefs of Staff, 26 Dec 2006), GL-8.

[5] Weddle, 141.

[6] FM 3-0, *Operations*, (Washington, DC: Headquarters Department of the Army, 2001), 5–9.

The Key Federals

[1] Weddle, 109–111.

[2] Weddle, 112–113 and Mark Boatner, *The Civil War Dictionary*, (NY: David McKay Company, 1959), 44–45.

[3] Richard Sauers, *The Burnside Expedition in North Carolina*, (Dayton, OH: Morningside House, 1996), 42–43.

[4] Boatner, 107–108.

[5] Peter Chaitin, *The Coastal War*, (Alexandria, VA: Time-Life Books, 1984), 16–17.

[6] Bruce Catton, *Mr. Lincoln's Army*, (Garden City, NJ: Doubleday & Company, 1951), 256.

[7] Sauers, 203.

[8] Rod Gragg, *Confederate Goliath*, (NY: Harper Perennial, 1992), 38.

[9] Chester Hearn, *The Capture of New Orleans*, (Baton Rouge: Louisiana State University, 1995), 134, 248, 255–257, and 266.

[10] Boatner, 109.

[11] Shelby Foote, *The Civil War: A Narrative; Red River to Appomattox*, Vol. III, (NY: Random House, 1974), 740.

[12] Gragg, 258.

[13] Weddle, 163.

[14] Spencer Tucker, *A Short History of the Civil War at Sea*, (Wilmington, DE: Scholarly Resources Inc, 2002), 3, 100; Weddle, 162–163; and Boatner, 218.

[15] Boatner, 224 and Weddle, 112.

[16] Boatner, 252.

[17] Daniel Ammen, "Du Pont and the Port Royal Expedition," in *Battles and Leaders of the Civil War*, Vol. I, (Edison, NJ: Castle, rpt 1887), 690.

[18] Weddle, 160, 165, and 167.

[19] Bruce Catton, *This Hallowed Ground*, (Garden City: Doubleday & Company, 1956), 85.

[20] Weddle, 213.

[21] Bern Anderson, *By Sea and By River: A Naval History of the Civil War*, (Westport, CT: Greenwood Press, 1962), 118.

[22] Hearn, 102–105 and Anderson, 118.

[23] Richard West, *Gideon Welles: Lincoln's Navy Department*, (NY: Bobbs-Merrill Company, 1943), 203.

[24] Ivan Musicant, *Divided Waters: The Naval History of the Civil War*, (Edison, NJ: Castle Books, 1995), 56, 58–59.

[25] Weddle, 157.

[26] Weddle, 180–181.

[27] Sauers, 30.

[28] Foote, Vol. I, 228.

[29] Musicant, "Divided," 87.

[30] Virgil Jones, *The Civil War at Sea*, Vol. I, (NY: Holt, Rinehart, Winston, 1961), 23.

[31] Musicant, "Divided," 407.

[32] Boatner, 418–419.

[33] Robert Browning, *Success Is All That Was Expected: The South Atlantic Blockading Squadron during the Civil War*, (Washington, DC: Brassey's, Inc, 2002), 91.

[34] Boatner, 661.

[35] Hearn, 97.

[36] Boatner, 591–592.

[37] Chaitin, 58.

[38] Ulysses Grant, *Personal Memoirs of U. S. Grant*, ed. E. B. Long, (NY: Da Capo Press, 1982), 300–301.

[39] Sauers, 123.

[40] Boatner, 750.

[41] Browning, 91.

[42] Boatner, 811.

[43] Catton, "Hallowed," 85.

[44] Musicant, "Divided," 59.

[45] Rush Hawkins, "Early Coastal Operations in North Carolina," in *Battles and Leaders of the Civil War*, Vol. I. (Edison, NJ: Castle, rpt 1887), 634.

[46] Musicant, "Divided," 86–87.

[47] Foote, Vol. III, 741 and Herman Hattaway and Archer Jones, *How the North Won*, (Urbana: University of Illinois Press, 1983), 660.

[48] Boatner, 831.

[49] Gragg, 107.

[50] Allan Nevins, *The War for the Union*, Vol. II, (NY: Charles Scribner's Sons, 1960), 191.

[51] Boatner, 831.

[52] Hearn, 33–34; Clarence Macartney, *Mr. Lincoln's Admirals*, (NY: Funk & Wagnalls Co, 1956), 10; and Boatner, 900–901.

The Key Confederates

[1] Boatner, 55.

[2] Boatner, 80; Clifford Dowdey, *The Seven Days*, (NY: Fairfax Press, 1978), 81; and Clifford Dowdey, *The Land They Fought For*, (Garden City, NJ: Doubleday & Company, 1955), 192.

[3] Hearn, 70–72 and 261.

[4] Gragg, 14–17.

[5] Gragg, 272.

[6] Chaitin, 156.

[7] Hearn, 107.

[8] Hearn, 118.

[9] Boatner, 501 and Edward Cotham, "The Battle of Galveston." *North & South*, Vol. IX: No. 6, Dec 2006, 30–31.

[10] Emory Thomas, *The Confederate Nation*, (NY: Harper & Row, 1979), 76–77; Tucker 9, 32–33; and Boatner, 503–504.

[11] Anderson, 121 and Hearn, 104–105 and 262.

[12] Virgil Jones, Vol. II, 319.

[13] R. Thomas Campbell, *Fire & Thunder: Exploits of the Confederate Navy*, (Shippenburg, PA: Burd Street Press, 1997), 97 and Robert Kerby, *Kirby Smith's Confederacy: The Trans-Mississippi South, 1863–1865*, (NY: Columbia University Press, 1972), 379 and 410–411.

14 Virgil Jones, Vol. I, 179.
15 Foote, Vol. 1, 117 and Boatner, 826.
16 Paul Branch, "The Life of Colonel Moses James White." *Ramparts*, Spring, 2004, Volume XI, Issue 1, 1–4.
17 Dowdey, "Land," 65.
18 Sauers, 101.
19 Boatner, 944.
20 Sauers, 101.
21 Sauers, 101.

The Blockade and the Navy Board
1 Hattaway and Jones, 127.
2 Hattaway and Jones 135 and Rowena Reed, *Combined Operations in the Civil War*, (Annapolis, MD: Naval Institute Press, 1978), 8.
3 Weddle, 107.
4 JP 5-0, IV-2.
5 Weddle, 107.
6 Weddle, 111.
7 Stephen Carney, *Gateway South: The Campaign for Monterey*, (Washington, DC: Center of Military History, US Army, 2005), 9.
8 Jack Bauer, *The Mexican War: 1846–1848*, (NY: MacMillan, 1974), 344 and Weddle, 27.
9 Weddle, 28.
10 Bauer, 345.
11 Robert Selph Henry, *The Story of the Mexican War*, (NY: Frederick Ungar, 1950), 210.
12 Weddle, 111.
13 Weddle, 28, 32–33, and 111.
14 Weddle, 109.
15 Foote, Vol. I, 115.
16 Weddle, 113.
17 Weddle, 113.
18 Weddle, 115.
19 Weddle, 116.
20 Weddle, 117 and Reed, 8–9.
21 Weddle, 120–121 and Musicant, "Divided," 63.
22 Weddle, 122.
23 Weddle, 123.

Hatteras Inlet: The Pattern is Formed
[1] Virgil Jones, Vol. I, 197.
[2] Foote, Vol. I, 115; Philip Van Doren Stern, *The Confederate Navy: A Pictorial History*, (Garden City, NJ: Doubleday & Company, 1962), 51; and Chaitin, 16.
[3] Virgil Jones, Vol. I, 193–197 and Van Doren Stern, 51.
[4] Foote, Vol. I, 115.
[5] Boatner 385; Foote, Vol. I, 115; and Van Doren Stern, 51.
[6] Van Doren Stern 51; Foote, Vol. I, 115; and E. A. Pollard, *The Lost Cause*, (NY: E. B. Treat & Company, 1867), 192–193.
[7] Boatner, 385.
[8] Foote, Vol. I, 115.
[9] Anderson, 48.
[10] Pollard, 193 and Van Doren Stern, 51.
[11] Hawkins, 634.
[12] Van Doren Stern, 51; Boatner, 385; Foote, Vol. I, 20; and Russell Weigley, *The American Way of War*, (Bloomington: University of Indiana Press, 1973), 99.
[13] Weigley, 99 and Foote, Vol. I, 120.
[14] Pollard, 193.
[15] Pollard, 192.
[16] Van Doren Stern, 51.
[17] Boatner, 385; Foote, Vol. I, 115–116; and Pollard, 193.
[18] Virgil Jones, Vol. I, 207.
[19] Chaitin, 16.
[20] Bruce Catton, *The Civil War*, (NY: The Fairfax Press, 1980), 74.
[21] Bruce Catton, *Reflections on the Civil War*, (Garden City, NJ: Doubleday & Company, 1981), 140.
[22] Catton, "Civil War," 74.
[23] Catton, "Lincoln's Army," 87.
[24] Anderson, 48.

Port Royal Sound: The Triumph of the Plan
[1] Foote, Vol. I, 116 and Weigley, 99.
[2] Catton, "Hallowed," 85; Foote, Vol. I, 116; Theodore Rosengarten, *Tombee: Portrait of a Cotton Planter*, (NY: William Morrow & Company, 1986), 213; Van Doren Stern, 54; and Anderson, 53–54.
[3] Catton, "Hallowed," 85 and Anderson, 53.
[4] Douglas Southall Freeman, *R. E. Lee,* Vol. I, (NY: Charles Scribners' Sons, 1934), 606;

Foote, Vol. I, 116–117; and Clifford Dowdey and Louis Manarin, *The Wartime Papers of R. E. Lee*, (NY: Bramhall House, 1961), 81.
[5] Foote, Vol. I, 117; Anderson, 54; and Weddle, 131.
[6] Weigley, 99–100.
[7] W. Scott, *South Carolina's Civil War: A Narrative History*, (Macon, GA: Mercer University Press, 2005), 38–39; Rosengarten, 212; Pollard, 193; and Foote, Vol. I, 117.
[8] Weddle, 130; Poole, 39; and Foote, Vol. I, 117.
[9] Foote, Vol. I, 117.
[10] Weddle, 132.
[11] Virgil Jones, Vol. I, 275.
[12] Anderson, 55 and Foote, Vol. I, 117–119.
[13] Virgil Jones, Vol. I, 278.
[14] Pollard, 194.
[15] Poole, 39; Foote, Vol. I, 119; and Chaitin, 20.
[16] Anderson, 57.
[17] Foote, Vol. I, 118–119.
[18] Weddle, 140–141; Foote, Vol. I, 119–120; Pollard, 194; Anderson, 57–58; and Thomas, "Confederate," 125.
[19] Emory Thomas, *Robert E. Lee*, (NY: W. W. Norton & Company, 1995), 212.
[20] Weigley, 101–102.
[21] Weddle, 140.
[22] Freeman, "Lee," Vol. I, 610 and Dowdey and Manarin, 82.
[23] Anderson, 59.
[24] Van Doren Stern, 54.
[25] Anderson, 61.
[26] Rosengarten, 219–221.
[27] Poole, 42–43.

Fernandina and Jacksonville
[1] Weddle, 113.
[2] Weddle, 116.
[3] Anderson, 38–39 and Browning 9, 21, and 25.
[4] Browning, 66–68.
[5] Porter, *Naval History of the Civil War*, (Secaucus, NJ: Castle, 1984), 77.
[6] Porter, "History," 77.
[7] Browning, 68.
[8] Porter, "History," 77.
[9] Browning, 66.

[10] Porter "History," 77 and Browning, 69.
[11] Browning, 70.
[12] Browning, 70–71.
[13] Browning, 71–72.
[14] Porter, "History," 78.
[15] Browning, 72.
[16] Browning, 74–75.
[17] Porter, "History," 78.
[18] Browning, 72–73.
[19] Browning, 73.
[20] Browning, 91–94.
[21] Browning, 163–164.
[22] Browning, 118 and 300.
[23] Hattaway and Jones, 142.

Fort Pulaski: Rifled Artillery's First Breach of Masonry

[1] Browning, 58.
[2] Q. A. Gillmore, "Siege and Capture of Fort Pulaski," in *Battles and Leaders of the Civil War,* Vol. I. (Edison, NJ: Castle, 1985), 1 and Kevin Dougherty, "Rifled Artillery's First Breach of Masonry," in *Forward Observer*, April 92, 6.
[3] Browning, 58.
[4] Browning, 60–63.
[5] Browning, 63–66.
[6] Gillmore, 2–3.
[7] Virgil Jones, Vol. II, 142.
[8] Gillmore, 7–9 and Browning, 92.
[9] Browning, 91.
[10] Porter, "History," 78 and Browning, 92.
[11] Gillmore, 9 and Browning, 92.
[12] Gillmore, 9–10.
[13] Gillmore, 8–10.
[14] Gillmore, 10–11.
[15] Daniel Brown, "Fort Pulaski," in *The Civil War Battlefield Guide*, Frances Kennedy, ed., (Boston: Houghton Mifflin Company, 1990), 36–40.
[16] Gillmore, 12.
[17] Weddle, 154 and Browning, 92–93.
[18] Weddle, 153 and Browning, 104–105.
[19] Browning, 125.

Roanoke Island: Amphibious Proving Ground
[1] Dowdey, "Land," 135.
[2] Muscicant, "Pursuit," 72.
[3] Foote, Vol. I, 230.
[4] Foote, Vol. I, 225.
[5] Thomas, "Nation," 121.
[6] Thomas, "Lee," 297.
[7] Hattaway and Jones, 111.
[8] Nevins, 90.
[9] Sauers, 152.
[10] Thomas, "Nation," 121–122 and Hattaway and Jones, 112.
[11] Sauers, 152.
[12] Van Doren Stern, 69.
[13] Chaitin, 22 and Thomas, "Nation," 121.
[14] Thomas, "Nation," 121–122 and Sauers, 162.
[15] Hawkins, 645.
[16] Chaitin, 19.
[17] Sauers, 40.
[18] Ivan Musicant, "Hot Pursuit Up the Sounds," in *Proceedings*, Oct 96, 68.
[19] Musicant, "Pursuit," 68–69.
[20] Musicant, "Pursuit," 69.
[21] Foote, Vol. I, 228 and A. E. Burnside, "The Burnside Expedition," in *Battles and Leaders of the Civil War*, Vol. I, (Edison, NJ: Castle, rpt 1887), 661.
[22] Musicant, "Pursuit," 69.
[23] Foote, Vol. I, 228.
[24] Foote, Vol. I, 228 and Catton, "Lincoln's Army," 256.
[25] Foote, Vol. I, 228–229 and Chaitin, 21.
[26] Burnside, 665–666.
[27] Foote, Vol. I, 229 and Chaitin, 23–24.
[28] Foote, Vol. I, 229.
[29] Musicant, "Pursuit," 70; Sauers, 143–145; Burnside, 667; Chaitin, 24; and Foote, Vol. I, 230.
[30] Hawkins, 642.
[31] Chaitin, 25.
[32] Chaitin, 24 and Tucker, 28.
[33] Chaitin, 25; Van Doren Stern, 69; Sauers, 172–173; and Pollard, 211.
[34] Anderson 63; Chaitin, 24; and Musicant, "Pursuit," 70.
[35] Hattaway and Jones, 112.
[36] Musicant, "Pursuit," 68.

[37] Sauers, 176–177.

[38] Chaitin, 24.

[39] Burnside, 667; Anderson, 63; and Musicant, "Pursuit," 72.

[40] Hawkins, 642 and Chaitin, 25–27.

[41] Burnside, 668.

[42] Burnside, 668.

[43] Chaitin, 27–30.

[44] Sauers, 202.

[45] Nevins, 90.

[46] Musicant, "Pursuit," 72.

[47] Chaitin, 30.

[48] Dowdey, "Land," 135–136.

[49] Foote, Vol. I, 232.

[50] Thomas, "Confederate," 123.

[51] Dowdey, "Land," 135.

[52] Scott Stuckey, "Joint Operations in the Civil War," in *Joint Forces Quarterly*, Autumn/Winter 1994–1995, 98–99.

[53] Anderson, 64.

New Bern: Expanded Logistical Impact of the Coastal War

[1] Sauers, 233.

[2] Sauers, 233.

[3] Archer Jones, 141.

[4] Sauers, 181 and Van Doren Stern, 69.

[5] Burnside, 668.

[6] Dowdey, "Land," 190.

[7] Chaitin, 35.

[8] Sauers, 233.

[9] Burnside, 668 and Sauers, 236–237.

[10] Chaitin, 35.

[11] Burnside, 668.

[12] Sauers, 240.

[13] Chaitin, 35.

[14] Chaitin, 36.

[15] Chaitin, 36–37.

[16] Chaitin, 37 and Burnside, 669.

[17] Sauers, 307.

Fort Macon: Final Victory of the Burnside Expedition

[1] Sauers, 309.

[2] Paul Branch, "The Confederate Seizure of Fort Macon," in *Ramparts*, Spring, 1998, Vol. V, Issue 1: 3.

[3] Branch, "White," 2 and Sauers, 309–310.

[4] Paul Branch, "The Confederate Defense of Fort Macon: Part 1—The Siege Begins," in *Ramparts*, Vol. VII, Issue 3, Fall 2000, 3 and Sauers, 310–312.

[5] Sauers, 309–314.

[6] Branch, "Siege," 3.

[7] Branch, "Siege," 4.

[8] Branch, "Siege," 4 and Sauers, 320–321.

[9] Branch, "Siege," 4 and Sauers, 319–320.

[10] Branch, "Siege," 4 and Sauers, 323–324.

[11] Branch, "Seige," 4 and Sauers, 329–330.

[12] Paul Branch, "The Confederate Defense of Fort Macon: Part 2—The Battle Begins," in *Ramparts*, Vol. VIII, Issue 1, Spring 2001, 2 and Sauers, 335–336.

[13] Branch, "Battle," 3.

[14] Branch, "Battle," 3 and Sauers, 337–338.

[15] Sauers, 340.

[16] Pollard, 231. In actuality, Wilmington remained open.

[17] Anderson, 65.

[18] Catton, "Civil War," 75.

[19] Sauers, 444.

[20] Burnside, 669 and Sauers, 365.

[21] Sauers, 462 and Chaitin, 39.

[22] Burnside, 669.

[23] Chaitin, 39.

The Peninsula Campaign: A Failure in Cooperation

[1] Catton, "Mr. Lincoln's Army," 87.

[2] Kevin Dougherty, *The Peninsula Campaign of 1862: A Military Analysis*, (Jackson: The University Press of Mississippi, 2005), 37.

[3] Hattaway and Jones, 93.

[4] Ronald Bailey, *Forward to Richmond: McClellan's Peninsular Campaign*, (Alexandria, VA: Time-Life, 1983), 81–83.

[5] T. Harry Williams, *Lincoln and His Generals*, (NY: Alfred A. Knopf, 1952), 72.

[6] Catton, "Army of the Potomac," 99.

[7] John Quarstein, *The Battle of the Ironclads*, (Charleston, SC: Arcadia, 1999), 11–13 and Musicant, "Divided," 157.

[8] Boatner, 560.

[9] Foote, Vol. I, 255.

[10] John Taylor Wood, "The First Fight of the Ironclads," in *Battles and Leaders of the Civil War*, Vol. I, (Edison: NJ: Castle, rpt 1887), 696.

[11] Reed, 102.

[12] Foote, Vol. I, 256–257.

[13] Musicant, "Divided," 157–160.

[14] Musicant, "Divided," 161–163 and Foote, Vol. I, 259–260.

[15] Catton, "Civil War," 77.

[16] Wood, 701.

[17] Musicant, "Divided," 174.

[18] Musicant, "Divided," 174–175.

[19] Foote, Vol. I, 261–262; Boatner, 560–561; and Catton, "Civil War," 77–80.

[20] Catton, "Army of the Potomac," 107; Catton, "Civil War," 64; Nevins, 48; and Williams, 78.

[21] Bruce Catton, *The Terrible Swift Sword*. (Garden City, NJ: Doubleday & Company, 1963), 263–264.

[22] Stephen Sears, *To the Gates of Richmond: The Peninsular Campaign*, (NY: Ticknor and Fields, 1992), 24.

[23] Williams, "Lincoln," 90.

[24] Warren Hassler, *General George B. McClellan: Shield of the Union*, (Baton Rouge: Louisiana State University Press, 1957), 86.

[25] George McClellan, "The Peninsular Campaign," in *Battles and Leaders of the Civil War*, Vol. II, (Edison, NJ: Castle, rpt 1887), 169.

[26] Sears, "Gates," 32.

[27] Catton, "Terrible Swift Sword," 273.

[28] Catton, "Terrible Swift Sword," 275.

[29] Nevins, 56.

[30] Dowdey, "Seven Days," 43–44.

[31] Dowdey, "Seven Days," 45.

[32] Porter, "History," 404.

[33] Foote, Vol. I, 796.

[34] Porter, "History," 404.

[35] Cullen, Joseph. *Richmond National Battlefield Park Virginia*. Available at http://www.nps.gov/history/history/online_books/hh/33/index.htm. Assessed May 5, 2009.

[36] Douglas Southall Freeman, *Lee's Lieutenants: A Study in Command*, Vol. I, (NY: Charles Scribners' Sons, 1942), 211.

[37] Sears, "Gates," 10.

[38] West, "Welles," 182.

Ship Island: Setting the Stage
[1] Musicant, "Divided Waters," 63.
[2] Weddle, 119–121.
[3] Sarah Dorsey, *Recollections of Henry Watkins Allen*, (NY: M. Doolady, 1866), 54; Robert Holzman, *Stormy Ben Butler*, (NY: The MacMillan Company, 1954), 62; and Musicant, "Divided Waters," 222.
[4] Zed Burns, *Ship Island and the Confederacy*, (Hattiesburg: University and College Press of Mississippi, 1971), 19.
[5] Vincent Cassidy and Amos Simpson, *Henry Watkins Allen of Louisiana*, (Baton Rouge: Louisiana State University Press, 1964), 72–73; William C. Davis, *Brother Against Brother*, (Alexandria, VA: Time-Life Books, 1983), 128; Dorsey, 55; and Hearn, 129.
[6] Burns, 7–8.
[7] Burns, 8–9.
[8] Burns, 13 and 20.
[9] Cassidy, 73 and Hearn, 129.
[10] Burns, 15–16.
[11] Boatner, 109.
[12] Reed, 58–59 and Burns, 25.
[13] Reed, 60–62.
[14] Hans Trefousse, *Ben Butler: The South Called Him BEAST!* (NY: Twayne Publishers, 1957), 92.
[15] Holzman, 60.
[16] Holzman, 59–60.
[17] Chaitin, 61; Musicant, "Divided Waters," 222–224; and Hearn, 128, 134–135.
[18] Hearn, 131.
[19] Hearn, 130.
[20] Foote, Vol. I, 361.
[21] Burns, 33.
[22] Chaitin, 55.
[23] James Hollandsworth, "What a Hell of a Place to Send 2000 Men 3000 Miles: Union Soldiers on Ship Island During the Civil War," *The Journal of Mississippi History*, Volume LXII, No. 2, (Summer 2000): 126.
[24] Hollandsworth, 127.
[25] Trefousse, 117 and Holzman, 70.
[26] Trefousse, 122–124.
[27] Hollandsworth, 125.

New Orleans: The Price of Unpreparedness

[1] Catton, "Civil War," 440–441.
[2] Virgil Jones, Vol. II, 61.
[3] Hearn, 7–8 and Chaitin, 54.
[4] Hearn 3, 73–80, 95.
[5] David Surdam, "The Union Navy's Blockade Reconsidered," *Naval War College Review*, Autumn 1998, Vol. LI, No. 4, 104.
[6] Hearn, 11, 16 and Chaitin, 55.
[7] Hattaway and Jones, 28.
[8] Hearn, 30–31.
[9] Hearn, 11.
[10] Hearn, 71.
[11] Catton, "Fury," 439 and Macartney, 24–25.
[12] Chaitin, 55.
[13] Hearn, 71.
[14] Hearn, 72 and Musicant, "Divided," 223.
[15] H. Allen Gosnell, *Guns on the Western Waters: The Story of River Gunboats in the Civil War*, (Baton Rouge: Louisiana State University Press, 1993), 38.
[16] Porter, "History," 91.
[17] Hearn, 84–95.
[18] Porter, "History," 91.
[19] David Porter, "The Opening of the Lower Mississippi." in *Battles and Leaders of the Civil War*, Vol. II, (Edison, NJ: Castle Books, rpt 1887), 23; Hearn, 96; and Chaitin, 55–57.
[20] Musicant, "Divided," 219–220 and Hearn, 97–98.
[21] Musicant, "Divided," 221.
[22] Hearn, 104–105; Musicant, "Divided," 220–22; and Tucker, 68.
[23] Hearn, 105–106.
[24] Hearn, 108.
[25] Dowdey, "Land," 153.
[26] Hearn, 109.
[27] Hearn, 109–116.
[28] Hearn, 121.
[29] Hearn, 122.
[30] Hearn, 109–117.
[31] Virgil Jones, Vol. II, 93–94.
[32] Musicant, "Divided," 227–228 and Hearn, 195.
[33] Virgil Jones, Vol. II, 70.
[34] Hearn, 122–124.

[35] Hearn, 135 and Musicant, "Divided," 226.

[36] Hearn, 141–47.

[37] Hearn, 147.

[38] Hearn, 147–150.

[39] Hearn, 147–148.

[40] Musicant, "Divided," 225 and Hearn, 168.

[41] Hearn, 168–169.

[42] Hearn, 172.

[43] Porter, "Opening," 35.

[44] Musicant, "Divided," 226–227 and Hearn, 180–186.

[45] Hearn, 199–200.

[46] Hearn, 201–203.

[47] Chaitin, 65–66.

[48] Hearn, 195.

[49] Tucker, 68, 72–73.

[50] Musicant, "Divided," 223–234.

[51] Musicant, "Divided," 235.

[52] Musicant, "Divided," 235 and Virgil Jones, Vol. II, 121–129.

[53] Musicant, "Divided," 235–235.

[54] Reed, 193–195.

[55] Tucker, 84.

[56] Musicant, "Divided," 236–237.

[57] Reed, 199.

[58] Macartney, 54.

[59] Tucker, 85–87 and James Duffy, *Lincoln's Admiral: The Civil War Campaigns of David Farragut*, (NY: John Wiley & Sons, Inc, 1997), 130, 134.

[60] Richard West, *Mr. Lincoln's Navy*, (NY: Longmans, Green and Company, 1957), 157.

[61] C. Vann Woodward, ed. *Mary Chesnut's Civil War*, (New Haven, CT: Yale University Press, 1981), 330.

Pensacola: The Confederacy is Stretched Too Thin

[1] Boatner, 641; Tucker 8; and Anderson, 16, 20–21.

[2] West, "Welles," 109.

[3] Porter, "History," 103 and West, "Navy," 25.

[4] Anderson, 24, 37; West, "Navy," 8–13, 20–28; and Boatner, 641.

[5] Boatner, 640–641, 720.

[6] Boatner, 641 and Chaitin, 8.

[7] Hattaway and Jones, 157

[8] Musicant, "Divided," 237–238 and Boatner, 641.

[9] West, "Welles," 182; Richard Beringer et al, *Why the South Lost the Civil War*, (Athens: The University of Georgia Press, 1986), 62; Musicant "Divided," 238; and Reed, 224.

[10] Reed, 221–222.

Galveston: A Federal Setback

[1] Reed, 225.

[2] Cotham, 20–21.

[3] Tucker, 137.

[4] Cotham, 21 and Duffy, 162.

[5] Cotham, 20 and Tucker, 138.

[6] Cotham, 21.

[7] Anderson, 136 and Boatner, 322.

[8] Cotham, 24; Duffy, 162; and Musicant, "Divided," 267.

[9] Cotham, 23.

[10] Cotham, 23.

[11] Cotham, 23 and Tucker, 138.

[12] Cotham, 22.

[13] Cotham, 25.

[14] Cotham, 26.

[15] Cotham, 26.

[16] Cotham, 27.

[17] Tucker, 138 and Cotham, 28.

[18] Tucker, 137–138.

[19] Musicant, "Divided," 268.

[20] Porter, "History," 270.

[21] Anderson, 205.

[22] Tucker, 121, 124–125 and Cotham, 30.

[23] Porter, "History," 271.

[24] Reed, 240–241.

[25] Reed, 240–241.

[26] Reed, 225.

Charleston: Too Strong From the Sea

[1] Weddle, 158.

[2] Tucker, 89.

[3] Tucker, 89–90 and Weddle, 143.

[4] Weddle, 159.

[5] Weddle, 156.

6 Tucker, 90–91 and Weddle, 177–178.
7 Tucker, 91.
8 Weddle, 156, 178.
9 Tucker, 91–92 and Weddle, 155, 160, and 164.
10 Weddle, 166–168.
11 Tucker, 92 and Weddle, 183–184.
12 Weddle, 157.
13 Tucker, 94 and Weddle, 184.
14 Weddle, 182.
15 Tucker, 93.
16 Tucker, 97–99 and Weddle,191–193, 195.
17 Tucker, 99–100 and Weddle, 188, 203–204.
18 Tucker, 101.
19 Tucker, 101.
20 Tucker, 101.
21 Tucker, 102 and Musicant, "Divided," 402–404.
22 Tucker, 108–109 and Musicant, "Divided," 406–407.

Mobile Bay: Damn the Torpedoes

1 Musicant, "Divided," 306–307.
2 Duffy, 222.
3 Musicant, "Divided," 307; Tucker, 141; and Anderson, 233–234.
4 Hattaway and Jones, 621 and Duffy, 230.
5 Virgil Jones, Vol. III, 230 and Chaitin, 142.
6 Musicant, "Divided," 309.
7 Musicant, "Divided," 309.
8 Chaitin, 143 and Musicant, "Divided," 310–311.
9 Musicant, "Divided," 313.
10 Chaitin, 145.
11 Virgil Jones, Vol. III, 242.
12 West, "Welles" 203.
13 Musicant, "Divided," 312.
14 Virgil Jones, Vol. III, 245–246.
15 Virgil Jones, Vol. III, 247–248.
16 Virgil Jones, Vol. III, 248–249.
17 Musicant, "Divided," 314.
18 Virgil Jones, Vol. III, 249.
19 Musicant, "Divided," 317 and Chaitin, 147.
20 Virgil Jones, Vol. III, 256.
21 Virgil Jones, Vol. III, 256 and Musicant, "Divided," 320–323.

[22] Boatner, 559.

[23] Virgil Jones, Vol. III, 260.

[24] Boatner, 298.

[25] Virgil Jones, Vol. III, 260.

[26] Musicant, "Divided," 324.

[27] Robert Doughty, *American Military History and the Evolution of Warfare in the Western World*, (Lexington, MA: D. C. Heath, 1996), 201 and Hattaway and Jones, 624.

[28] Grant, 519.

Fort Fisher: The Final Chapter

[1] Gragg, 3.

[2] Chris Fonvielle, *The Wilmington Campaign: The Last Rays of Departing Hope*, (Shippenburg, PA: Stackpole, 2001), 79.

[3] Stuckey, 100.

[4] Chaitin, 158.

[5] William Lamb, "The Defense of Fort Fisher," in *Battles and Leaders of the Civil War*, vol 4, (Edison, NJ: Castle, 1985, rpt 1887), 642.

[6] Gragg, 17.

[7] Fonvielle, 41–42 and Nevins, 189.

[8] Gragg, 17–21.

[9] Gragg, 21.

[10] Lamb, "Battles and Leaders," 643.

[11] Fonvielle, 60–61.

[12] Nevins, 190.

[13] Chaitin, 158–159.

[14] Hattaway and Jones, 659.

[15] Chaitin, 159.

[16] Gragg, 41.

[17] Chaitin, 159; Fonvielle, 102–103, 120; and Stuckey, 101.

[18] Stuckey, 101 and Gragg, 46–47.

[19] Chaitin, 157.

[20] Stuckey, 101.

[21] Chaitin, 157–158.

[22] Fonvielle, 105.

[23] Fonvielle, 99.

[24] Fonvielle 105.

[25] Gragg, 47–49, 61 and Stuckey, 101.

[26] Gragg, 49; Fonvielle, 139; and Stuckey, 101.

[27] Gragg, 51.

[28] Gragg, 52.

[29] Foote, Vol. III, 719.

[30] Gragg, 53.

[31] Nevins, 190.

[32] Chaitin, 161.

[33] Chaitin, 161 and Nevins, 190.

[34] William Lamb, "The Confederates Repulse an Attack on Fort Fisher," in *The Blue and the Gray*, Henry Steele Commanger, ed. (NY: The Fairfax Press, 1982), 839.

[35] Foote, Vol. III, 719 and Lamb, "Blue and Gray," 840.

[36] Gragg, 73 and Chaitin, 161.

[37] Gragg, 74 and Fonvielle, 139–140.

[38] Chaitin, 161 and Fonvielle, 154.

[39] Stuckey, 101–102; Fonvielle, 161–172; and Chaitin, 161–62.

[40] Chaitin, 161.

[41] Foote, Vol. III, 720.

[42] Fonvielle, 189; Foote, vol 1, 721; Chaitin, 162; and Hattaway and Jones, 659.

[43] Lamb, "Blue and Gray," 842.

[44] Lamb, "Blue and Gray," 646.

[45] Gragg, 74.

[46] Gragg 107; Stuckey 102; and Foote, vol 3, 741.

[47] Chaitin, 163; Fonvielle, 196-197; and Foote, vol 3, 741.

[48] Fonvielle, 197 and Foote, vol 3, 741.

[49] Foote, vol 3, 740 and Chaitin, 164, 169.

[50] Fonvielle, 193.

[51] Fonvielle, 198–199.

[52] Fonvielle, 194.

[53] Pollard, 673 and Gragg, 26–27.

[54] Fonvielle, 88.

[55] Chaitin, 163–164.

[56] Chaitin, 163; Gragg, 108; Foote, vol 3, 741; and Lamb, "Battles and Leaders," 647.

[57] Foote, vol 3, 741–742.

[58] Foote, vol 3, 742; Gragg 188; Chaitin, 164; and Lamb, "Battles and Leaders," 647.

[59] Fonvielle, 234–236; Foote, vol 3, 743; and Chaitin, 164.

[60] Stuckey, 103.

[61] Lamb, "Battles and Leaders," 647–648.

[62] Chaitin, 164–165.

[63] Chaitin, 165 and Fonvielle, 237.

[64] Stuckey, 103.

[65] Fonvielle, 257.

[66] Chaitin, 167–168.

[67] Boatner, 294.

[68] Chaitin, 169.

[69] Gragg, 195.

[70] Gragg, 212–213.

[71] Gragg, 215–217 and Fonvielle, 279–280, 292.

[72] Gragg, 226–227; Chaitin, 168–170; and Foote, vol 3, 746.

[73] Chaitin, 170.

The Coastal War and the Elements of Operational Design

[1] JP 3-0, IV-3.

[2] JP 3-0, IV-6.

[3] JP 3-0, IV-7.

[4] JP 3-0, IV-8.

[5] Weddle, 161–162.

[6] Weddle, 177.

[7] JP 3-0, IV-8.

[8] Porter, "History," 77.

[9] Browning, 66.

[10] Hattaway and Jones, 157.

[11] Surdam, 104.

[12] JP 3-0, IV-10.

[13] Carl von Clausewitz, *On War,* Ed. Michael Howard and Peter Paret, (Princeton, NJ: Princeton University Press, 1976), 595.

[14] Clausewitz, 596.

[15] JP 3-0, IV-11.

[16] Weddle, 113.

[17] JP 3-0, IV-12.

[18] JP 3-0, IV-12.

[19] JP 3-0, IV-13— IV-14.

[20] JP 3-0, IV-13.

[21] JP 3-0, IV-14.

[22] JP 3-0, IV-14 — IV-15.

[23] JP 3-0, IV-15 — IV-16.

[24] JP 3-0, IV-16.

[25] JP 3-0, IV-16.

[26] Weddle, 169-171.

[27] JP 3-0, IV-17.
[28] JP 3-0, IV-17.
[29] JP 3-0, IV-17.
[30] JP 3-0, IV-18.
[31] JP 3-0, A-2.
[32] Stuckey, 98–99.
[33] Stuckey, 94.
[34] Stuckey, 104.
[35] Chaitin, 163.
[36] Nevins, 192.
[37] Gragg, 109.
[38] Lamb, "Battles and Leaders," 654.
[39] JP 3-0, IV-18– IV-19.
[40] Weddle, 162.
[41] Weddle, 183.
[42] Weddle, 182–183.
[43] Weddle, 116.
[44] Weddle, 120–121.
[45] JP 3-0, IV-20.
[46] Weddle, 143.
[47] Weddle, 140.
[48] Weddle, 143–144.
[49] Weddle, 143.
[50] Anderson, 61.

BIBLIOGRAPHY

Ammen, Daniel. "Du Pont and the Port Royal Expedition," in *Battles and Leaders of the Civil War*, vol 1. Edison, NJ: Castle, rpt 1887, p. 670–691.

Anderson, Bern. *By Sea and By River: A Naval History of the Civil War*. Westport: Greenwood Press, 1962.

Bailey, Ronald. *Forward to Richmond: McClellan's Peninsular Campaign*. Alexandria, VA: Time-Life, 1983.

Bauer, Jack. *The Mexican War: 1846–1848*. New York: MacMillan, 1974.

Beringer, Richard, et al. *Why the South Lost the Civil War*. Athens: The University of Georgia Press, 1986.

Boatner, Mark. *The Civil War Dictionary*. New York: David McKay Company, 1959.

Branch, Paul. "The Confederate Defense of Fort Macon: Part 1—The Siege Begins." *Ramparts*, Vol. VII, Issue 3, Fall 2000, 1–5.

Branch, Paul. "The Confederate Defense of Fort Macon: Part 2—The Battle Begins." *Ramparts*, Vol. VIII, Issue 1, Spring 2001, 1–4.

Branch, Paul. "The Confederate Seizure of Fort Macon." *Ramparts*, Spring, 1998, Volume V, Issue 1, 1–4.

Branch, Paul. "The Life of Colonel Moses James White." *Ramparts*, Spring, 2004, Volume XI, Issue 1, 1–4.

Brown, Daniel, "Fort Pulaski," in *The Civil War Battlefield Guide*, Frances Kennedy, ed. Boston: Houghton Mifflin Company, 1990.

Browning, Robert. *Success Is All That Was Expected: The South Atlantic Blockading Squadron during the Civil War*. Washington, DC: Brassey's, Inc, 2002.

Burns, Zed. *Ship Island and the Confederacy*. Hattiesburg: University and College Press of Mississippi, 1971.

Burnside, A. E. "The Burnside Expedition," in *Battles and Leaders of the Civil War*, vol 1. Edison, NJ: Castle, rpt 1887, p. 660–670.

Campbell, R. Thomas. *Fire & Thunder: Exploits of the Confederate Navy*. Shippenburg, PA: Burd Street Press, 1997.

Carney, Stephen. *Gateway South: The Campaign for Monterey*. Washington, DC: Center of Military History, US Army, 2005.

Cassidy, Vincent and Amos Simpson. *Henry Watkins Allen of Louisiana*. Baton Rouge: Louisiana State University Press, 1964.

Catton, Bruce. *Mr. Lincoln's Army*. Garden City, NJ: Doubleday & Company, 1951.

Catton, Bruce. *The Civil War*. NY: The Fairfax Press, 1980.

Catton, Bruce. *The Terrible Swift Sword*. Garden City, NJ: Doubleday & Company, 1963.

Catton, Bruce. *This Hallowed Ground*. Garden City, NJ: Doubleday & Company, 1956.

Catton, Bruce. *Reflections on the Civil War*. Garden City, NJ: Doubleday & Company, 1981.

Chaitin, Peter. *The Coastal War*. Alexandria, VA: Time-Life Books, 1984.

Clausewitz, Carl von. *On War*. Ed. Michael Howard and Peter Paret. Princeton, NJ: Princeton University Press, 1976.

Cotham, Edward. "The Battle of Galveston." *North & South*. Vol 9: No 6, Dec 2006, 20–31.

Cullen, Joseph. *Richmond National Battlefield Park Virginia*. Available at www.nps.gov/history/history/online_books/hh/33/index.htm. Assessed May 5, 2009.

Davis, William C. *Brother Against Brother*. Alexandria, VA: Time-Life Books, 1983.

Dorsey, Sarah. *Recollections of Henry Watkins Allen*. New York: M. Doolady, 1866.

Dougherty, Kevin, "Rifled Artillery's First Breach of Masonry," in *Forward Observer*, Apr 92, 6-8.

Dougherty, Kevin. "The Coastal War in North and South Carolina: An Analysis of the Evolution of Joint Naval-Army Operations 1861–1865." Danville, VA: The Blue & Gray Education Society, 2002.

Dougherty, Kevin. *The Peninsula Campaign of 1862: A Military Analysis.* Jackson: The University Press of Mississippi, 2005.

Doughty, Robert. *American Military History and the Evolution of Warfare in the Western World.* Lexington, MA: D. C. Heath, 1996.

Dowdey, Clifford. *The Land They Fought For.* Garden City, NJ: Doubleday & Company, 1955.

Dowdey, Clifford. *The Seven Days.* New York: Fairfax Press, 1978.

Dowdey, Clifford and Louis Manarin. *The Wartime Papers of R. E. Lee.* New York: Bramhall House, 1961.

Duffy, James. *Lincoln's Admiral: The Civil War Campaigns of David Farragut.* New York: John Wiley & Sons, Inc, 1997.

FM 3-0, *Operations.* Washington, DC: Headquarters Department of the Army, 2001.

Fonvielle, Chris. *The Wilmington Campaign: The Last Rays of Departing Hope.* Shippenburg, PA: Stackpole, 2001.

Foote, Shelby. *The Civil War: A Narrative.* 3 vols. New York: Random House, 1958–1974.

Freeman, Douglas Southall. *Lee's Lieutenants: A Study in Command.* 3 vols. New York: Charles Scribners' Sons, 1942–1944.

Freeman, Douglas Southall. *R. E. Lee,* vol 1. New York: Charles Scribners' Sons, 1934.

Gillmore, Q. A. "Siege and Capture of Fort Pulaski." in *Battles and Leaders of the Civil War,* vol 1. Edison, NJ: Castle, 1985, p. 1–12.

Gosnell, H. Allen. *Guns on the Western Waters: The Story of River Gunboats in the Civil War.* Baton Rouge: Louisiana State University Press, 1993.

Gragg, Rod. *Confederate Goliath.* New York: Harper Perennial, 1992.

Grant, Ulysses. *Personal Memoirs of U. S. Grant.* Ed. E. B. Long. New York: Da Capo Press, 1982.

Hassler, Warren. *General George B. McClellan: Shield of the Union.* Baton Rouge: Louisiana State University Press, 1957.

Hattaway, Herman and Archer Jones. *How the North Won.* Urbana: University of Illinois Press, 1983.

Hawkins, Rush, "Early Coastal Operations in North Carolina," in *Battles and Leaders of the Civil War,* vol 1. Edison, NJ: Castle, rpt

1887, p. 632–659.

Hearn, Chester. *The Capture of New Orleans*. Baton Rouge: Louisiana State University, 1995.

Henry, Robert Selph. *The Story of the Mexican War*. New York: Frederick Ungar, 1950.

Hollandsworth, James. "What a Hell of a Place to Send 2000 Men 3000 Miles: Union Soldiers on Ship Island During the Civil War," *The Journal of Mississippi History*, Volume LXII, No. 2, (Summer 2000), 123–39.

Holzman, Robert. *Stormy Ben Butler*. New York: The MacMillan Company, 1954.

Johnson, Charles, "An Amphibious Force Captures Roanoke Island," in *The Blue and the Gray*, Henry Steele Commanger, ed. New York: The Fairfax Press, 1982, p. 797–802.

Joint Pub 3-0, *Operations*. Washington, DC: Joint Chiefs of Staff, 17 Sept 2006.

Joint Pub 5-0, *Joint Operational Planning*. Washington, DC: Joint Chiefs of Staff, 26 Dec 2006.

Jones, Archer. *Civil War Command & Strategy*. New York: The Free Press, 1992.

Jones, Virgil. *The Civil War at Sea*. 3 vols. New York: Holt, Rinehart, Winston, 1961.

Kerby, Robert. *Kirby Smith's Confederacy: The Trans-Mississippi South, 1863–1865*. New York: Columbia University Press, 1972.

Lamb, William, "The Defense of Fort Fisher," in *Battles and Leaders of the Civil War*, vol 4, Edison, NJ: Castle, 1985, rpt 1887: p. 642–654.

Lamb, William, "The Confederates Repulse an Attack on Fort Fisher," in *The Blue and the Gray*, Henry Steele Commanger, ed. NY: The Fairfax Press, 1982, p. 838–843.

McClellan, George. "The Peninsular Campaign," in *Battles and Leaders of the Civil War*, vol 2, Edison: NJ: Castle, rpt 1887: p. 160–188.

Macartney, Clarence. *Mr. Lincoln's Admirals*. New York: Funk & Wagnalls Co, 1956.

Magee, Mickey. "The Road to Fort Macon." *Ramparts*. Summer 2000, Volume VII, Issue 2, 1–4.

Musicant, Ivan. *Divided Waters: The Naval History of the Civil War.* Edison, NJ: Castle Books, 1995.

Musicant, Ivan. "Hot Pursuit Up the Sounds," in *Proceedings*, Oct 96, p. 68–72.

Nash, Howard. *Stormy Petrel: The Life and Times of General Benjamin F. Butler 1818–1893.* Rutherford, NJ: Fairleigh Dickinson University Press, 1969.

Nevins, Allan. *The War for the Union*, vol 2. New York: Charles Scribner's Sons, 1960.

Pollard, E. A. *The Lost Cause.* New York: E. B. Treat & Company, 1867.

Poole, W. Scott. *South Carolina's Civil War: A Narrative History.* Macon, GA: Mercer University Press, 2005.

Porter, David. "The Opening of the Lower Mississippi." *Battles and Leaders of the Civil War,* Vol 2. Edison, NJ: Castle Books, 1985: p. 22–55.

Porter, David. *Naval History of the Civil War.* Secaucus, NJ: Castle, 1984.

Quarstein, John. *The Battle of the Ironclads.* Charleston, SC: Arcadia, 1999.

Reed, Rowena. *Combined Operations in the Civil War.* Annapolis, MD: Naval Institute Press, 1978.

Rosengarten, Theodore. *Tombee: Portrait of a Cotton Planter.* New York: William Morrow & Company, 1986.

Sauers, Richard. *The Burnside Expedition in North Carolina.* Dayton, OH: Morningside House, 1996.

Sears, Stephen. *To the Gates of Richmond: The Peninsular Campaign.* New York: Ticknor and Fields, 1992.

Stuckey, Scott. "Joint Operations in the Civil War," in *Joint Forces Quarterly*, Autumn/Winter 1994–1995, 92–105.

Surdam, David. "The Union Navy's Blockade Reconsidered." *Naval War College Review*, Autumn 1998, Vol LI, No. 4, 85–107.

Thomas, Emory. *Robert E. Lee.* New York: W.W. Norton & Company, 1995.

Thomas, Emory. *The Confederate Nation.* NewYork: Harper & Row, 1979.

Time-Life Books, editors. *The Blockade: Runners and Raiders.*

Alexandria, VA: Time-Life Books, 1983.

Trefousse, Hans. *Ben Butler: The South Called Him BEAST!* New York: Twayne Publishers, 1957.

Tucker, Spencer. *A Short History of the Civil War at Sea.* Wilmington, DE: Scholarly Resources Inc, 2002.

Van Doren Stern, Philip. *The Confederate Navy: A Pictorial History.* Garden City, NJ: Doubleday & Company, 1962.

Weddle, Kevin. *Lincoln's Tragic Admiral: The Life of Samuel Francis Du Pont.* Charlottesville: University of Virginia Press, 2005.

Weigley, Russell. *The American Way of War.* Bloomington: University of Indiana Press, 1973.

West, Richard. *Gideon Welles: Lincoln's Navy Department.* New York: Bobbs-Merrill Company, 1943.

West, Richard. *Mr. Lincoln's Navy.* New York: Longmans, Green and Company, 1957.

Williams, T. Harry. *Lincoln and His Generals.* New York: Alfred A. Knopf, 1952.

Wood, John Taylor. "The First Fight of the Ironclads," in *Battles and Leaders of the Civil War,* vol 1. Edison: NJ: Castle, rpt 1887: p. 692–711.

Woodward, C. Vann, ed. *Mary Chesnut's Civil War.* New Haven, CT: Yale University Press, 1981.

INDEX